First World War

and Army of Occupation

War Diary

France, Belgium and Germany

I0301959

48 DIVISION
145 Infantry Brigade,
Brigade Machine Gun Company
11 January 1916 - 31 October 1917

WO95/2764/2

The Naval & Military Press Ltd
www.nmarchive.com
Published in association with The National Archives

Published by

The Naval & Military Press Ltd

Unit 10 Ridgewood Industrial Park,

Uckfield, East Sussex,

TN22 5QE England

Tel: +44 (0) 1825 749494

www.naval-military-press.com

www.nmarchive.com

This diary has been reprinted in facsimile from the original. Any imperfections are inevitably reproduced and the quality may fall short of modern type and cartographic standards.

Contents

Document type	Place/Title	Date From	Date To
Heading	145th Machine Gun Coy Jan 1916 To Oct 1917		
Heading	48th Division 145th Infy Bde 145th Machine Gun Coy. Jan 1916-1917 Oct		
Heading	145th Brigade 48th Division Company Formed In France 11.1.15 145th Brigade Machine Gun Company 11th January To 29th February 1916 Dec 1917		
War Diary	Couin	11/01/1916	21/01/1916
War Diary	Hebuterne	21/01/1916	27/01/1916
War Diary	Couin	29/01/1916	02/02/1916
War Diary	Hebuterne	03/02/1916	29/02/1916
Miscellaneous	To Officer i/c A.G. Office Base	01/03/1916	01/03/1916
Heading	145th Brigade 48th Division 145th Brigade Machine Gun Company March 1916		
War Diary	Hebuterne	01/03/1916	31/03/1916
Heading	145th Brigade 48th Division 145th Brigade Machine Gun Company April 1916		
Miscellaneous	Herewith At C2118		
War Diary	Hebuterne	01/04/1916	30/04/1916
Heading	145th Brigade 48th Division 145th Brigade Machine Gun Company May 1916		
War Diary	Hebuterne	25/04/1916	17/05/1916
War Diary	Beauval	18/05/1916	31/05/1916
Heading	145th Brigade 48th Division 145th Brigade Machine Gun Company June 1916		
War Diary	Coulonvillers	01/06/1916	14/06/1916
War Diary	Hebuterne	15/06/1916	21/06/1916
War Diary	Couin	22/06/1916	23/06/1916
Heading	145th Inf. Bde. 48th Div. War Diary 145th Machine Gun Company July 1916		
War Diary	Mailly Maillet	01/07/1916	03/07/1916
War Diary	Couin	04/07/1916	05/07/1916
War Diary	Sailly	05/07/1916	05/07/1916
War Diary	Bivouacs In The Dell	06/07/1916	12/07/1916
War Diary	Sailly	13/07/1916	15/07/1916
War Diary	Senlis	14/07/1916	17/07/1916
War Diary	Bouzincourt	18/07/1916	20/07/1916
War Diary	Usna Redoubt	20/07/1916	25/07/1916
War Diary	Bouzincourt	26/07/1916	26/07/1916
War Diary	Lealvillers	26/07/1916	27/07/1916
War Diary	Beauval	27/07/1916	28/07/1916
War Diary	Cramont	29/07/1916	31/07/1916
Miscellaneous	Appendices		
Map	Map		
Miscellaneous	Special Order Of The Day By General Sir Douglas Haig. Commander-In-Chief British Armies In France	17/07/1916	17/07/1916
Miscellaneous	Special Order Of The Day By General Sir Douglas Haig.G.C.B. K.C.I.E. K.C.V.O A.D.C Commander-In-Chief British Armies In France	18/07/1916	18/07/1916
Miscellaneous	Message	04/07/1916	04/07/1916
Miscellaneous	O.C. Battalions Bde. M.G. Coy. 145th T.m. Battery	21/07/1916	21/07/1916

Miscellaneous	145th Inf. Bde.	22/07/1916	22/07/1916
Heading	145th Brigade 48th Division 145th Brigade Machine Gun Company August 1916		
War Diary	Cramont (Lemenage)	01/08/1916	08/08/1916
War Diary	Beauval	09/08/1916	09/08/1916
War Diary	Varennes	10/08/1916	10/08/1916
War Diary	Bouzincourt	11/08/1916	12/08/1916
War Diary	Usna Redoubt	13/08/1916	18/08/1916
War Diary	Bouzincourt	19/08/1916	23/08/1916
War Diary	Lake View (w:17.d.7.0)	23/08/1916	25/08/1916
War Diary	Lake View	25/08/1916	28/08/1916
War Diary	Bouzincourt Bus-Les-Artois	28/08/1916	31/08/1916
Heading	145th Brigade 48th Division 145th Brigade Machine Gun Company September 1916		
War Diary	Bus-Les-Artois	01/09/1916	04/09/1916
War Diary	Bus-Les-Artois & Mailly-Maillet	05/09/1916	09/09/1916
War Diary	Bus-Les-Artois	10/09/1916	10/09/1916
War Diary	Bus-Les-Artois Beauval	11/09/1916	18/09/1916
War Diary	Fienvillers	18/09/1916	29/09/1916
War Diary	Humbercourt	30/09/1916	30/09/1916
Heading	145th Brigade 48th Division 145th Brigade Machine Gun Company October 1916		
War Diary	Warlincourt	01/10/1916	20/10/1916
War Diary	Les Annelles	21/10/1916	31/10/1916
Heading	145th Brigade 48th Division 145th Brigade Machine Gun Company November 1916		
Heading	War Diary Of 145 Machine Gun Company From 1st Nov 1916 To 30th Nov 1916		
War Diary	Millencourt	01/11/1916	01/11/1916
War Diary	Millencourt Lozenge Wood Martinpuich	02/11/1916	02/11/1916
War Diary	Martinpuich Le Sars	03/11/1916	20/11/1916
War Diary	Martinpuich Le Sars and Contalmaison	20/11/1916	30/11/1916
Map	Map		
Heading	145 M.G. Coy. Appendix Is War Diary For Nov 1916		
Heading	145th Brigade 48th Division 145th Brigade Machine Gun Company December 1916		
Heading	War Diary Of 145 Machine Gun Company For December 1916		
War Diary	Contalmaison Martinpuich Le Sars	01/12/1916	15/12/1916
War Diary	Becourt	15/12/1916	28/12/1916
War Diary	Bresle	28/12/1916	30/12/1916
Miscellaneous	Appendix "A" Reference to Map		
War Diary		01/12/1916	31/12/1916
Map	Map		
Heading	War Diary Of 145th Machine Gun Company From Jan 1st 1917 To Jan 31st 1917		
War Diary	Bresle	01/01/1917	09/01/1917
War Diary	Frucourt	10/01/1917	29/01/1917
War Diary	Hamel	30/01/1917	31/01/1917
War Diary	Bresle	02/01/1917	09/01/1917
War Diary	Frucourt	10/01/1917	28/01/1917
War Diary	Hamel	29/01/1917	31/01/1917
Heading	War Diary Of 145th Machine Gun Company From February 1st 1917 To February 28th 1917		
War Diary	Hamel	01/02/1917	02/02/1917
War Diary	Cappy (no 5b Camp)	02/02/1917	06/02/1917

War Diary	Cappy	07/02/1917	28/02/1917
Miscellaneous	Appendix "A" 145th Machine Gun Company		
Miscellaneous	Ref Appendix "B"		
Miscellaneous		14/02/1917	14/02/1917
Miscellaneous	Relief Orders		
Map	Map		
Miscellaneous	Appendix "B" 145 Machine Gun Company		
Heading	War Diary Of 145 Machine Gun Company From March 1st 1917 To March 31st 1917		
War Diary	Bois D' Achille	01/03/1917	14/03/1917
War Diary	Cappy	15/03/1917	20/03/1917
War Diary	Peronne	21/03/1917	26/03/1917
War Diary	Buire	27/03/1917	30/03/1917
War Diary	Hamel	31/03/1917	31/03/1917
Miscellaneous	Appendix "B" 145th Machine Gun Company		
War Diary	Peronne	22/03/1917	22/03/1917
War Diary	Cartigny	23/03/1917	28/03/1917
Map	Map		
Miscellaneous	Scheme Machine Gun Barrage		
Heading	War Diary Of 145th Machine Gun Company From April 1st 17 To April 30th 17		
War Diary	Hamel	01/04/1917	03/04/1917
War Diary	Villers Faucon	04/04/1917	30/04/1917
Miscellaneous	Appendix "A" 145th Machine Gun Company		
Heading	War Diary Of 145th Machine Gun Company From May 1st 1917 To May 31st 1917		
War Diary	Alder Spinney (Roisel)-Peronne	01/05/1917	04/05/1917
War Diary	Peronne	04/05/1917	11/05/1917
War Diary	Peronne Combles	12/05/1917	12/05/1917
War Diary	Combles Reincourt Les Bapaume	13/05/1917	14/05/1917
War Diary	Hermies Demicourt	15/05/1917	31/05/1917
Miscellaneous	Appendix "A" 145th Machine Gun Company		
Map	Map		
Heading	War Diary Of 145th Machine Gun Company From June 1st 1917 To June 30th 1917		
War Diary	Hermies-Demicourt	01/06/1917	30/06/1917
Miscellaneous	Appendix "A" 145 Machine Gun Company		
Heading	War Diary Of 145th Machine Gun Company From July 1st 1917 To July 31st 1917		
War Diary	Hermies Demicourt	01/07/1917	01/07/1917
War Diary	Velu	02/07/1917	03/07/1917
War Diary	Bihucourt	04/07/1917	04/07/1917
War Diary	Bailleulmont	05/07/1917	09/07/1917
War Diary	St. Omer Moulle	10/07/1917	10/07/1917
War Diary	Moulle	11/07/1917	30/07/1917
War Diary	Ref Trench Map St. Julien 28 NW2	31/07/1917	31/07/1917
Heading	War Diary Of 145th Machine Gun Company From 1st July 1917 To 31st July 1917		
Miscellaneous	Appendix "A" 145 Machine Gun Company		
Heading	War Diary Of 145th Machine Gun Company From 1st July To 31st July 1917		
Operation(al) Order(s)	145 M.G. Company Operation Order No. 1	19/07/1917	19/07/1917
Miscellaneous	Instructions. In Conjunction With 145th M.G. Coy. O.O. No.1	20/07/1917	20/07/1917
Miscellaneous	Allocation Of Duties		
Miscellaneous	145 M.G.C. "F" Battery (c 16d 7505)	31/07/1917	31/07/1917

Miscellaneous	145 M.G.C. "G" Battery (C 16d 1525)	31/07/1917	31/07/1917
War Diary	Belgium & France 1:40000 Sheet 28 A 29c Central	01/08/1917	01/08/1917
War Diary	Map Ref For Operations 28.N.W.Z. St Julien	01/08/1917	31/08/1917
Heading	War Diary Of 145th Machine Gun Company From August 1st 1917 To August 31st 1917		
Heading	War Diary Of 145 Machine Gun Company From 1st August To 31st August 1917		
Operation(al) Order(s)	145th M.G. Company Order No. 2	04/08/1917	04/08/1917
Operation(al) Order(s)	145th M.G. Company Order No. 3	07/08/1917	07/08/1917
Map	Map		
Operation(al) Order(s)	145th M.G. Company Operation Order No. 4	11/08/1917	11/08/1917
Operation(al) Order(s)	145th M.G. Company Operation Order No. 8	15/08/1917	15/08/1917
Operation(al) Order(s)	145th M.G. Company Operation Order No. 5	12/08/1917	12/08/1917
Miscellaneous	145th M.G. Company Order No. 5 Administrative Orders.	15/08/1917	15/08/1917
Miscellaneous	Appendix I Communication		
Miscellaneous	145th M.G. Company Order No. 5/1	14/08/1917	14/08/1917
Operation(al) Order(s)	145th M.G. Company Order No. 7	25/08/1917	25/08/1917
Miscellaneous	145th M.G. Company Order No. 7/1	26/08/1917	26/08/1917
Miscellaneous	Indirect Overhead Fire		
Heading	War Diary Of 145th Machine Gun Company From Sept 1st 1917 To Sept 30th 1917		
War Diary	Road Camp St Jan Der Biezen	01/09/1917	06/09/1917
War Diary	Road Camp St Jan Der Biezen Belgium	07/09/1917	15/09/1917
War Diary	Clerques A Villiage About 12 Miles West Of St. Omer France	16/09/1917	16/09/1917
War Diary	Clerques	17/09/1917	26/09/1917
War Diary	Clerques Brielen Line (Pockappelle) 1:10000 Edition 4	27/09/1917	27/09/1917
War Diary	Line	28/09/1917	30/09/1917
Heading	War Diary Of 145th Machine Gun Company From Oct 1st 1917 To Oct 31st 1917		
War Diary	St. Julien (Ref Map Poelcappelle 1:10000	01/10/1917	09/10/1917
War Diary		27/09/1917	10/10/1917
War Diary	St Julien	27/09/1917	00/10/1917
War Diary	Dambre Camp Near Vlamertinghe (Sheet 27)	11/10/1917	12/10/1917
War Diary	En Route To Jan-Ter Biezen	12/10/1917	12/10/1917
War Diary	Jan Ter Biezen	13/10/1917	14/10/1917
War Diary	Camblain L'Abbe (Lens II)	14/10/1917	17/10/1917
War Diary	Aux Reitz Sheet 51b (A8 C50)	18/10/1917	19/10/1917
War Diary	Aux Reitz (A8 C50)	20/10/1917	31/10/1917

www.ingramcontent.com/pod-product-compliance
Lightning Source LLC
Chambersburg PA
CBHW082009220426
43670CB00014B/2588
* 9 7 8 1 4 7 4 5 2 6 9 7 5 *

Instructions regarding War Diaries and Intelligence Summaries are contained in F. S. Regs., Part II. and the Staff Manual respectively. Title Pages will be prepared in manuscript.

WAR DIARY
or
INTELLIGENCE SUMMARY
(Erase heading not required.)

Army Form C. 2118

Place	Date	Hour	Summary of Events and Information	Remarks and references to Appendices
AUX REITZ (7 8 c 50)	OCT 31	4.30pm	Nos 1 and 3 sections proceeded to the line and relieved 8 guns of 143rd M.G. Coy. in the line – Relief was complete by 10pm. The night was very quiet.	SHW

S.H.W[illegible] Captn
O/C 145 M.G.C.

31st October 1917

1875 Wt. W593/826 1,000,000 4/15 J.B.C. & A. A.D.S.S./Forms/C. 2118.

Instructions regarding War Diaries and Intelligence Summaries are contained in F. S. Regs., Part II. and the Staff Manual respectively. Title pages will be prepared in manuscript.

WAR DIARY
or
INTELLIGENCE SUMMARY.

(Erase heading not required.)

Army Form C. 2118.

Place	Date	Hour	Summary of Events and Information	Remarks and references to Appendices
AUX REITZ ~~[illegible]~~ ~~[illegible]~~ (A 8 c 5 0)	OCT 20		Training. Weather excellent	SHEET 51B [illegible]
	OCT 21		Sunday. Divine Service - Weather very good	[illegible]
	OCT 22.		Weather wet. Two hours training - Baths	[illegible]
	OCT 23		Training continued.	[illegible]
	OCT 24		Training about 2 hours. Remainder of day spent on improving Camp, making paths & roads. Weather wet.	[illegible]
	OCT 25		Training continued but interrupted by storms.	[illegible]
	OCT 26.		Training.	[illegible]
	OCT 27.		Training.	[illegible]
	OCT 28		Training, wet weather.	[illegible]
	OCT 29.		Training during morning, afternoon spent on making roads etc. in Camp.	[illegible]
	OCT 30		All guns were tested on range, prior to taking them into the line.	[illegible]

Army Form C. 2118.

WAR DIARY
or
INTELLIGENCE SUMMARY.
(Erase heading not required.)

Instructions regarding War Diaries and Intelligence Summaries are contained in F. S. Regs., Part II. and the Staff Manual respectively. Title pages will be prepared in manuscript.

Place	Date	Hour	Summary of Events and Information	Remarks and references to Appendices
			[illegible] company [illegible]	
			the following day [illegible]	
			convey blankets & packs to CAMBLAIN L'ABBE [illegible]	
			[illegible] to the following	
CAMBLAIN L'ABBE (LENS 11)			Evening – The company marched to CAMBLAIN	
			L'ABBE arriving at 4 am. Billets were good	
			Following [illegible] and the fact that the	
			blankets and packs had not arrived sleep	
			was difficult	[illegible]
	OCT 15		Rest – Weather improved	[illegible]
	OCT 16		Training & cleaning up [illegible]	[illegible]
	OCT 17		Training	[illegible]
AUX REITZ	OCT 18		Company moved to AUX REITZ (Sheet 51B A8c50)	[illegible]
Sheet 51B (A8c50)	OCT 19		Training	

Army Form C. 2118.

WAR DIARY
or
INTELLIGENCE SUMMARY.
(Erase heading not required.)

Instructions regarding War Diaries and Intelligence Summaries are contained in F. S. Regs., Part II. and the Staff Manual respectively. Title pages will be prepared in manuscript.

Place	Date	Hour	Summary of Events and Information	Remarks and references to Appendices
			[illegible]	SHEET 27
			[illegible] with [illegible] [illegible] them	[illegible]
JAN TER BIEZEN	OCT 13		Regt owing to [illegible] [illegible]	
			could be [illegible]	[illegible]
ON MOVE	14		Brigade moved to AUBIGNY [illegible]	
			[illegible] CAMBLAIN L'ABBE	
			[illegible] officers and [illegible] OR [illegible]	
			the first train to [illegible]	
			transport left ROAD CAMP at 8.30 am [illegible]	
			at 10am [illegible] HOPOUTRE SIDING [illegible]	
			[illegible] taken [illegible]	
			a Battn. [illegible] the Company entrained for	
			LIGNY AU FAUCHELLES (LENS 11) [illegible]	
			at about 5pm the Coy [illegible]	[illegible]
			[illegible] the [illegible]	

(A7092). Wt. W12839/M1293. 750,000. 1/17. D. D. & L., Ltd. Forms/C.2118/14.

Instructions regarding War Diaries and Intelligence Summaries are contained in F. S. Regs., Part II. and the Staff Manual respectively. Title pages will be prepared in manuscript.

WAR DIARY
or
INTELLIGENCE SUMMARY.
(Erase heading not required.)

Army Form C. 2118.

Place	Date	Hour	Summary of Events and Information	Remarks and references to Appendices
EN ROUTE TO JAN-TER BIEZEN	OCT 12		The weather was very [illegible] rain fell [illegible] the march [illegible] the billeting officer [illegible] billets in barns in the [illegible] of [illegible] He had some difficulty in persuading the Camp Adjutant, though there were [illegible], that fatigued men would be better [illegible] than if they had to pitch their tents in a very muddy field on a [illegible] night. On arrival at JAN TER BIEZEN the Y.M.C.A. by arrangement with the billeting officer helped the Coy greatly by supplying hot tea & biscuits for the men on arrival, at a very moderate charge	Sh. 27 EAW

(A7092). Wt. W12839/M1293. 750,000. 1/17. D. D. & L., Ltd. Forms/C.2118/14.

Instructions regarding War Diaries and Intelligence Summaries are contained in F. S. Regs., Part II. and the Staff Manual respectively. Title pages will be prepared in manuscript.

WAR DIARY
or
INTELLIGENCE SUMMARY.
(Erase heading not required.)

Army Form C. 2118.

Place	Date	Hour	Summary of Events and Information	Remarks and references to Appendices
DAMBRE CAMP	OCT 11		~~[illegible]~~ Day spent [illegible] [illegible] up. Weather very bad	[illegible]
NEAR VLAMERTINGHE (Sheet 27)	OCT 12		1 N.C.O. [illegible] to AUBIGNY area with a Brigade Billeting party. [illegible] [illegible] [illegible] [illegible] (Sheet [illegible]) to arrange billets for the [illegible] of the first [illegible]. The party left at [illegible] one company [illegible] [illegible] [illegible] [illegible] their destination at [illegible] [illegible] [illegible] [illegible] the [illegible] [illegible] the [illegible] route they joined the company [illegible] had passed [illegible] the [illegible] [illegible]	[illegible]

(A7092). Wt. W12839/M1293. 750,000. 1/17. D. D. & L., Ltd. Forms/C.2118/14.

Army Form C. 2118.

WAR DIARY
or
INTELLIGENCE SUMMARY.
(Erase heading not required.)

Instructions regarding War Diaries and Intelligence Summaries are contained in F. S. Regs., Part II. and the Staff Manual respectively. Title pages will be prepared in manuscript.

Place	Date	Hour	Summary of Events and Information	Remarks and references to Appendices
ST JULIEN	SEPT 27 – OCT		At best [illegible] of these were returned to salvage [illegible] [illegible] 3 additional [illegible] 1 additional [illegible] was returned to salvage dump. A German [illegible] was returned to D.A.D.O.S. [illegible] fired [illegible] 27th – 10 Oct 73,850 rounds. Total casualties 1 officer wounded – 1 officer [illegible] 3 O.R. killed 20 O.R. wounded 7 O.R. [illegible] 10 O.R. sick. Not one man went sick the morning of the relief in spite of the severe time they had been through [illegible]	POELCAPPELLE 1:10000 [illegible]

Instructions regarding War Diaries and Intelligence Summaries are contained in F. S. Regs., Part II. and the Staff Manual respectively. Title pages will be prepared in manuscript.

WAR DIARY
or
INTELLIGENCE SUMMARY.
(Erase heading not required.)

Army Form C. 2118.

Place	Date	Hour	Summary of Events and Information	Remarks and references to Appendices
	SEPT 27 OCT 10		27/9 to 10/10/17 Summary. The benefits derived from the two tours of duty were that the [illegible] turned out and [illegible] was [illegible] on the part of the N.C.O. [illegible] not to 25%. Infantry carriers were found [illegible]. The establishment of [illegible] laid down was a [illegible] found to be 100% [illegible]. Work of the transport however was excellent. In spite of the condition of the ground there was no [illegible]. [illegible] was completely destroyed [illegible] Red River [illegible] [illegible] Boxes were destroyed by [illegible]	[illegible]

(A7092). Wt. W12839/M1293. 750,000. 1/17. D. D. & L., Ltd. Forms/C.2118/14.

Instructions regarding War Diaries and Intelligence Summaries are contained in F. S. Regs., Part II. and the Staff Manual respectively. Title pages will be prepared in manuscript.

WAR DIARY
or
INTELLIGENCE SUMMARY.

(Erase heading not required.)

Army Form C. 2118.

Place	Date	Hour	Summary of Events and Information	Remarks and references to Appendices
	Oct 8 (contd)		[illegible]	
			joining [illegible]	[illegible]
	Oct 9		[illegible]	
			[illegible]	
			[illegible]	
			[illegible]	
			[illegible]	
			[illegible] infantry [illegible]	
			[illegible]	
			[illegible]	
			[illegible]	
			sections withdrew [illegible]	
			[illegible]	[illegible]

Instructions regarding War Diaries and Intelligence Summaries are contained in F. S. Regs., Part II. and the Staff Manual respectively. Title pages will be prepared in manuscript.

WAR DIARY
or
INTELLIGENCE SUMMARY.
(Erase heading not required.)

Army Form C. 2118.

Place	Date	Hour	Summary of Events and Information	Remarks and references to Appendices
			LANGEMARK LINES [illegible] HUBNER (D 16 5?) [illegible] VON TIRPITZ FARM (D 7 ?). [illegible] forward [illegible] tripods and ammunition [illegible] from 143 [illegible] Coy. [illegible]	[illegible]
	OCT 8		[illegible] 30 [illegible] 8? [illegible] LANGEMARK [illegible] ALBATROS [illegible] R.F.C. 143 [illegible] R.F.C. [illegible] LANGEMARK LINE	[illegible]

(A7092). Wt. W12839/M1293. 750,000. 1/17. D. D. & L., Ltd. Forms/C.2118/14.

Army Form C. 2118.

WAR DIARY
or
INTELLIGENCE SUMMARY.
(Erase heading not required.)

Instructions regarding War Diaries and Intelligence Summaries are contained in F. S. Regs., Part II. and the Staff Manual respectively. Title pages will be prepared in manuscript.

Place	Date	Hour	Summary of Events and Information	Remarks and references to Appendices
	OCT 4	[illegible]	At 11.30 pm [illegible]	
			to the [illegible] (which they [illegible])	[illegible]
	OCT 5		[illegible]	
			[illegible] 113 [illegible]	
			REIGERSBURG CAMP (Sheet 28 H 6 d) [illegible]	
			[illegible]	[illegible]
	OCT 6		[illegible]	[illegible]
	OCT 7		[illegible] Brigade [illegible] Brigade [illegible]	
			The section (No 3) attached to 113 [illegible]	
			[illegible]	
			(C 1 R D). [illegible]	
			place [illegible]	
			2 3 [illegible] — TWEED [illegible] (C 25 1 8 7)	
			WINCHESTER FARM (D 2 a 5 3) WELLINGTON (D 2 b 2 1) ALBATROSS (D 2 d 3 3).	[illegible]
			[illegible]	

(A7092). Wt. W12839/M1293. 750,000. 1/17. D. D. & L., Ltd. Forms/C.2118/14.

Army Form C. 2118.

WAR DIARY
or
INTELLIGENCE SUMMARY.
(*Erase heading not required.*)

Instructions regarding War Diaries and Intelligence Summaries are contained in F. S. Regs., Part II. and the Staff Manual respectively. Title pages will be prepared in manuscript.

Place	Date	Hour	Summary of Events and Information	Remarks and references to Appendices
			usual until 4.30 am when the 1st half [illegible]	
			[illegible] in the front [illegible] 143rd [illegible]	
			support. Several targets were engaged [illegible]	
			[illegible] definitely knocked out [illegible]	
			[illegible] but casualties were [illegible] and [illegible]	
			killed and 7 wounded — [illegible]	
			[illegible] knocked out [illegible]	
			[illegible]	
			[illegible] 3/4 [illegible] were fired.	
			At 2.15 pm [illegible]	
			of the two [illegible] knocked [illegible]	
			7 guns on the LANGEMARK LINE. Box [illegible]	
			[illegible]	
			[illegible] to 143 Brigade [illegible]	[illegible]

(A7092). Wt. W12839/M1293. 750,000. 1/17. D. D. & L., Ltd. Forms/C.2118/14.

8

Instructions regarding War Diaries and Intelligence Summaries are contained in F. S. Regs., Part II. and the Staff Manual respectively. Title pages will be prepared in manuscript.

WAR DIARY
or
INTELLIGENCE SUMMARY.
(Erase heading not required.)

Army Form C. 2118.

Place	Date	Hour	Summary of Events and Information	Remarks and references to Appendices
	OCT 3 cont'd		We were kept [illegible] during the day [illegible] in the attack of the 143rd Inf Bde on the [illegible] morning. We [illegible] [illegible] in the 17th [illegible] to bring their battery of [illegible] [illegible] [illegible] [illegible] [illegible] [illegible] [illegible] [illegible] [illegible] [illegible]	[illegible]
	OCT 4.		at 4.30 am [illegible] passed [illegible] 143 [illegible] 143 Inf Bde. [illegible] the [illegible] was withdrawn from the line the [illegible] [illegible] [illegible] [illegible] [illegible] [illegible] [illegible] [illegible] [illegible] [illegible] [illegible] [illegible] [illegible] [illegible] line. During the night 3/4 [illegible] this was carried out [illegible]	[illegible]

(A7092). Wt. W12839/M1293. 750,000. 1/17. D. D. & L., Ltd. Forms/C.2118/14.

1

Army Form C. 2118.

WAR DIARY
or
INTELLIGENCE SUMMARY.
(*Erase heading not required.*)

Instructions regarding War Diaries and Intelligence Summaries are contained in F. S. Regs., Part II. and the Staff Manual respectively. Title pages will be prepared in manuscript.

Place	Date	Hour	Summary of Events and Information	Remarks and references to Appendices
	OCT 2ND		WINCHESTER FARM (D2 a 53) was fired on during the night 1/2 800 rounds. During this morning 4,500 rounds were fired on the same place in conjunction with the H.A. 350 rounds were fired at an E.A. Our gun position at FLORA COT (D1a23) was shelled during the ~~night~~ day – no casualties.	POELCAPPELLE 1:10000
				MWT
	OCT 3		During the night 2/3 the four guns in the front line which had had the hardest time were withdrawn two changing places one at MON DU HIBOU the other at ST JULIEN and two returning to Coy H.Q. at ALBERTA. No 4 Section took their place in the line – guns being handed over in the line. 2Lt CHERRY took over No 4 Section in the line vice 2/Lieut HUNT slightly gassed.	MWT

(A7092). Wt. W12839/M1293. 750,000. 1/17. D. D. & L., Ltd. Forms/C.2118/14.

WAR DIARY
or
INTELLIGENCE SUMMARY.
(*Erase heading not required.*)

Army Form C. 2118.

Instructions regarding War Diaries and Intelligence Summaries are contained in F. S. Regs., Part II. and the Staff Manual respectively. Title pages will be prepared in manuscript.

Place	Date	Hour	Summary of Events and Information	Remarks and references to Appendices
	OCT 1 (CONTD.)		different teams, provide runners and in their spare time employed in salvage work. During the day enemy aeroplanes were engaged 5,000 rounds were fired in all. 4,000 rounds were fired as mentioned above in conjunction with H.A. In the former case the aeroplanes were undoubtedly prevented from flying low over our lines. At 9 p.m. the company with the aid of a working party of 1/5 Gloucesters man handled 120,000 rounds from ST JULIEN to C 6 d 6 4 - about 900 yards	TO BELG ARP 1:10,000 [illegible]
	OCT 2		During the night of the 1/2 one of the 2 guns at FLORA COT was moved into position at V.[illegible]25 c 6 3. and 3,000 rounds was expended in harassing fire. At stand to machine guns fired 4,000 rounds on Enemy back areas.	[illegible]

(A7092). Wt. W12839/M1293. 750,000. 1/17. D. D. & L., Ltd. Forms/C.2118/14.

1

Instructions regarding War Diaries and Intelligence Summaries are contained in F. S. Regs., Part II. and the Staff Manual respectively. Title pages will be prepared in manuscript.

WAR DIARY
or
INTELLIGENCE SUMMARY.
(Erase heading not required.)

Army Form C. 2118.

Place	Date	Hour	Summary of Events and Information	Remarks and references to Appendices
St JULIEN (REF MAP POELCAPPELLE 1:10,000	1 OCT 1917		Company H.Qrs - Alberta (800x West of St Julien) - During the night 30 Sept/1 Oct the machine guns fired 3,000 rounds searching & traversing areas where movement had been seen. Our M.G's in the front line anticipated a quiet night. Two guns only were detailed for carrying out firing. These were connected by telephone to the [illegible] Artillery and efforts were made to co-operate with the H.A. our observers having reported that the enemy were inclined to leave concrete positions while they were being shelled. Position of these guns was C.12.d 11. During this period the infantry carriers attached [illegible] reported to Coy H.Q. Their principal work was to draw rations & carry [illegible]	[illegible]

(A7092). Wt. W12839/M1293. 750,000. 1/17. D. D. & L., Ltd. Forms/C.2118/14.

CONFIDENTIAL

Vol 21

WAR DIARY

OF

145th MACHINE GUN COMPANY.

FROM OCT: 1st 1917 TO OCT: 31st 1917.

G H Wright

CAPT. O.C. 145TH M.G. COMPANY.

Instructions regarding War Diaries and Intelligence Summaries are contained in F. S. Regs., Part II. and the Staff Manual respectively. Title pages will be prepared in manuscript.

WAR DIARY
or
INTELLIGENCE SUMMARY.
(Erase heading not required.)

Army Form C. 2118.

Place	Date	Hour	Summary of Events and Information	Remarks and references to Appendices
	Sept 29		Belt boxes were taken over. 2/Lt COUCHMAN & No2 relieved 2/Lt JOHNSON & No3. The latter returned to positions vacated by the former. This relief was not so well carried out. Casualties 1 O.R. Killed 2 O.R. gassed. [illegible initials]	
	30.		Nothing to report in line. [illegible initials]	
			4,500 rounds – with some tracer fired at hostile aircraft at night. [illegible initials]	
			[illegible signature] Lieut. for O.C. 145 M.G. Coy.	

(A7092). Wt. W12839/M1293. 750,000. 1/17. D. D. & L., Ltd. Forms/C.2118/14.

Instructions regarding War Diaries and Intelligence Summaries are contained in F. S. Regs., Part II. and the Staff Manual respectively. Title pages will be prepared in manuscript.

WAR DIARY
or
INTELLIGENCE SUMMARY.
(Erase heading not required.)

Army Form C. 2118.

Place	Date	Hour	Summary of Events and Information	Remarks and references to Appendices
			The night was quiet – Coy H.Q. was at ALBERTA (C 11 c). The flanks were well guarded.	
			The guns in the front line were in position in shell holes – houses were non existent. [initials]	
Line.	Sept 28		2/Lt CHERRY relieved 2 guns of 32nd M.G. Coy at FLORA COT (D 1 a)	
			A counter attack was feared on the right and the artillery fire on both sides was heavy. Arrangements to meet this were – The R. BERKS were in reserve and ready to counter attack if necessary – 2/Lt SALMON with 2 guns was placed under orders of O.C. R. BERKS.	
			One of the Coy guns was knocked out.	
			2nd Lieut JOHNSON took bearings on 3 enemy M.G. guns which were dealt with by our heavies. [initials]	
	29.		Line fairly quiet. Our artillery very active.	
			2/Lt SALMON & No 1 Section relieved 2/Lt HUNT and numbers 4 Section – the latter returned to the CANAL BANK.	

Army Form C. 2118.

WAR DIARY
or
INTELLIGENCE SUMMARY.
(Erase heading not required.)

Instructions regarding War Diaries and Intelligence Summaries are contained in F. S. Regs., Part II. and the Staff Manual respectively. Title pages will be prepared in manuscript.

Place	Date	Hour	Summary of Events and Information	Remarks and references to Appendices
CLERQUES BRIELEN LINE (Poelcappelle) 1.10.000 Edition A	Sept 27th		No 4 Section moved to CANAL BANK Guns Remainder of Company & transport left CLERQUES at 3am and marched to ARDRUICQ where it entrained & proceeded to BRIELEN BELGIUM No 4 Section under 2/Lt W.V. HUNT proceeded to the line and relieved 2 Guns of 215 M.G. Coy at STROPPE FARM (D1d) and 2 Guns of 215 M.G. Coy at VON TIRPITZ. (D7b) 2 Guns under 2/Lt JOHNSON relieved 2 Guns of 198 M.G. Coy at HUBNER FARM. (D1c) 2/Lt COUCHMAN & 4 Guns took up positions as follows 2 guns at JEWS HILL (C12d) 1 ARTILLERY HOUSE (C12 & 34) and 1 at MON DU HIBOU (C6c) 2/Lt SALMON & 4 Guns took up 2 positions in CANOPUS TRENCH (C17) and 1 at ALBERTA (C11c) and 1 at REGINA CROSS (C11a) Belt Boxes were taken over - [illegible] was well carried out [illegible]	

(A7092). Wt. W12839/M1293. 750,000. 1/17. D. D. & L., Ltd. Forms/C.2118/14.

Instructions regarding War Diaries and Intelligence Summaries are contained in F. S. Regs., Part II. and the Staff Manual respectively. Title pages will be prepared in manuscript.

WAR DIARY
or
INTELLIGENCE SUMMARY.
(Erase heading not required.)

Army Form C. 2118.

Place	Date 1917	Hour	Summary of Events and Information	Remarks and references to Appendices
CLERQUES	Sept 21		Nos 1, 3 & 4 Sections training under section officers. No 2 section & No 1 carried out scheme as on the 17th inst on the field firing range.	SHW
	Sept 22		Church parade only.	SHW
	Sept 23		No 4 & 1st Sections Field firing scheme as on the 21st. Remainder of company on 30 yards range with rifles, revolvers & guns.	SHW
	Sept 24		Nos 1 & 2 Sections Field firing on the range as on the 21st. Remainder of company on 30 yards range with rifles, revolvers & guns.	
			No 4 section's transport started by road ~~for BRIELEN - BELGIUM~~ ~~Pass~~ to A 22 d 8.8 (Sheet 28 BELGIUM & FRANCE)	SHW
	Sept 25		No 4 Section entrained at AUDRUICQ and proceeded to BRIELEN - BELGIUM where they came under the orders of the 58th Division. The remainder of the company carried on with training.	SHW
	Sept 26		6 limbers left at 3am destination RESEL HOEK - BELGIUM. 1, 2 & 3 Sections training. Orders came that we were to proceed to BRIELEN.	SHW

(A7092). Wt. W12839/M1293. 750,000. 1/17. D. D. & L., Ltd. Forms/C.2118/14.

Army Form C. 2118.

WAR DIARY
or
INTELLIGENCE SUMMARY.
(Erase heading not required.)

Instructions regarding War Diaries and Intelligence Summaries are contained in F. S. Regs., Part II. and the Staff Manual respectively. Title pages will be prepared in manuscript.

Place	Date 1917	Hour	Summary of Events and Information	Remarks and references to Appendices
CLERQUES.	Sept 17.		Two sections were trained in Elementry drill, and some firing on a 30 yards range was carried out. During this period i.e. up to the 25th inst. the company was generally employed in tactical schemes with Battalions, Brigade or Division, when not on these schemes attention was paid principally to Elementry Drill. Two sections were employed in a Field firing scheme firing live rounds. two guns at a time gave supporting overhead fire to Infantry companies practising the attack	[illegible]
	Sept 18		The whole Company practised the attack with the Brigade, pack animals were used, and all men carried full loads	[illegible]
	Sept 19.		A light days work. Elementry drill & Lectures.	[illegible]
	Sept 20.		A Scheme practiced with the Brigade. 145th Brigade defended an area which was attacked by two other Brigades of the Division, our guns were put in defensive positions	[illegible]

(A7092). Wt. W12839/M1293. 750,000. 1/17. D. D. & L., Ltd. Forms/C.2118/14.

Instructions regarding War Diaries and Intelligence Summaries are contained in F. S. Regs., Part II. and the Staff Manual respectively. Title pages will be prepared in manuscript.

WAR DIARY
or
INTELLIGENCE SUMMARY.
(Erase heading not required.)

Army Form C. 2118.

Place	Date 1917	Hour	Summary of Events and Information	Remarks and references to Appendices
ROAD CAMP ST JAN DER BIEZEN BELGIUM	Sept 14		As on the 9th six limbers left for CLERQUES a village about 12	
	~~[illegible]~~		miles WEST of ST. OMER, FRANCE	
	Sept 15		The remainder of the company entrained at PROVEN leaving there at 2 pm and arriving at AUDRUICQ at 11.30 pm. The men had no proper meal during the day except breakfast, so on arrival at AUDRUICQ arrangements were made with the SALVATION ARMY hut there for tea &c. a very good meal was arranged at a very moderate price.	
CLERQUES a village about 12 miles WEST of ST. OMER FRANCE	Sept 16		All the company arrived in CLERQUES and were in their billets – which were very comfortable barns and lofts for the men, except for the transport men, these had to bivouac in the open, as the weather was fine and warm however it was not a great inconvenience – at 6 am. The day was spent in resting. In the evening the officers reconnoitred the training area. This proved to be very good ample room for range work and manoeuvring	

(A7092). Wt. W12839/M1293. 750,000. 1/17. D. D. & L., Ltd. Forms/C.2118/14.

Army Form C. 2118.

Instructions regarding War Diaries and Intelligence Summaries are contained in F. S. Regs., Part II. and the Staff Manual respectively. Title pages will be prepared in manuscript.

WAR DIARY
or
INTELLIGENCE SUMMARY.
(*Erase heading not required.*)

Place	Date	Hour	Summary of Events and Information	Remarks and references to Appendices
	1917			
ROAD CAMP	7th		Training as on the 3rd.	
ST JAN	8th		Sunday Church Parade	
DER BIEZEN - BELGIUM	9th		Training for two sections as on the 3rd inst. Two sections per day for a period up to the 16th inst. carried out schemes. The average scheme — 145 I.B. supposed to be attacking and M Gs were ordered to consolidate on a certain line. Teams had to carry full loads. Section Officers & Sergeants had to work out angles, and see that the fire of their guns crossed with the fire of the guns on their flanks; & team commanders had to prepare sketches & range cards. Barrage drill and 30 yards range work carried out	HWS
	10th		do	HWS
	11th		do	HWS
	12th		do	HWS
	13th		do	HWS

(A7092). Wt. W12839/M1293. 750,000. 1/17. D. D. & L., Ltd. Forms/C.2118/14.

Instructions regarding War Diaries and Intelligence Summaries are contained in F. S. Regs., Part II. and the Staff Manual respectively. Title pages will be prepared in manuscript.

WAR DIARY
or
INTELLIGENCE SUMMARY.
(Erase heading not required.)

Army Form C. 2118.

145 Machine Gun Coy.

Place	Date	Hour	Summary of Events and Information	Remarks and references to Appendices
ROAD CAMP	1917			
ST JAN DER BIEZEN	Sept 1		Period of training commenced. Cleaning up gun equipment	SHW
	2		Fine weather. The whole Brigade paraded for C of E service on field N of ROAD CAMP	SHW
	3		Training continued. The parades for the day were the average for a period up to the 8th inst. Reveille 6.30 am. Breakfast 7 Dinners 12.30 pm. Teas 4.30 pm. 7.45 – 8.15 PHYSICAL TRAINING. 8.40 – 9.15 am. Inspection & home gas drill & how, snapping rifles & revolvers 9.15 am to 12.15 pm. Elementary drill. 2 to 2.30 CEREMONIAL drill 2.30 to 3 pm Lecture on range cards. 3 to 4 pm Football.	SHW
	4th		Training on the same lines as above. Two guns mounted each night as an "anti aircraft" subsection.	SHW
	5th		Training as on the 3rd.	SHW
	6th		do.	SHW

(A7092). Wt. W12839/M1293. 750,000. 1/17. D. D. & L., Ltd. Forms/C.2118/14.

Vol 20

CONFIDENTIAL

WAR DIARY

OF

145th MACHINE GUN COMPANY.

FROM Sept 1st 1917 To Sept 30th 1917.

[signature] O.C.
145 M.G. Coy.

INDIRECT OVERHEAD FIRE.

No............M.G. Coy. No............Section. Date.................................. Map used.................................. Officer i/c Firing..................................

ELEVATION.								CLEARANCE OVER OWN TROOPS.					DIRECTION.	REMARKS.			
Gun No.	Target.	Range to Target in Yards	Contours in Yards: Gun A	Contours in Yards: Target	V.I. in Yards	Q.E. in Minutes — Table 3 (A) or 3 (B)	Range for Q.E. in Yards — Table 1, Col. 2	Contour of own troops in Yards B	Range to own troops in Yards	Traj. Height in Yards — Table 2 C	Clearance obtained by Note (1) below	Clearance required in Yards	Compass Bearing or D.D. Reading	Time of firing	No. of rounds fired	Checked by	General.
1 4	D.i.b 30	2300	15	15		360	2300						46 - 49 49 - 52				
5 8	V25.c635	2200	15	15		322	2200						52 - 55 55 - 59				
1 4	D.i.b 30 50	2400	15	15		401	2400						45 - 48 48 - 51				
5 8	V25c 8060	2300	15	15		360	2300						51 - 54 54 - 58				
1 4	D.i.b 30 50	2600	15	15		496	2600						48 - 51 51 - 54				
5 8	V25d 2575		15	15		496	2600	–	1860	155	155	80	54 - 57 57 - 60				

NOTES.—(1) CLEARANCE in yards = A – B plus or minus C according as trajectory tables give positive or negative values of C.
(2) IMMEDIATELY before firing Q.E. must be corrected, if necessary, for atmospheric influences. SEE TABLE 5.
(3) For lateral wind allowance. SEE TABLE 4.
(4) If obstruction exists between gun and target, and its highest point cannot be seen, ascertain if shots will clear by substituting "obstruction" for "own troops" in clearance columns above, and find clearance by rule in NOTE (1). Minimum clearance required equals half height of cone for range to obstruction.

C.O. Company will be at HILL TOP at ZERO and proceeds to CHEDDER VILLA just before ZERO plus 5 hours.
Company H.Q. will be at CORNER COP (Reserve gunners will be the

7. The closest touch will be kept with the Infantry and especially with Battalion Commanders.

INSTRUCTIONS AND ADMINISTRATIVE ORDERS TO FOLLOW.

Issued at 3.20 a.m.

[signature] Lieut.,
for Commanding 145 M.G. Company.

Copies to:-
1. 145 Inf. Bde.
2. G.O.C. 48th. Divn.
3-7 Officers.
8. File
9-10 War Diary.
11 215 M.G. Company (for information.)

APPENDIX. N° 9.

[illegible]. Copy No. 2...

145th Machine Gun Company Order No 7/1.

26:8:17.

Ref. Special Map (POELCAPPELLE Edn. 1.)

1. [illegible] and 2 Sections under Lieuts [illegible] and [illegible], respectively, will be known as "A" Battery.
Lieut. Moss will command the battery.
The battery will move to positions in rear of concrete dugout at [illegible] 18 c 00.35. on the night 26/27 August, and dig in.

2. From ZERO to ZERO plus 25 mins. the battery will fire "F" barrage
From ZERO plus 35 mins. to ZERO plus 3 hrs. 30 mins. "G" barrage
From ZERO plus 3hrs. 30 mins to ZERO plus 4 hrs 30 mins. upon the S.O.S. line (D 1 b 90.65. to V 25 d 4 .4.)
And again from ZERO plus 5 hrs 5 mins to ZERO plus 5 hours 25 mns.
This completes the barrages.
If, however, the S.O.S. is sent up the battery will open fire upon the S.O.S. line.
Fire table herewith to those concerned.
The battery will receive orders from Divn. as to their disposal on completion of their task.

3. (a) No 3 Section will advance from the Assembly positions to be notified later) with the reserve company of the OXFORDS.
Nos 9 & 10 guns will be under 2nd Lieut KING and Nos 11 & 12 unde Sergt. SIMS. They will take up positions as follows:-
NO 9 GUN (approx) D 1 a 55.85. -- Direction of fire N.W. down the STROOMBEEK VALLEY, with an alternative line of fire in the direction of the cemetery (V 25 c).
NO 10 GUN.(approx)D 1 c 5.8. -- Direction of fire due East.up the STROOMBEEK VALLEY, with an alternative direction due North.
(b) NOS 11 & 12 GUNS under Sergt SIMS will move to dugouts (appr) at D 1 c 65.40.) No 11 Gun will fire in a northerly direction across the front of the DOTTED BLUE LINE. No 12 Gun will fire in a south easterly direction across the front of the DOTTED BLUE LN Both these guns will be prepared to bring fire to bear upon a series of dugouts in D 1 d .
(c) When 2nd Lieut. KING and SERGT SIMS ~~Have~~ have got into touch 2nd Lieut KING will again take over the charge of four guns.

4. No 4 Section will move up, Nos 13 and 14 Guns under 2nd. Lieut COUCHMAN, Nos 15 and 16 guns under Sergt. MORGAN, from assembly positions (to be notified later) with the reserve company of the BERKS. The following positions will be taken up:-
(b) No 13 GUN to dugout at D 7 b 20.61. --Direction of fire N.
NO 14 GUN to dugout at D 7 b 10.63. This gun will deal with the right flank. Special attention is to be paid to VALE HOUSE (D 7b
(c) NOS 15 and 16 guns to dugout at D 7 b 35.40. These guns will also deal with the right flank. Special attention will be paid to line of dugouts running from approx. D 7 b 50.55. to D 7 b 80.33. and to the trench in D 8 a east of(CLIFTON HOUSE)

(d) When 2nd Lieut COUCHMAN and Sergt MORGAN have got into touch 2nd Lieut COUCHMAN will take over the command of the four guns.
(e) The right flank of the BERKS cannot be supported too much by machine guns, very strict attention must be paid to it. The dugouts and trench to which guns have been alloted to pay attention to are of a dangerous nature, as the enemy might possibly form up there for a counter-attack. The high ground on the right will, likewise be watched.

5. Officers who consider that the situation demands a change in the dispositions of the guns are at perfect liberty to carry out what they think best.

/ [illegible]

APPENDIX 8

145 M.G. Company Order No. 7. Copy No. 10

Ref. Special Map (POELCAPPELLE Edn. 8.) 25:8:17.

1. The Division, with 61st Divn. on the right and the 11 Divn. on the left will attack on 27th August.

2. ZERO will be notified later and will be in daylight.

3. The 143 Inf. Bde on the right and 144 Inf. Bde on the left will push forward and capture the DOTTED RED LINE which runs east of the LANGEMARCK LINE.

4. This Brigade will attack at ZERO plus 5 hours the third objective (DOTTED BLUE) line of farms--VON TIRPITZ (D 7 d) -- STROPPE (D 1 c) -- HUBNER (D 1 c).

5. For these attacks the left Divn. will deal with VIEILLES MAISONS (J 6 b) and FLORA COT (D 1 a), and trenches joining these places. On the night 23/28 August the Brigade will take over the normal boundary.

6. The Brigade will be in Divisional reserve during the attack by 143 and 144 Brigades.

7. The Brigade will attack as follows:-

ASSAULTING BATTALIONS.) R.BERKS on the right.
----------------------) OXFORDS on the left.
RESERVE BATTALIONS.) GLOSTERS on the right.
----------------------) BUCKS on the left.

The dividing line between the Battalions will be (approx) an imaginary line drawn from SPRINGFIELD (J 12 b) to a point mid-way between GENOA (D 1 c) and STROPPE FARM (D 1 c).

8. All objectives will be consolidated and held.

9. The Brigade will consolidate the Objective as an Outpost line of resistance, as specially sited and prepared for a further advance.

10. The main line of resistance is being consolidated on the GHELUVELT-LANGEMARCK LINE.
A second line on the WINNIPEG-LANGEMARCK ROAD.

11. The Brigade will make strong points at VON TIRPITZ FARM (D 7 b) --STROPPE FARM (D 1 c) -- HUBNER FARM (D 1 c).

12. The R.BERKS and OXFORDS will move to the Assembly Positions, east of the STEENBEEK, (from the CANAL BANK) arriving between ZERO plus 3 hours and ZERO plus 4 hours.

13. Should the Assaulting Brigades not reach their Objectives 145 Inf. Bde will be prepared to assist. Too much detail cannot be laid down with regard to this, it will be purely a matter for those on the spot to use their own initiative.

14. Four tanks have been alloted to the 48th. Division.

15. No 4 Section will be attached to the R.BERKS and No. 3 Section to the OXFORDS. No ~~secret~~ barrage maps, notes on operations will taken forward by Officers or O.R.s with these two sections. Nos 1 and 2 Sections will carry out barrage work.

16. BRIGADE REPORT CENTRE HILL TOP AT ZERO, CHEDDER VILLA at ZERO 5
BATTALION COMMAND POSTS. R.BERKS . Concrete dugout C 12 C 45.85 on the St. Julien-Poelcappelle Road.
OXFORDS. Concrete dugout C 6 c 8.2. about 100 yards S.E. of MON DU HIBOU.

Issued at....
Distribution:-
1-2 War Diary. 3-8 Coy. Officers. 9 File.
10 215 M.G.Company (For information.)

[signature] Lieut.,
for Comdg. 145 M.G.Company.

3. "E" Battery will, if the situation permits, salve belt boxes left by 117 M.G. Coy, in their present positions.
In the event of a lull by our artillery the Battery will open fire on suspected hostile battery positions with a view to preventing the guns from being withdrawn.
The ten belt boxes brought forward will be used for repelling counter-attacks.

4. REPORTS. Positions will be marked on maps supplied and the detailed questions set down on the back of the aforesaid maps will be answered. These reports will be rendered immediately positions are taken up.

(Signed) G.A.WEBB. Lieut.,
for Captain.,
Comdg. 145th M.G. Company.

Issued at ...... 8 p.m.

Copies to.
1-2 War Diary.
3-6 Sections.
7. 145th Inf: Brigade.
8. D.M.G.O. 48th Divn.
9-10 Spare.

APPENDIX No 7.

SECRET. Copy No.......... .

145th M.G. Company Order No.5/1.

14.8.17.

Reference. POELCAPPELLE. 1:10,000. (Edition 5).

1. (a) "F" Battery.

2/Lieut. INWOOD and 13 & 14 guns will at zero minus two hours be in position in the vicinity and south of ALBERTA (C 11 c).
He will advance with the fourth wave of the Gloucesters as far as the GREEN LINE, at this point he will drop about 200 yds. behind the fourth wave. He will arrive at the PINK LINE at zero plus 1 hour 40 minutes and dig in with a view of repelling counter-attacks.
One gun will be at D 7 a 65(approx), and the other gun at D 7 a 17 (approx). The field of fire of the latter gun should be true north.

(b) 2/Lieut. SELBIE and 15 & 16 guns will at zero minus two hours take up position in rear of the fourth wave of the Bucks approx: position ALBERTA (C 11 c).
He will advance with the fourth wave of the Bucks and proceed to dugouts in the immediate north of SPRINGFIELD (C 12 b).
He will be prepared to cover the left flank of our right attack or fill any gap by bringing fire to bear on it.
At zero plus 50 minutes he will proceed to take up new positions. One gun at C 6 d 62.(approx) firing south-east along the OLD GERMAN LINE.
The other will take up position at C 6 b 73.

(c) 2/Lieut. CLUTTON and No.3 Section will be in Brigade reserve with the Berks. He will be at approximately C 11 d central by zero minus two hours.
He will move with the rear party of the Berks as far as HILLOCK FARM (C 12 a central) and await further orders.

"E" Battery.

2. (a) "E" Battery will move forward not earlier then zero plus 30 minutesand not later than zero plus four hours. The officers will choose the best moment for getting through the enemy barrage.
The officers of "E" Battery will reconnoitre positions for their guns while they (the guns) are coming forward.
2/Lieut. TAUNTON, (on the left), with ~~five~~ three guns rendezvous at HILLOCK FARM (C 12 a central) and move to positions to be reconnoitred by him.
Three guns to be in concrete dugouts immediately north of SPRINGFIELD FARM (C 12 b central).
These guns will cover the GREEN LINE.
Two guns will be at MON DU HIBOU (C 6 c 14.) (Capt Jeffreys)

(b) Lieut. ORCHARD will advance with three guns to JANET FARM (C 12 b 44). He will reconnoitre positions for two guns in the vicinity of C 12 d 98, and for one gun at WINNEPEG. (D 7 c 28).

(c) All the guns in (b) and the guns at MON DU HIBOU (a) will cover their respective flanks.

APPENDIX I

COMMUNICATION.

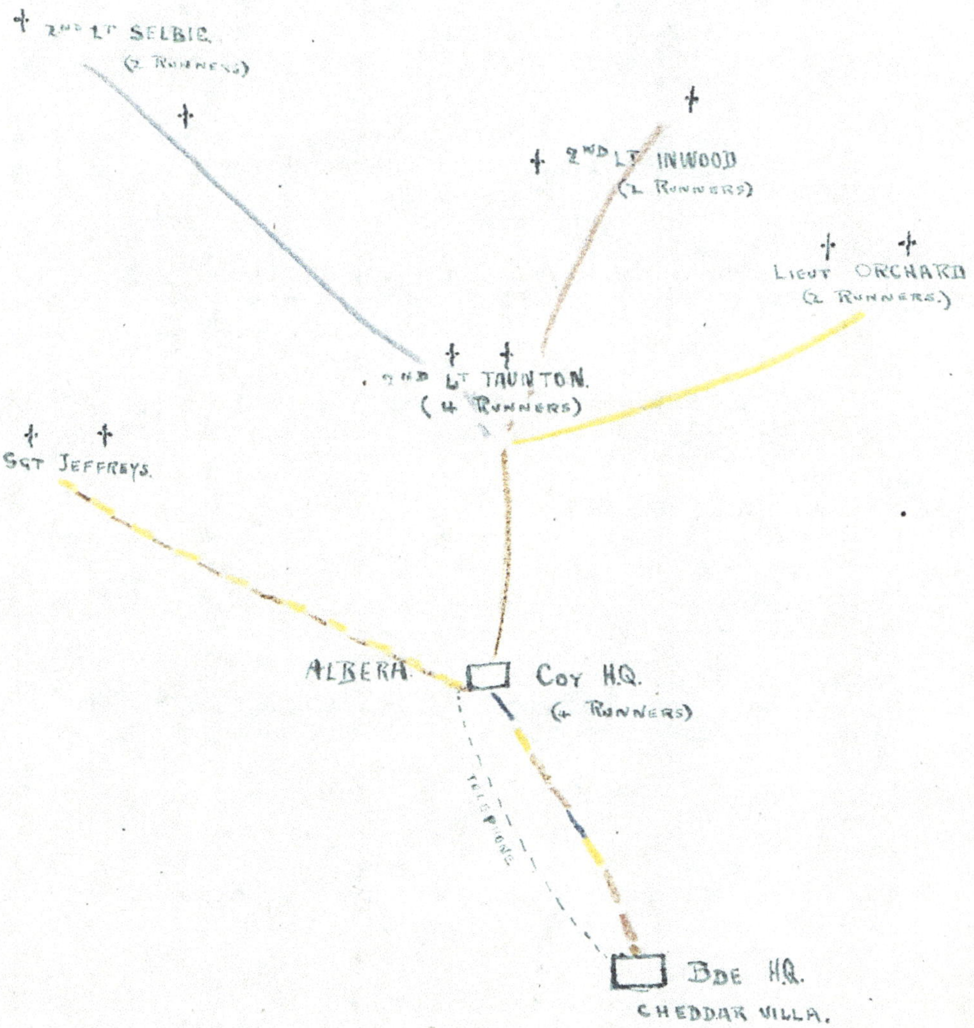

ISSUED WITH ADMINISTRATIVE ORDERS
IN CONJUNCTION WITH.
145 M.G.Coy O.O. No 5.

SECRET. Copy No.1 ....

145th M.G. Company Order No.5. Administrative Orders.

15.8.17.

1. RATIONS & WATER. Rations for consumption on "Z" Day will be carried by the ½ Coy. proceeding to the line to-day on the man and in bulk for the ½ Company now in the line.
The bulk "Z" Days rations will be taken up on the gun limbers.

RATIONS & WATER FOR CONSUMPTION ON "Z" PLUS 1 DAY will be made up as follows:-
20 bags of 4 complete rations, marked "4 MEN".
1 bag of 7 rations marked O.C.,
1 bag of 7 rations marked Lieut. TAUNTON.
The remainder in bulk.
Water and the above will be taken up on pack ponies on "Z" Day to C 17 b 5.2. (where CANOPUS TRENCH cuts the road.)
The C.S.M will distribute the rations at this point.

2. Officers and Sergt. Jefferys will retain requisite number of r runners and will return the remainder of the carriers to ALBERTA on completion of duties.
Lieut. ORCHARD will, however, send his surplus to dugouts in CANOPUS TRENCH vacated by him.
Lieut. ORCHARD will send his report to CANOPUS where the N.C.O in charge (to be detailed later,) will be responsible that message is forwarded to Coy. H.Q. at ALBERTA.

3. RESERVE GUNNERS will be at the disposal of the C.O. at Coy.H.Q. Officers will indent on him to replace casualties.

4. MEDICAL ARRANGEMENTS.
Right half................Relay post ....C 22 c 25.
Left half................Relay post.....C 16 d 25.
Corps Walking wounded ....H 3 d 5 8.
Advcd. Dressing Station................C 25 b 30.
Bearer post............................C 21 c 42.
Lines of Evacuation
Right half road through CHEDDAR VILLA.(C 17 c 70.
Left half Duckboard Track to BUFF ROAD.

5. R.E. DUMP is at C 17 d 52.

6. Officers will report their arrival at assembly positions to Coy. H.Q.

7. LOADS. Team Commr. Verey lights, Verey Pistol, spare parts case, cleaning rod. No.1. Gun. No.2. Tripod. No.3. Petrol tins with water, belt box and condenser. 3 carriers 3 belt boxes each. Officers batmen 2shovels. Sergt. Jefferys 2 shovels.

8. DRESS: Fighting order, 2 sandbags per man. Biscuit and cheese ration and "Z" days rations.

9. AMMUNITION. Indents will be sentto Coy. H.Q.

10. COMMUNICATION. See Appendix I attached.
Issued at 1.30 a.m.

(Signed) G.A.WEBB. Lt.,
for O.C., 145th M.G. Company.

Copies to
1-2 War Diary. 6. C.S.M.
3. Lt. INWOOD. 7. C.Q.M.S.
4. Lt. SELBIE. 8. Lt. TAUNTON.
5. Lt. CLUTTON. 9. Lt. ORCHARD.
10. Spare.

6. Company H.Q. will be at ALBERTA (C 11 c).
Brigade H.Q. will be at CHEDDAR VILLA (C 17 c 05).

7. Action in detail and administrative arrangements to follow.

(Signed) G.H.WRIGHT, Capt.,
O.C., 145th M.G. Company.

Copies to
1-2 War Diary.
3-6 Sections.
7. 145th Inf: Bde.
8. D.M.G.O. 48th Div.
9. Spare.

APPENDIX No 6

SECRET.

Copy No..............

145th M.G. Company Order No.5.

Ref: POELCAPPELLE. 1:10,000 (Edition 5)

In the Field.
12.8.17.

1. (a) The Brigade will attack on Z day.
(b) The Brigade will capture two objectives, and will push out an outpost line in front of the second objective, map attached.
(c) The enemy counter-attack may be expected in 3 to 4 hours ~~in~~ time.
(d(109th Brigade will be on the right, and 34th Brigade on the left.
(e) The Brigade will attack on a 3 Battn. front: Right to Left - Gloucesters - Bucks - Oxfords. The Royal Berks will be in reserve.
(f) The first waves will deploy E of the STEENBEEKE, covered by the 143rd Brigade.
(g) 1st WAVE will deal with the line of gun-pits and farms W of LANGMARCK & WINNEPEG ROAD.
2nd WAVE. at zero plus 35 will capture GREEN LINE.

A pause of 20 minutes on theright and 1 hour 55 mins. on the left will follow, during which there will be smoke barrages.

3rd & 4th WAVES will deal with PINK & BLUE LINES.
The right flank will attack pink and blue lines at zero plus 1 hour 20 minutes.
The left flank will attack pink and blue lines at zero plus 3 hours.

When the right moves forward the Bucks will form a defensive flank on the SHORT GREEN & DOTTED RED LINE.

The 3rd WAVE will actually take the DOTTED BLUE LINE.
The 4th WAVE will consolidate the PINK LINE.

(h) In the PINK LINE four strong points will be made from Right to Left:- BERKS FORT - GLOUCESTER FORT - BUCKS FORT - OXFORD FORT.

2. Nos. 1 & 2 sections (now in the line) will be known as "E" Battery.
"E" Battery will move forward and consolidate the ground in and behind the GREEN LINE.

3. The remaining 8 guns. (Nos.3 & 4 sections) will be known as "F" Battery, and will be at the disposal of the G.O.C.

4. The four strong points in the pink line will have 1 Vickers gun each. The guns will move in rear of the 4th wave.
The Bucks Fort may be employed temporarily for the defence of the temporary line formed by the Bucks.

5. Reserve Section with the Berks will move to vicinity of HILLOCK FARM (C 12 a central.) Point to be selected by 2/Lieut. CLUTTON.

/6. Company H.Q.

APPENDIX NO 5

SECRET. Copy No.............

145th M.G. Company Order No.8. 15.8.17

1. The half Company will move, less Transport, H.Q. details and the 35%, to the line today.
The half Company will parade at 11.20 a.m. in full fighting order and proceed in two stages.
The half Company will pass the starting point H 3 d 37½ at 11.52 and proceed by SLEEPER ROAD and road running N.E. through H 6 b and proceed to REIGERSBURG CAMP (H 6 b) where it will remain until 11 p.m.

2. 2/Lieut. Hugman, Corpl. Geary and Pte. Rowland will meet the Staff Captain at Bde. H.Q. at 10.20 a.m.

3. At 11 p.m. the Company will cross the CANAL 100 yards in rear of the 14th Royal Berks for moving into the line.
ROUTE. Trench board track to road C 25 c 83, down LONG ROAD to Southern track at I 1 b 27.

4. Two cooks will accompany the ½ Company to REIGERSBURG CAMP returning after tea.

5. Further details will follow.
A special map is issued herewith to Transport Officer.

Issued at 1 a.m.

(Signed) G.A.WEBB, Lieut.,
for O.C., 145th M.G. Company.

Copies to
1-2 War Diary.
3 Transport Officer.
4. Lt. INWOOD.
5. Lt. SALBIS.
6. Lt. CLUFTON.
7. C.S.M.

APPENDIX NO 4

SECRET. Copy No...1.....

145th M.G. Company Operation Order No.4.

11.3.17.

Ref: Trench Map, St. JULIEN 28. N.W. 2.

1.
RELIEF. Nos. 1 & 2 Sections will relieve Nos. 3 & 4.
One Sergeant, two team commanders and six men will relieve two teams at REGINA CROSS.

2/Lieut. LAUGHTON, batman, two runners (attached men) three team commanders and nine men will relieve 2/Lt. CLUTTON and three guns at ALBERTA.

Lieut. ORCHARD, batman, two runners, three team commanders and nine men will relieve 2/Lt. INWOOD and three guns at CANOPUS TRENCH.

2.
TIME. Relief will take place tomorrow 12th as soon after dusk as possible.
Party will leave transport lines at 3 p.m.

3.
RESERVE PARTY.
A reserve of 1 N.C.O, three gunners and two runners will be at the disposal of O.C., 143rd M.G. Company.
These men are not to be used for any severe work, and are there solely with the object of replacing casualties.
The N.C.O. and men will report to O.C., 143 M.G. Coy, at HILL TOP dugouts.

4.
TACTICAL REPORTS.
Tactical reports will be made to O.C., 143 M.G. Company, and orders will be taken from him.

5. Relief complete will be reported to O.C., 143 M.G. Company at HILL TOP, and to O.C., 145th M.G. Company on arrival at transport lines.

6. The 2nd i/c will arrange that the returning party has hot food and a rum ration on arrival.

7. Rations and water will be brought up with the teams. The rations and water will be sent up afterwards to C 21 b 68.
(N.B. Empty petrol tins must be returned.)

8. TRANSPORT. One limber will accompany the two sections.

9.
TAKING OVER. Guns, stores, etc., will be taken over, receipts are not required, but a careful examination of all stock is to be made.

10.
GUIDES. Guides will not be required.

(Signed) G.H. WRIGHT., Captain,
O.C., 145th M.G. Company.

Copies to
1-2 War Diary. ✓
3. O.C., 143M.G. Coy.
4-7 Sections.
8 Transport Officer.
9 File.

1:10 000 PILKEM. POSITIONS OF GUNS AUG 5TH – AUG 8TH

APPENDIX No 3

APPENDIX NO 2.

SECRET.

Copy No....9....

145th M.G. Company Order No.5.

Ref: French Map. St. JULIEN 28. N.W. 2. 7.8.17.

1.

RELIEFS. Nos. 3 & 4 sections under 2/Lts CLUTTON & INWOOD will relieve Nos. 1 & 2 sections under 2/Lt. SELBIE and Lt. ORCHARD.

1 N.C.O and 4 men (spare runners) and 4 runners will relieve those now at Company H.Q.

The relief will take place on the 8th August. The runner at CANAL BANK will remain in "statu quo".

The above party will parade at 1.30 p.m. the 8th inst, and will proceed to ZOUAVE VILLA (C 30 c 71).

Two cooks will accompany this party, and make teas on arrival at ZOUAVE VILLA.

2.

GUIDES. One guide per team and one Company H.Q. guide will be at ZOUAVE VILLA at 6 p.m.

3.

DISTRIBUTION.

Nos. 9 & 10 teams under Sgt. O'NEILL will relieve Nos. 1 & 2 teams under Sgt. JEFFERY at REGINA CROSS ROADS (C 11 a 87.)

Nos. 11, 12 & 13 teams under 2/Lt. CLUTTON will relieve Nos. 3, 4 & 5 teams under 2/Lt. SELBIE at ALBERTA (C 11 c 87.)

Nos. 14, 15 & 16 teams under 2/Lt. INWOOD will relieve Nos. 6, 7 & 8 teams under Lt. ORCHARD in the vicinity of CORNER COT. (C 17 b 64.)

4.

RATIONS & WATER.

Rations will if possible be taken with the sections. If impossible they will be at Cross Roads (C 22 c 68), at the usual time. Water will be taken with the sections.

5.

TRANSPORT. One limber will accompany the two sections.

6.

HANDING OVER. Guns, tripods, etc., will be handed over, as well as all trench stores. Receipts will be handed in to O.R. by noon the 9th inst.

7.

S.A.A. DUMPS.

ALBERTA (C 11 c 88).

COMPANY H.Q. (C 16 c 58.)

8.

COMPANY H.Q. Company H.Q. will be at C 16 c 58.

ISSUED AT 8 a.m.

(Signed) G.A.WEBB. Lieut.,
for O.C., 145th M.G. Company.

Copies to:
1. D.M.G.O.
2. O.C. Company.
3. No.1 Section.
4. No.2 "
5. No.3 "
6. No.4 "
7. Transport Officer.
8-9 War Diary.

RATIONS & WATER. 143 & 144 Coys. will send rations, made up for gun teams, to Q.M. Stores 145th Coy, as early as possible daily. Rations will be at Cross Roads J 22 c 6.5. each evening at 6 p.m.
Water will be brought up from billets.
Empty petrol cans MUST be returned.

10.
TRANSPORT. Transport by limber, 6 horses will be necessary.

11.
HANDING OVER. Belt boxes and Tripods will NOT be exchanged.

12.
S.A.A. DUMPS. ALBERTA J 11 c 8.8.
COY. H.Q.

ISSUED AT 11.30 pm. Lieut.,
Comdg. 145th M.G. Company.

Copies to
1. D.M.G.O. 48th Divn.
2. D.M.G.O. 88th "
3. 117th M.G. Company.
4. 228th M.G. Company.
5. 143rd. M.G. Company.
6. 144th M.G. Company.
7. 145th Inf: Brigade.
8. No.1 Section.
9. No. 2 Section.
10. Transport Officer
11-13 War Diary.

APPENDIX No I   Copy No 11

SECRET.   145th M.G. Company Order No. 3.

Ref: Trench Map St. Julien 28 N.W. 2.   4.8.17.

1.
RELIEF. 8 guns of 145th M.G. Company, 4 guns of 143rd M.G. Coy, and 4 guns of the 144th Machine Gun Company under the O.C., 145th M.G. Coy., will relieve the 117th and 228th M.G. Coys., on the 39th Divl, front on the night 5/6th.

2.
COY. H.Q. Company Headquarters will be at C 16 c 5.2. beside 145th Brigade H.Q.

3.
4 GUNS OF 145 COY, & 2 GUNS 144th COY. 2/Lt. MAY with 4 guns of 145 Company will meet two guns of 144th Company at the CHURCH ARMY HUT at the Cross roads near A 30 central (Sheet 28) at 1.30 p.m. on the 5th inst. The whole will then proceed to ESSEX FARM C 25 a 5.9. arriving there at 3 p.m.
A guide from 228th M.G. Coy., will meet him there and lead the party to Cross roads at C 22 c 3.2. where further guides supplied by the 228th Coy, will lead the teams to gun positions.
Carrying parties will be arranged later.
These 6 guns will relieve 6 guns of 228th M.G. Coy, in CAMPHOR AVENUE and CALF RESERVE (C 16 d)

4.
8 GUNS OF 145th COY. & 2 GUNS 144 COY. No.1 & 2 sections of the 145th Coy, and 2 guns of 144th Coy, under an officer, and carrying parties to be detailed later will leave 145th M.G.Coy's Transport lines at 1.30 p.m. and proceed to ZOUAVE VILLA at ~~6 p.m.~~ C 30 c 71.
Two cooks will accompany this party and arrange teas on arrival.
Team guides from 117th M.G. Company will meet these teams at ZOUAVE VILLA at 6 p.m. and proceed as far forward as possible in daylight. The ridge must not be crossed in daylight.
Nos. 1 & 2 guns of 145th Coy, under Sgt. JEFFREY will relieve 2 guns of 117th Coy, at REGINA CROSS ROADS C 11 a 6.7.
Nos. 3 4 & 5 guns of 145th Coy, under 2/Lt. SELFIS will relieve 4 guns of 117th Coy, at ALBERTA C 11 c 8.7.
Nos. 6.7 & 8 guns of 145th Coy, will, under Lt. ORCHARD relieve 4 guns of 117th Coy, in the vicinity of CORNER COT. C 17 b 6.4.
One gun of 144th Coy, will relieve 1 gun of 117th Coy, at ADAMS FARM. C 10 b 3.3.
The officer of 144th Coy. will remain at Coy. H.Q., with 1 gun
RELIEFS TO BE REPORTED ON COMPLETION TO COY. H.Q.

~~5.~~ REPORTS.
5.

6.
VERY LIGHTS, BOMBS. All teams will arrange to have VERY LIGHTS & BOMBS.

7.
COMMUNICATIONS. A runners post will be established at Dugout No. 99/ West Bank CANAL, near Bridge 6a to connect Coy.H.Q. with Transport lines and D.M.G.O.
Each officer will have two runners.

8.
RECONNAISSANCE. 2/Lt. MAY will take first opportunity to reconnoitre four positions on HALF-CORNER RIDGE, and report to Coy. H.Q. on completion.

/RATIONS & WATER.

CONFIDENTIAL

APPENDICES Nos 1 to 9.

to

WAR DIARY

of

145 Machine Gun Company

From 1st August to 31st August 1917.

2nd Sept 1917.

Vol 19

CONFIDENTIAL

WAR DIARY

— OF —

145th MACHINE GUN COMPANY

FROM AUGUST 1st 1917 TO AUGUST 31st 1917.

[signature]
OC
145 M.G. Coy.

Instructions regarding War Diaries and Intelligence Summaries are contained in F. S. Regs., Part II. and the Staff Manual respectively. Title pages will be prepared in manuscript.

WAR DIARY
or
INTELLIGENCE SUMMARY.
(Erase heading not required.)

Army Form C. 2118.

113 Machine Gun Coy.

Place	Date	Hour	Summary of Events and Information	Remarks and references to Appendices
	Aug 31st (Contd)		The Company had been in action since the opening of the offensive on July 31st, the total Casualties being:-	

	KILLED	WOUNDED	WD. REM'D	MISSING
OFFICERS	1	4	1	-
SERGEANTS	-	4	-	-
O.R.s (Gunners)	5	40	16	-
Attached (Carr.)	6	11	1	2
	12	59	18	2

Reinforcements received during same period.

OFFICERS 6

O.R. 49.

Place	Date	Hour	Summary of Events and Information	Remarks and references to Appendices
	Aug 31st		Strength of Company - 13 Officers 181 O.R. (Gunners) 52 Attached.	

[signature]

(A7092). Wt. W12839/M1293. 750,000. 1/17. D. D. & L., Ltd. Forms/C.2118/14.

Army Form C. 2118.

WAR DIARY
or
INTELLIGENCE SUMMARY.
(Erase heading not required.)

Instructions regarding War Diaries and Intelligence Summaries are contained in F. S. Regs., Part II. and the Staff Manual respectively. Title pages will be prepared in manuscript.

14th Machine Gun Company

Place	Date	Hour	Summary of Events and Information	Remarks and references to Appendices
	Aug 28		Battery guns were placed at disposal of G.O.C. [illegible] and remained in "Status quo". These guns [illegible] at dusk.	
			No 3 Section. The two guns in vicinity of [illegible] moved up slightly. The other gun team of No 3 Section reported to F Battery position having lost the Company and remained there. The fourth gun was lost.	
			No 4 Section. Two guns remained in immediate readiness at F1 Battery position – the two that had been missing were found and put in immediate readiness at F1 Battery position. All guns were withdrawn on night 28/29th, & returned to DAMBRE CAMP. [signature]	
	29		Resting. [signature]	
	30	4 AM	Marched to ROAD CAMP ST JAN DE BIEZEN [signature]	
	31		Training. [signature]	

(A7092). Wt. W12839/M1293. 750,000. 1/17. D. D. & L., Ltd. Forms/C.2118/14.

Instructions regarding War Diaries and Intelligence Summaries are contained in F. S. Regs., Part II. and the Staff Manual respectively. Title pages will be prepared in manuscript.

WAR DIARY
or
INTELLIGENCE SUMMARY.
(*Erase heading not required.*)

Army Form C. 2118.

145 Machine Gun Coy

Place	Date	Hour	Summary of Events and Information	Remarks and references to Appendices
	Aug 26 (Contd)		under 2/Lt A.H. SALMON & 2/Lt J.S. ALEXANDER (the latter being Battery Commander) moved up to Battery positions. Night very wet. Casualties 1 OR (1 [illegible]) wounded. No 3 & 4 sections under 2/Lt S.R. KING & 2/Lt A.W. [illegible] moved to assembly positions in vicinity of MOUSE TRAP FARM. [signature]	APPENDIX No 9 O No 7/1
	Aug 27		The rain which had fallen during the night made going very difficult. Zero was at 1.55 pm. Barrage guns fired as per programme. Casualties 3 OR Wounded. Four guns with 1/4th Oxf & Bucks L.I. and four with 1/4th R. Berks lost touch when moving forward. Only two guns got into action with the 1/4th Oxf & Bucks L.I. in vicinity of MON DU HIBOU, & none with the 1/4th R. Berks. Two were in immediate readiness by A Battery position. The causes of the above were straggling and lack of NCOs due to heavy losses during the month. [signature]	

8.

(A7092). Wt. W12839/M1293. 750,000. 1/17. D. D. & L., Ltd. Forms/C.2118/14.

Army Form C. 2118.

Instructions regarding War Diaries and Intelligence Summaries are contained in F. S. Regs., Part II. and the Staff Manual respectively. Title pages will be prepared in manuscript.

WAR DIARY
or
INTELLIGENCE SUMMARY.
(Erase heading not required.)

145 [illegible] Coy

Place	Date	Hour	Summary of Events and Information	Remarks and references to Appendices
	AUG 18th		On the night of the 18th/19th the remaining six guns were relieved [illegible] to the Camp at (Sheet 28 B27c). The strength of the Company before moving into action was: 11 Officers 244 OR [illegible] attached. Casualties: 1 Officer killed 6 OR killed, 3 Officers wounded 31 OR wounded including attached and 2 OR missing. [signature]	
	19–22		Training [signature]	
	23		Took 30,000 rounds to form barrage dump at ALBERTA [signature]	
	24		Took 130,000 rounds to form barrage dump at ALBERTA [signature]	
			Took [illegible] 28,000 rounds to ST JULIEN [signature]	
	25		Training [signature]	
	26		Night 26/27th. Company moved into the line. No 1 and 2 sections	APPENDIX [illegible]

(A7092). Wt. W12839/M1293. 750,000. 1/17. D. D. & L., Ltd. Forms/C.2118/14.

Instructions regarding War Diaries and Intelligence Summaries are contained in F. S. Regs., Part II. and the Staff Manual respectively. Title pages will be prepared in manuscript.

WAR DIARY
or
INTELLIGENCE SUMMARY.
(Erase heading not required.)

Army Form C. 2118.

145 Machine Gun Coy

Place	Date	Hour	Summary of Events and Information	Remarks and references to Appendices
			two of the enemy and took nine prisoners and organised the MG defence with his three guns on an approximate line C12c77 – C12a22. He also got two other guns sent [illegible], the teams having become casualties, also he brought into action a German Light Machine Gun on this line and eventually recovered two missing guns. He rendered a report to Company Headquarters, saw all wounded attended to and dead buried.	
			Positions of guns at Zero hour and approximate positions taken up are shown on map	
	Aug 17th		No alteration. The Brigade was relieved on the night of the 17th/18th. Ten guns were relieved by guns of the 143rd and 144th MG Coys. Delay in relieving the remaining guns was caused by the relieving section of the 143 MG Coy sustaining heavy casualties on the way up.	

Instructions regarding War Diaries and Intelligence Summaries are contained in F. S. Regs., Part II. and the Staff Manual respectively. Title pages will be prepared in manuscript.

WAR DIARY
or
INTELLIGENCE SUMMARY.
(Erase heading not required.)

Army Form C. 2118.

145 Machine Gun Coy

Place	Date	Hour	Summary of Events and Information	Remarks and references to Appendices
			the No 1 and returned to HQ. LIEUT ALEXANDER [illegible] reported as Officer the Reserve section was sent to take charge of these guns. The two guns at REGINA CROSS under the charge of Sgt. JEFFERY advanced until Sgt JEFFERY and one team [illegible] were wounded and one gun smashed. A private took charge and brought the gun into position at C 5 d 4.2. This private finding himself in an exposed position withdrew later to C 11 b 1.7. LIEUT. ORCHARD and two guns went forward and succeeded in getting as far as C 12 d 2.2. where he was held up by rifle & M.G. fire. One of his guns was left behind at CANOPUS TRENCH. The guns from ALBERTA and centre guns under 2/LIEUT. TAUNTON advanced to approximately C 12 c 4.9. 2/LIEUT. TAUNTON was wounded here; these 3 guns found themselves in the melée. Cpl MALPASS took charge and displayed great gallantry. He shot	

(A7092). Wt. W12839/M1293. 750,000. 1/17. D. D. & L., Ltd. Forms/C.2118/14.

Army Form C. 2118.

Instructions regarding War Diaries and Intelligence Summaries are contained in F. S. Regs., Part II. and the Staff Manual respectively. Title pages will be prepared in manuscript.

WAR DIARY
or
INTELLIGENCE SUMMARY.
(Erase heading not required.)

145 Machine Gun Coy

Place	Date	Hour	Summary of Events and Information	Remarks and references to Appendices
	AUG 16 Contd		and rifle fire. After crossing the STEENBEEK, 2/LIEUT. INWOOD was killed, and Sgt WAITE although wounded brought the teams on and was wounded for the second time, however, he got them into position at C12C 68 + C12C 76 (appro) Sgt WAITE came back to company headquarters and reported, and volunteered to return to duty but was not permitted to do so. No 15 + 16 Guns under 2/LIEUT. SELBIE advanced as laid down until held up by enemy M.G. and rifle fire 2/LIEUT SELBIE being wounded.	
			The teams in reserve the O.C. found completely disorganized at approximately zero + 3 hours in shell holes, still in the enemy barrage at assembly point. He got two teams together brought them forward + put them at C 11 b 5.4. This was outside the enemy's barrage, as was evident the attack was not a success he left these teams here under the charge of	

(A7092). Wt. W12839/M1293. 750,000. 1/17. D. D. & L., Ltd. Forms/C.2118/14.

Instructions regarding War Diaries and Intelligence Summaries are contained in F. S. Regs., Part II. and the Staff Manual respectively. Title pages will be prepared in manuscript.

WAR DIARY
or
INTELLIGENCE SUMMARY.
(Erase heading not required.)

Army Form C. 2118.

14th Machine Gun Coy

Place	Date	Hour	Summary of Events and Information	Remarks and references to Appendices
	AUG 16 (cont)		especially by the reserve section, of which last were 2/LIEUT CLUTTON & the section sergeant. Zero was 4.45 AM. The attack was not successful, machine guns took up positions on a line from C12 a 4.4 – C12 d 1/6. The infantry advanced & found 4 concrete battery positions held by the enemy had not been affected by the barrage and as a result several machine guns & rifles came into action against them causing considerable delay to the advance — ipso facto the barrage went on leaving them too far behind. The final result was that even the first objective was not obtained.	
			General outline of the action & Machine Guns:–	APR No 7 O.5/1.
			No 13 & 14 Guns under 2/LIEUT. INHOOD advanced as laid down in orders & after crossing the STEENBEEKE came into enemy machine gun	

Army Form C. 2118.

WAR DIARY
or
INTELLIGENCE SUMMARY.
(Erase heading not required.)

Instructions regarding War Diaries and Intelligence Summaries are contained in F. S. Regs., Part II. and the Staff Manual respectively. Title pages will be prepared in manuscript.

145 Machine Gun Coy

Place	Date	Hour	Summary of Events and Information	Remarks and references to Appendices
	AUG 9. 10. 11.		Two Sections in line with 143rd Brigade, under Command of CAPTN WILLAT 143RD M.G. COY. Remainder of Company Training.	
	12.		Two sections in line, ~~two sections in training~~. relieved	APPEN. No 4 OO No 4
	13.		Two sections in line, two sections training	
	14		Two sections in line, two sections training	
	15		The ½ Company moved up to REIGERSBURG CAMP where 3 OR were wounded (shell fire).	APP. No 5 OO No 6
			On the night of the 15th/16th the Company moved into position in the line, the journey up being uneventful. At the assembly positions the enemy put down a light barrage. There was a certain amount of delay in settling down, & reports that did arrive at the assembly point were late, in one case just before zero.	APP. No 6 OO No 5.
	16		As the result of the barrage, some casualties were sustained.	

(A7092). Wt. W12839/M1293. 750,000. 1/17. D. D. & L., Ltd. Forms/C.2118/14.

Instructions regarding War Diaries and Intelligence Summaries are contained in F. S. Regs., Part II. and the Staff Manual respectively. Title pages will be prepared in manuscript.

WAR DIARY
or
INTELLIGENCE SUMMARY.
(Erase heading not required.)

Army Form C. 2118.

143 M.G. Coy

Place	Date	Hour	Summary of Events and Information	Remarks and references to Appendices
	AUG. 7 (CONTD.)		enemy shelling was very heavy. S.O.S. rockets were fired to which our Batty replied. ~~XXX~~ 18,000 rounds were fired during the night.	F.L.W.?
	8th		Weather fine - heavy thunderstorm at 8pm.	
			Arrangements for belt filling were improved at Batty position. Dump established at C15 b 90.05. an enemy dugout taken as a belt filling centre from which a track was taped to the Batty for runners with ammunition. 60,000 rounds with 20 carriers was sent up, limbers brought up ammn. to C15 d 1.2. During the night enemy M.G. fire was active.	
			Relief was carried out in accordance with O.O. No 3 attached.	APPENDIX No 2. O. No 3.
			Casualties 1 O.R. killed, 2 O.R. wounded, ~~1 O.R. gassed~~.	
			Total Casualties 1 Officer killed, 1 Officer Shell Shock, 4 O.R. killed, 8 O.R. wounded, ~~1 O.R. gassed~~. Captain G. H. WRIGHT handed over command to Captain WILLAT 143rd M.G. Coy who retained 2 sections of this company.	

(A7092). Wt. W12839/M1293. 750,000. 1/17. D. D. & L., Ltd. Forms/C.2118/14.

Instructions regarding War Diaries and Intelligence Summaries are contained in F. S. Regs., Part II. and the Staff Manual respectively. Title pages will be prepared in manuscript.

WAR DIARY
or
INTELLIGENCE SUMMARY.
(Erase heading not required.)

Army Form C. 2118.

105 M.G. Company

Place	Date	Hour	Summary of Events and Information	Remarks and references to Appendices
	AUG 6th (Cont'd.)		Shelled and was therefore moved to C16c9595. Owing to the loss of two officers this Batty was not in position in time to carry out harassing fire the following night. Enemy shelling heavy, few aeroplanes in evidence.	HW
	7th		Weather fair. 2,000 rounds were fired on an enemy screen from C6a21 to C6d85. Batty was laid on ZERO line 60° True Bearing. For the night No 6 Gun was taken as the centre Gun and Batty distributed 4 degrees. Each gun to traverse 6° on an approx. line from C6a21 to C12b81. Object: ration Parties &c. The Batty had also orders to fire on this target in the event of the S.O.S. being sent up. This was too thin to be called a barrage. Average range 2650. Same elevation 8°40' on all guns. Close touch had to be kept with Bn. Commds in case patrols were pushed out. During the night	

(A7092). Wt. W12839/M1293. 750,000. 1/17. D. D. & L., Ltd. Forms/C.2118/14.

Instructions regarding War Diaries and Intelligence Summaries are contained in F. S. Regs., Part II. and the Staff Manual respectively. Title pages will be prepared in manuscript.

WAR DIARY
or
INTELLIGENCE SUMMARY.
(Erase heading not required.)

Army Form C. 2118.

Place	Date	Hour	Summary of Events and Information	Remarks and references to Appendices
	5 AUG (Contd.)		carried up approximately No1 Tripod, No 2 Gun, Team Comm. Spare Parts, Cleaning Rod & condenser & Verey Lights, Carriers Nos 1 & 2 3 belt boxes each, No 3 Belt Box & Tin of water, No 4 Rations & Empty Petrol Tin. Shelling fairly continuous throughout the night. Fair	RWI
	6TH		Weather. Very misty in morning, later fine. O.C. Coy had no difficulty in visiting guns & crossing STEENBEEK without being seen. The guns in CORNER COT vicinity had concrete dugouts. The guns at ALBERTA large concrete dugouts. The guns at REGINA CROSS in Enemy concrete Battery Positions. See map attached showing dispositions. All the teams therefore had good cover from shell fire. On the O.Cs return he found that the attached sections had been heavily shelled and 2ND LT T.G. [redacted] MAY (143rd M.G.Coy) & 2 O.R killed 2ND LT W. BETTS went down with shell shock same evening. This Battery was in an area considerably	App. NO 3 MAP PILKEM 1:10,000 att.

(A7094). Wt. W12839/M1293. 750,000. 1/17. D. D. & L., Ltd. Forms/C.2118/14.

Instructions regarding War Diaries and Intelligence Summaries are contained in F. S. Regs., Part II. and the Staff Manual respectively. Title pages will be prepared in manuscript.

WAR DIARY
or
INTELLIGENCE SUMMARY.
(Erase heading not required.)

Army For[m]

145 [illegible]

Place	Date	Hour	Summary of Events and Information	Remarks and references to Appendices
BELGIUM & FRANCE 1:40.000 SHEET 28 A 29 c central	1st AUG		SITUATION on Divl. Front. Line of Resistance W. Bank of STEENBEEK – OUTPOSTS on E. Side. Strength of Company Officers 12 O.R. 170 attached 64. The Company returned to Transport Lines A29c central. Everybody was wet through and the accommodation – bad bivouac sheets did not allow the men to get dry for two days owing to continual rain. Result 12 men sick for several days. Gaw	
MAP REF FOR OPERATIONS 28 N.W.2 ST JULIEN.	2nd 3rd }		Bad weather continued – no training possible. Gaw	
	4th		Weather improved & men were dry though they had not had a comfortable rest. Gaw	GWJ
	5th		Weather fine. Half the Company & sections attached proceeded to the line. Roads pretty good. Transport (limbers) got up reasonably close to front System. 145 Inf Bde H.Q. did not remain as stated in O.O. No 2. at C16c58 C.22.c.7.8. but returned to HILL TOP. Transport got away quietly, but teams were heavily shelled. Casualties 1 Killed 3 Wounded. Relief was complete by 2 a.m. Roads	APPENDIX I O.O. No 2.

145 M.G.C. "G" BATTERY (C16 d.1525) Date: 31/7/17 Map: 28 N.W.2. 1/10,000

Gun No.	Target	ELEVATION: Range	Contour: Gun m.	Contour: Target m.	Q.E. ° ′	CLEARANCE: Troops contour m.	Troops range yds.	Clearance yds.	Clearance required yds.	DIRECTION: Magnetic °	REMARKS: Time from zero +	Rate per hour per gun	Rounds fired	Checked by	General
9		1800	29	15	5 52					51 to 55					
10										50 54					
11	FIRST OBJECTIVE:	1850	"	"	3 6					49 53					
12	Line from C11 d 8080									48 52	2.00 to 3.40	1800			
13	to C 11 b 1040									47 51					
14										46 50					
15		1900	"	"	3 20					45 49					
16										44 48					
9										59 to 61					
10										58 60					
11										57 59					
12	SECOND OBJECTIVE	2600	29	20	8 4					56 58	3.40 to 4.05	3750			
13	Line from C12 b 1872									55 57					
14	to C6 c 6232									54 56					
15										53 55					
16										52 54					
9										58 to 61					
10										56 59					
11		2600	29	20	8 4					54 57					
12	THIRD OBJECTIVE:									52 55	4.05 to 6.20	1500			
13	Line from C12 b 1873	2650	"	16	8 25					50 53					
14	to C 6 c 0085									48 51					
15		2700	"	16	8 53					46 49					
16										44 47					

145 M.G.C "F" BATTERY (C 16 d7505) Date: 31/7/17 Map: 28 N.W.2 1/10,000

Gun No.	Target	ELEVATION Range	Contour Gun m.	Contour Target m.	Q.E ° ′	CLEARANCE Troops contour m	Troops range yds	Clearance yds	Clearance required yds	DIRECTION Magnetic °	REMARKS Time from Zero +	Rate per hour per gun	Rounds fired	Checked by	General
1		1850	27	15	3 45					54 to 58					Ranges increased by 150x beyond target.
2										53 57					
3	FIRST OBJECTIVE:	1800			3 32					52 56					
4	Line from C11 a 8080									50 54	2.00 to 3.40	1800			
5	to C12 c 5540	1750			3 21					48 52					
6										47 51					
7		1700			3 12					46 50					
8										45 49					
1										60 to 62					
2										59 61					
3										58 60					
4	SECOND OBJECTIVE:	2500	27	20	7 16					57 59	3.40 to 4.05.	3750			
5	Line from C12 b 1873									56 58					
6	to C12 b 7212									55 57					
7										54 56					
8										53 55					
1										67 to 71					
2										65 69					
3		2550	27	20	7 41					63 67					
4	THIRD OBJECTIVE:									61 65	4.05 to 6.20	1500			
5	Line from C12 b 1873									59 63					
6	to D7 c 2450	2500	..	.	7 16					57 61					
7										55 59					
8										53 57				[illegible]	[illegible signature]

A L L O C A T I O N   O F   D U T I E S .

BATTERY COMMRS. (1) To locate the sites for battery positions, by compass To lead up tapelayers (supervising their own signallers, and their own runners.
(2) To meet sections and direct them to their allotted positions and supervist the making of emplacements and ammunition supply.
(3) To get into communication with other battery commanders("F" or "G" as the case may be) and Bde. Fwd. Station.
(4) To get the infantry tp place out a screen (see para. 7 M.G. O.O. No.1.
(5) To command the battery, USING THEIR OWN INITIATIVE.
(6) On capture of solid GREEN LINE to return to the prearranged rendezvous.

SECTION OFFICERS. (1) To get their sections into position being guided by the tape.
(2) To select the actual gun positions, not further than 10 yards apart, obtain directions, and check elevations.
(3) To get into communication with Battery Commanders.
(4) To supervise supply, informing Coy.H.Q. of urgent needs by returning runners. All communications not sent by returning runners MUST be sent through Battery Commanders.
(5) TO CONTROL THE GUNS taking times from Battery Comrs.
(6) To return empty belts as often as possible.

C.S.M. (1) To maintain ammunition, water, oil, ets., supply from Coy.H.Q. to sections.
(2) To keep a record of casualties.
(3) To keep runners and spare men filling belts.

C.Q.M.S. (1) To maintain good ration and general supply from Coy. rear H.Q. to Advanced H.Q.

N.C.O.s

(Signed) G.A.WEBB. Lt.,
for O.C., 145th M.G. Company.

6.
BATTERY COMMRS. SIGNALS.

The following signals will be used by Battery Commrs.

RED .... CEASE FIRE.
GREEN .... FIRE.
YELLOW .... 2nd ELEVATION.
WHITE & RED
STRIPES ... 3rd ELEVATION.

7.
ELEVATION CARDS.

Cards with elevations and directions for lifts have been issued to all Officers, all sergeants, all corpls, all gun Nos.1-4.

8.
LETTERS.

Officers will ensure that no N.C.O. or man takes any letters into action.

INSTRUCTIONS.

In conjunction with 145th M.G. Coy. O.O. No.1 20th July. 1917.

Ref: Map. Trench Map. 28. N.W. 2.

1.
MOVE FROM HILL TOP TO GERMAN LINE.

Battery Commanders will emerge from Tunnels immediately the order has been received from 117th Brigade, a accompanied by tapelayers, batmen, and Battery Commanders' runners, and will proceed with all speed to sites for Batty positions, where boards will be placed thus:-

"F" Battery "G" Battery

Five minutes after the Battery Commanders have left, batteries will emerge from Tunnels and advance in artillery formation, rear point of leading sections to be 100 yards in front of the first point of rear sections.
"F" Battery will emerge first.
Nos. 1 & 4 sections will lead respective batteries.
Section Commanders of Nos.1 & 4 sections will lead their sections taking direction from the tape.
Section Commanders of Nos. 2 & 3 will be in rear of their sections, thus being able to keep all on the move.
Nos. 2 & 3 sections will take their direction from Nos. 1 & 4, and on arrival at GERMAN SECOND LINE will e bear inwards.

The Battery Commanders will meet sections on arrival and supervise positioning of guns.
No guns to be further apart than 10 yards.

The Nos.1 will mark emplacements "V.G.1, &c.,
"F" Battery 1-8 R to L. "G" Battery 9-16, R to L.

2.
CONSTITUTION OF SECTIONS.

Each section will consist of:-
1 Sergt. 1 Corporal
14 Gunners 16 Carriers.

<u>LOADS</u>
Sergt. 1 belt box and aiming posts, Corpls. 1 belt box, shovel and pick. No.1 Tripod and clinometer. No.2.Gun. No.3 Spare parts box and condenser. No.4 Water, oil and shovel. Remainder and section officers batmen, 3 belt boxes each. Total boxes per section 47.
With Battery Commanders:
2 runners at 2 boxes each..........4
1 batman at 2 boxes 2
Total with battery 100.

3.
CARRIERS.

Section officers will send back all carriers together and will send back word to C.S.M. as to the number of belt boxes that have arrived.

4.
DUTIES ON

On arrival at emplacements sections will at once proceed with making open emplacements, deepen trench at gun position and make recesses for ammunition. Section officers will not communicate with Coy.H.Q. except as in para. 3 or through Battery Commanders. When the carriers have come up the second time they will receive orders from Section Officers as to return to Coy. H.Q.
Used belts will be returned to Coy. H.Q. as often as possible.

5.
COY..H.Q.

The C.S.M. will be entirely responsible for ammunition, oil water and general supply from Coy. H.Q. to Batteries. He will see that the runners and spare men at H.Q. fill all used belts with the belt filling machines.

5\. FIRING. Firing will take place from zero plus 2 hours until zero plus 6 hours 20 minutes. See Appendix 1.

6\. COMMUNICATION.
(1) Group Commander. to Divl. Hdqrs. Telephone.
(2) Group Commander to Batteries. Relay.
(3) Battery Commanders to Section Commanders. Visual.
(4) Lieut. TAUNTON will act as Liaison Officer and will accompany 117th Brigade.
(5) Brigade forward station will be at C 16 d 2025.

7\. INSTRUCTIONS. Guns will not be more than 10 yards apart.
Battery Commanders will ask nearest infantry to place a chain of men at 5 yard interval on either flank 300 yards in front of their batteries, and also 50 yards on either flank to prevent runners and wounded running into the danger zone.

8\. LOCATIONS.

Water Dump.	Company dugouts in HILL TOP SYSTEM.	
S.A.A. Dump	39th Divl.	I 2 a 19.
	116th Brigade	C 21 d 43.
	117th Brigade	C 21 c 26.
	Forward Dump	Cross Road Farm. C 22 c 37.

(Signed) G.A.WEBB. Lt.
for O.C., 145th M.G. Company.

APPENDIX "B"

SECRET.

145 M.G. C ompany Operation Order No.1.

Map Ref: Trench Map. St. Julien. 28 N.W. 2.

19.7.1917.

1. GENERAL. The Company is attached to the 39th Division for the opening operations, and will assist with barrages, the object of which will be to prevent the enemy from withdrawing his artillery.

The Company will rejoin the 48th Division on the capture of the SOLID GREEN LINE.

2. ORGANISATION. The Group (consisting of two Batteries, "F" and "G",) will be under the Command of O.C., Company, and will be known as "B" Group.

The two Batteries will be as under:-

F. Battery.	G. Battery.
Lt. ORCHARD.	2/Lt. MOSS.
Nos.1 & 2 Sections.	Nos.3 & 4 Sections.
2/Lt. CLUTTON & Lt. ALEXANDER.	2/Lt. SELBIE & Lt. GREEN.

3. ASSEMBLY POSITIONS.

Nos.1 & 2 sections will be accommodated for X/Y night in HILL TOP SYSTEM. Dugouts 27 - 32 will be used.

Nos.3 & 4 sections will be accommodated in dugouts in the CANAL BANK for X/Y night, and will proceed to HILL TOP on zero morning, reaching there by zero minus 2 hours.

4. ZERO DAY. The Company will leave HILL TOP when ordered to do so by the 117th Brigade (after the capture of the BLUE LINE) as under:-

"F" Battery.................... C.16 d 7505.

"G" Battery.................... C 16 d 1525.

Group Headquarters will remain at HILL TOP TUNNELS with 116th Brigade later proceeding to Brigade Forward Station at C 16 d 2025.

/ FIRING.

CONFIDENTIAL

APPENDIX "B"
to
WARDIARY
— of —

145th Machine Gun Company

From 1st July 1917 to 31st July 1917

2nd August 1917

Army Form C. 2118.

WAR DIARY
or
INTELLIGENCE SUMMARY.
(Erase heading not required.)

Instructions regarding War Diaries and Intelligence Summaries are contained in F. S. Regs., Part II. and the Staff Manual respectively. Title pages will be prepared in manuscript.

145 Machine Gun Company.

Place	Date	Hour	Summary of Events and Information	Remarks and references to Appendices

APPENDIX "A" (Contd)

Date	Effective strength for previous day		Strength increase during day		Strength decrease during day		To hospital during day		Rejoined from hospital		Total in hospital		To course leave etc during day		Rejoined from course leave etc		Total on course leave etc		Killed		Wounded		Missing		Available for duty		Effective strength	
July	Off	OR	Off	OR	Off	OR	Off	OR	Off	OR	Off	OR	Off	OR	Off	OR	Off	OR	Off	OR	Off	OR	Off	OR	Off	OR	Off	OR
17	11	174				1		1				7					2	11							9	151	11	173
18	11	174		2				1				8					2	11							9	152	11	175
19	11	175										8					2	11							9	152	11	175
20	11	175										8					2	11							9	152	11	175
21	11	175										8			1	2	1	9							10	154	11	175
22	11	175										8					1	9							10	154	11	175
23	11	175		2								8			1	3		6							11	157	11	177
24	11	177						1				9						6							11	156	11	177
25	11	177										9	1				1	6							10	156	11	177
26	11	177				1						8					1	6							10	156	11	176
27	11	176				1				1		6				1	1	5							10	158	11	175
28	11	175	1	2						1		5		1		1	1	5							11	161	12	177
29	12	177				1				1		4				1	1	4				1			11	162	12	176
30	12	176								4		-				1	1	3							11	167	12	176
31	12	176		1								-				1	1	2							11	169	12	176

[signature] O.C. 145 Machine Gun Coy

(A7092). Wt. W12839/M1293. 750,000. 1/17. D. D. & L., Ltd. Forms/C.2118/14.

Instructions regarding War Diaries and Intelligence Summaries are contained in F. S. Regs., Part II. and the Staff Manual respectively. Title pages will be prepared in manuscript.

WAR DIARY
or
INTELLIGENCE SUMMARY.
(Erase heading not required.)

Army Form C. 2118.

145 Machine Gun Company.

Place	Date	Hour	Summary of Events and Information	Remarks and references to Appendices

APPENDIX "A"

Date	Effective strength for previous day Off	Effective strength for previous day OR	Strength increase during week Off	Strength increase during week OR	Strength decrease during week Off	Strength decrease during week OR	To Hospital during day Off	To Hospital during day OR	Rejoined from Hospital Off	Rejoined from Hospital OR	Total in Hospital Off	Total in Hospital OR	To Course Leave etc during day Off	To Course Leave etc during day OR	Rejoined from Course Leave etc Off	Rejoined from Course Leave etc OR	Total on Course Leave etc. Off	Total on Course Leave etc. OR	Killed Off	Killed OR	Wounded Off	Wounded OR	Missing Off	Missing OR	Available for duty Off	Available for duty OR	Effective Strength Off	Effective Strength OR	Remarks
1	11	176						2				8				2	2	15							9	147	11	176	
2	11	176				1		1		1		7		1			2	16				1			9	146	11	175	
3	11	175				1		2		2		7		3		2	2	16							9	145	11	174	
4	11	174										7					2	16							9	146	11	174	
5	11	174										7					2	16							9	147	11	174	
6	11	174										7					2	15							9	147	11	174	
7	11	174						1		2		6					2	15							9	149	11	174	
8	11	174										6				1	2	14							9	149	11	174	64 OR attached for duty from [illegible]
9	11	174										6					2	14							9	147	11	174	
10	11	174										6				1	2	13							9	150	11	174	
11	11	174						1				7		1		3	2	11							9	152	11	174	
12	11	174										7					2	11							9	152	11	174	
13	11	174										7					2	11							9	152	11	174	
14	11	174										7					2	11							9	152	11	174	
15	11	174										7					2	11							9	152	11	174	
16	11	174										7					2	11							9	152	11	174	

(A7092). Wt. W12839/M1293. 750,000. 1/17. D. D. & L., Ltd. Forms/C.2118/14.

1

CONFIDENTIAL

APPENDIX "A"

to

WARDIARY

of

145th Machine Gun Company

From 1st July 1917 to 31st July 1917

2nd August 1917

Army Form C. 2118.

Instructions regarding War Diaries and Intelligence Summaries are contained in F. S. Regs., Part II. and the Staff Manual respectively. Title pages will be prepared in manuscript.

WAR DIARY
or
INTELLIGENCE SUMMARY.

(Erase heading not required.)

145 M.G. Coy

Place	Date	Hour	Summary of Events and Information	Remarks and references to Appendices
	July 31st		No difficulty was experienced in maintaining the supply of ammunition & water. One gun was destroyed by shell fire and one slightly damaged. [signature]	

Instructions regarding War Diaries and Intelligence Summaries are contained in F. S. Regs., Part II. and the Staff Manual respectively. Title pages will be prepared in manuscript.

WAR DIARY
or
INTELLIGENCE SUMMARY.
(Erase heading not required.)

Army Form C. 2118.

45 Machine Gun Coy.

Place	Date	Hour	Summary of Events and Information	Remarks and references to Appendices
	July 31		zero plus 2 hours but owing to the fact that the orders for moving forward were not received from 117th Brigade until zero plus 1 hour 40 minutes it was impossible to commence at the official time. Both batteries however were able to fire the second & third part of the barrage (zero plus 3 hours 40 minutes to zero plus 4 hours 5 minutes, and zero plus 4 hours 5 minutes to zero plus 6 hours 20 minutes) The Company should have rejoined the 4th Division on the capture of the Solid Green line. As this was not taken the Company remained in position until orders for its relief were received from the 39th Division. At zero plus 16 hours 25 minutes a wire was received from the Div M.G. Officer of the 39th Division to the effect that the Company would be relieved forthwith by the 228th M.G. Company. Owing to difficulties of the situation the relief did not take place until 6 am the following morning, when the Company proceeded back to the Transport lines. The total casualties during the day were Killed (1 O.R.) Died of shock (1 Attd), Wounded 18 (M.G.) Wounded 4 (Attd) With the exception of the delay in commencing the whole of the operations carried out by the Coy were very satisfactory. Gow	

(A7092). Wt. W12839/M1293. 750,000. 1/17. D. D. & L., Ltd. Forms/C.2118/14.

Army Form C. 2118.

Instructions regarding War Diaries and Intelligence Summaries are contained in F. S. Regs., Part II. and the Staff Manual respectively. Title pages will be prepared in manuscript.

WAR DIARY
or
INTELLIGENCE SUMMARY.

(*Erase heading not required.*)

145 Machine Gun Coy.

Place	Date	Hour	Summary of Events and Information	Remarks and references to Appendices
	July 22		were as follows:- MOULLE, ST OMER - ST MOMELIN - ZEGGERSCAPPEL - WORMHOUDT HERZEELE - WATOU - POPERINGHE PROVEN Road. G.a.w.	
			Day spent in cleaning up personal equipment + arranging bivouacs. G.a.w.	
	23		Very hot day, enemy shelled the vicinity of the Camp about 11.30 pm.	
	24		Training, including barrage drill G.a.w.	
	25		Training G.a.w.	
	26		Training G.a.w.	
	27		Training G.a.w.	
	28		Training G.a.w.	
	29 30		Training & On night of 29th/30th Nos 1 + 2 sections moved into dug-outs in the HILLTOP SYSTEM (C 21 d) preparatory to the forthcoming operations (vide appendix B) G.a.w. Nos 3 + 4 sections moved into dug-outs on the CANAL BANK (C 26 d 88)	G.a.w.
REF TRENCH MAP ST JULIEN 28 NW 2	31		At 1 am Nos 3 + 4 sections proceeded to join the remainder of the Coy at HILLTOP SYSTEM. At zero hour 3.50 am the company took part in the operations of the 39th Div. The role allotted to the Coy was to create a barrage as indicated in para 1. of O.O No 1 from CALF RESERVE TR in the second German line. The barrage was to have commenced at	

(A7092). Wt. W12839/M1293. 750,000. 1/17. D. D. & L., Ltd. Forms/C.2118/14.

Instructions regarding War Diaries and Intelligence Summaries are contained in F. S. Regs., Part II. and the Staff Manual respectively. Title pages will be prepared in manuscript.

WAR DIARY
or
INTELLIGENCE SUMMARY.
(*Erase heading not required.*)

Army Form C. 2118.

145 Machine Gun Coy.

Place	Date	Hour	Summary of Events and Information	Remarks and references to Appendices
ST OMER – MOULLE	July 10		Detrained at ST OMER at about 7am. & marched to MOULLE arrived there about 12.30pm. GAW	
			The remainder of Coy. arrived about 4.30pm. GAW	
MOULLE	11		Training continued GAW	
	12		Training. GAW	
	13		Training. GAW	
	14		Operations carried out in conjunction with 116th Inf. Brigade. A barrage scheme similar to that proposed for the coming offensive. GAW	
	15		Training Continued. GAW	
	16		Weather changing, some rain. Training carried on. GAW	
	17		Training GAW	
	18		Training was considerably hampered owing to heavy rainstorms. GAW	
	19		Training. GAW	
	20		Transport left MOULLE at 8am & proceeded to Camps near POPERINGHE. The journey occupied two days. The first night was spent at WORMHOUDT GAW	
	21		The Coy. less transport moved from MOULLE at 1pm. & proceeded in buses to Camps near POPERINGHE (Map Ref. A29c55. 1/40000 Sheet 28) arriving there about 2am on morning of 22nd July. Route taken by buses	

(A7092). Wt. W12839/M1293. 750,000. 1/17. D. D. & L., Ltd. Forms/C.2118/14.

Instructions regarding War Diaries and Intelligence Summaries are contained in F. S. Regs., Part II. and the Staff Manual respectively. Title pages will be prepared in manuscript.

WAR DIARY
or
INTELLIGENCE SUMMARY.
(*Erase heading not required.*)

Army Form C. 2118.

145 Machine Gun Coy.

Place	Date	Hour	Summary of Events and Information	Remarks and references to Appendices
HERMIES - DEMICOURT	July 1		Bright day, enemy exceptionally quiet. Company relieved in the line during night 1/2nd July by 9th M G Company. 1 NCO & man remained with 9th MG Coy in each position for 24 hours to instruct incoming teams as to their duties. Remainder of Coy moved to Transport lines West of VELU WOOD. G.a.w	
VELU.	2.		Coy at Transport lines. Day spent in cleaning guns etc. & personal equipment. G a.w.	
	3		Moved off to BIHUCOURT Area at 3.45 pm arrived BIHUCOURT at 7.30 pm. G.a.w	
BIHUCOURT	4		Moved from BIHUCOURT at 6pm & proceeded to BAILLEULMONT for a period of training. G.a.w	
BAILLEULMONT	5		Training during afternoon. G.a.w	
	6		Training. G.a.w.	
	7.		Training continued. Orders received about 8pm to stand by for move however no orders were received to move during the night. 64 OR were attached to Coy. for instructional purposes. G.a.w	
	8		Coy. standing by for move. No orders received up to present. G.a.w	
	9		Nos 1, 2, 3 Sections & H.Q. proceeded at 4pm to BEAUMETZ-RIVIERE to entrain. The remainder came by a later train same day. G.a.w	

(A7092). Wt. W12839/M1293. 750,000. 1/17. D. D. & L., Ltd. Forms/C.2118/14.

CONFIDENTIAL

Vol 18

WAR DIARY

OF

145th MACHINE GUN COMPANY.

FROM JULY 1st 1917 TO JULY 31st 1917

[illegible] Lieut
OC 145 Machine Gun Coy

Instructions regarding War Diaries and Intelligence Summaries are contained in F. S. Regs., Part II. and the Staff Manual respectively. Title pages will be prepared in manuscript.

WAR DIARY
or
INTELLIGENCE SUMMARY.
(*Erase heading not required.*)

Army Form C. 2118.

145 Machine Gun Company.

Place	Date	Hour	Summary of Events and Information	Remarks and references to Appendices

APPENDIX "A" (Contd)

June	Effective strength for previous day		Strength increase during day		Strength decrease during day		To Hospital during day		Rejoined from Hospital		Total in Hospital		To Course leave etc during day		Rejoined from Course leave etc.		Total on Course leave etc.		Killed		Wounded		Missing		Available for duty		Effective Strength		Remarks
	Off	OR	Off	OR	Off	OR	Off	OR	Off	OR	Off	OR	Off	OR	Off	OR	Off	OR	Off	OR	Off	OR	Off	OR	Off	OR	Off	OR	
16	9	178										7					2	6							7	159	9	178	
17	9	178										7			1		1	6							8	159	9	178	
18	9	178						2				9					1	6							8	157	9	178	
19	9	178		1						2		7		7			1	13							8	153	9	179	5 OR. att from [illegible] to replace 5 OR to Course 14.6.17.
20	9	179				1						6					1	13							8	153	9	178	
21	9	178				1		1				6		4			1	17							8	148	9	177	
22	9	177				1						6		1			1	18							8	146	9	176	
23	9	176	1					2		1		7					1	18							9	145	10	176	
24	10	176								2		5		1			1	19							9	146	10	176	
25	10	176										5		1		1	1	19							9	146	10	176	
26	10	176								1		4				3	1	16							9	150	10	176	
27	10	176										4		6			1	22							9	144	10	176	
28	10	176	1	1		1		1				5					1	22							10	143	11	176	
29	11	176										5	1			5	2	17							9	144	11	176	5 OR att [illegible]
30	11	176						1				6					2	17							9	147	11	176	

[illegible]
O.C.
145 Machine Gun Coy.

(A7092). Wt. W12839/M1293. 750,000. 1/17. D. D. & L., Ltd. Forms/C.2118/14.

Instructions regarding War Diaries and Intelligence Summaries are contained in F. S. Regs., Part II. and the Staff Manual respectively. Title pages will be prepared in manuscript.

WAR DIARY
or
INTELLIGENCE SUMMARY.

(*Erase heading not required.*)

Army Form C. 2118.

45 Machine Gun Company

Place	Date	Hour	Summary of Events and Information	Remarks and references to Appendices

APPENDIX "A"

Date	Effective strength for previous day Off	Effective strength for previous day OR	Strength increase during day Off	Strength increase during day OR	Strength decrease during day Off	Strength decrease during day OR	To Hospital during day Off	To Hospital during day OR	Rejoined from Hospital Off	Rejoined from Hospital OR	Total in Hospital Off	Total in Hospital OR	To Course leave etc. during day Off	To Course leave etc. during day OR	Rejoined from Course leave etc. Off	Rejoined from Course leave etc. OR	Total on Course, Leave etc. Off	Total on Course, Leave etc. OR	Killed Off	Killed OR	Wounded Off	Wounded OR	Missing Off	Missing OR	Available for duty Off	Available for duty OR	Effective Strength Off	Effective Strength OR
June 1	11	173		3								6					1	3							10	162	11	176
2	11	176		6	1	1				1		4					1	3							9	161	10	181
3	10	181			1							4					1	3							8	162	9	181
4	9	181						1				5					1	3							8	157	9	181
5	9	181				1		1				6					1	3				1			8	165	9	180
6	9	180				2						5					1	3				1			8	164	9	178
7	9	178						1				6					1	3							8	163	9	178
8	9	178		1						1		5				1	1	2							8	166	9	179
9	9	179										5					1	2							8	166	9	179
10	9	179						1				6		2			1	4							8	163	9	179
11	9	179		1								6	1	4		2	2	6							7	162	9	180
12	9	180				2		3		2		6		1			2	7							7	159	9	178
13	9	178	-	-	-	-		1			-	7					2	7							7	158	9	178
14	9	178		1		1		1				7					2	7							7	158	9	178
15	9	178		1		1						7				1	2	6				2	-		7	159	9	178

Instructions regarding War Diaries and Intelligence Summaries are contained in F. S. Regs., Part II. and the Staff Manual respectively. Title pages will be prepared in manuscript.

WAR DIARY
or
INTELLIGENCE SUMMARY.
(Erase heading not required.)

Army Form C. 2118.

145 Machine Gun Company.

Place	Date	Hour	Summary of Events and Information	Remarks and references to Appendices
HERMIES - DEMICOURT	June 29 (Contd)		shrapnel during night, 1 O.R. wounded.	
	30		Very dull day some rain. Nothing to report.	

(A7092). Wt. W12839/M1293. 750,000. 1/17. D. D. & L., Ltd. Forms/C.2118/14.

Instructions regarding War Diaries and Intelligence Summaries are contained in F. S. Regs., Part II. and the Staff Manual respectively. Title pages will be prepared in manuscript.

WAR DIARY
or
INTELLIGENCE SUMMARY.
(Erase heading not required.)

Army Form C. 2118.

148 Machine Gun Coy.

Place	Date	Hour	Summary of Events and Information	Remarks and references to Appendices
HERMIES – DEMICOURT	June 23		Fine day. Enemy quiet. No firing took place. Rcw	
	24		The usual night firing took place from guns at 1.2.3.4.5 & 8 on targets at K26 b&d K20 b&d, K21 a & c K26 b K27 b & c. No 8 ceased fire at midnight owing to infantry patrols going out. 9000 rounds were expended. Rcw	
	25		Our M.G. fired on enemy tracks & trenches in K2 c & d K15 a & b K20 b&d K21 a & c K26 b K27 a b & c. Total number of rounds fired 6000. Firing took place from positions 1.2.3. & 4. Rcw	
	26		Fine & bright, good visibility, aerial activity, enemy quiet. Guns at positions 3 5 & 6 fired on North end of SPOIL HEAP, & on tracks & trenches in K20 a & b, K20 b & d during the night. 4550 rounds fired. Rcw	
	27		Fine day, enemy shelled vicinity of VELU heavily, throughout the morning. Nothing to report, except slight hostile aerial activity. Rcw	
	28		Bright day, A/A Gun at 8 position fired 900 rounds during the day. Rcw	
	29		Fine weather. During the night No 5 gun fired on enemy tracks in K21 a & c, Rounds expended 1500. No 7 gun shelled with	

(A7092). Wt. W12839/M1293. 750,000. 1/17. D. D. & L., Ltd. Forms/C.2118/14.

Instructions regarding War Diaries and Intelligence Summaries are contained in F. S. Regs., Part II. and the Staff Manual respectively. Title pages will be prepared in manuscript.

WAR DIARY
or
INTELLIGENCE SUMMARY.
(Erase heading not required.)

Army Form C. 2118.

145 Machine Gun Coy

Place	Date	Hour	Summary of Events and Information	Remarks and references to Appendices
HERMIES - DEMICOURT	June 18 (Cont)		fired on enemy's tracks & trenches in K2 b & d, K20 b & d, K21 a & c K26 b. K27 a b & c. 18,000 rounds were expended. Intersection relief took place.	
	19		Some thunderstorms. Very quiet. Nothing to report.	
	20		Much cooler & few showers. Guns at positions 5 & 8 continued their fire during the night.	
	21		Weather clearing & much fresher, with occasional showers. 18,000 rounds expended against enemy tracks & trenches in K21 a & c, K20 b & d K2 b & d. K26 b K27 a b & c from positions 1,2,3,4,5 & 8. Some retaliation of enemy M.Gs. from SPOIL HEAP. Gun at No 5 position was put out of action owing to the Check Lever bracket breaking completely away from the right side plate. This gun was replaced by a gun from reserve.	
	22		Fine weather, cool breeze. As for the night 21/22nd enemy's tracks were fired on from positions 1.2.4.5 & 8. At the request of 06 Right Battn. No 3 gun did not fire on K26 b as arranged. Patrols out.	

(A7092). Wt. W12839/M1293. 750,000. 1/17. D. D. & L., Ltd. Forms/C.2118/14.

Instructions regarding War Diaries and Intelligence Summaries are contained in F. S. Regs., Part II. and the Staff Manual respectively. Title pages will be prepared in manuscript.

WAR DIARY
or
INTELLIGENCE SUMMARY.
(Erase heading not required.)

Army Form C. 2118.

145 Machine Gun Coy

Place	Date	Hour	Summary of Events and Information	Remarks and references to Appendices
HERMIES–DEMICOURT	June 14		No 8 position received some shelling + two men were wounded, one of whom remained at duty. Hot weather continued. Intersection relief took place. Arrangements were made between O.C. the Battn in left subsection of the line + Officer i/c of Nos 5 6 7 + 8 guns to bring fire to bear against German trenches in K9b + K9a from No 6 position. [initials]	
	15		Very hot. During the night 15/16th enemy was again harassed by guns at Nos 1 2 3 4 5 + 6 positions + his tracks in K15 a + b. K15 a + b K21 a + c K26 d K27 c + a new trench in K26 b were engaged. 11.350 rounds were expended. [initials]	
	16		Very hot. Enemy very quiet. Some hostile aircraft activity. Enemy tracks were fired on during the night as on previous night + in addition K20 b + d received attention, a total of 14000 rounds being expended against them. [initials]	
	17		Hot. Night firing took place against enemy tracks as on previous night. 13000 rounds were expended. [initials]	
	18		Thunderstorms. Enemy very quiet. Guns at positions 1 2 4 5 + 8	

(A7092). Wt. W12839/M1293. 750,000. 1/17. D. D. & L., Ltd. Forms/C.2118/14.

Army Form C. 2118.

Instructions regarding War Diaries and Intelligence Summaries are contained in F. S. Regs., Part II. and the Staff Manual respectively. Title pages will be prepared in manuscript.

WAR DIARY
or
INTELLIGENCE SUMMARY.
(Erase heading not required.)

145 Machine Gun Coy

Place	Date	Hour	Summary of Events and Information	Remarks and references to Appendices
HERMIES – DEMICOURT	June 10		positions, still remained on their barrage lines, and communication with 127 Brigade still maintained. There was however, no occasion for firing. [initials]	
	June 11	2AM	Heavy thunderstorm, brighter weather during day. On night of 11th/12th June, it was reported that enemy had a working party in K2c, and fire was brought to bear on it from No 8 position (J12d04) Firing also took place from No 2 position on hostile M.G. in K27c. The digging operations of 127 Brigade having been completed, notification was received that assistance was no longer required. [initials]	
	12		Extremely hot. Night firing was carried out from positions at J30d38 and J30b76 to harass the enemy along his approaches to the SLAG HEAP in K20a95 & K20b07. As in the previous night fire was directed against K2c from No 8 position at J12d04. [initials]	
	13.		Very hazy, poor visibility clearing towards evening. Enemy heavily shelled J21b between 4pm & 7pm. From 10.30pm to 2.30am, our M.G. at No 2 position & a gun at J30d38 were directed against enemy trenches & tracks in K20b, 16 belts being fired. [initials]	

(A7092). Wt. W12839/M1293. 750,000. 1/17. D. D. & L., Ltd. Forms/C.2118/14.

Army Form C. 2118.

Instructions regarding War Diaries and Intelligence Summaries are contained in F. S. Regs., Part II. and the Staff Manual respectively. Title pages will be prepared in manuscript.

WAR DIARY
or
INTELLIGENCE SUMMARY.

(*Erase heading not required.*)

145 Machine Gun Coy

Place	Date	Hour	Summary of Events and Information	Remarks and references to Appendices
HERMIES -DEMICOURT	7th (cont'd)		To give assistance, if required, to 127th Brigade who were digging a new line in front of their old one on night 8th/9th June, seven new indirect fire platforms were constructed, two at J30d88 three from J30b75 to J30b76 one at K19c06 and one at J24d76. A direct lateral line was laid to Forward H.Q at J30d88. [initials]	~~[illegible]~~
	8		Ten guns were in position by 10.30 pm to bring indirect fire to bear on German trenches from K26d.098 to K27c27. As the work by the 127th Brigade was uninterrupted by the enemy, no call for barrage fire was received. Bright day, threatening showers and cloudy during noon & evening. Very quiet. [initials]	
	9		Ten guns remained on their barrage lines	
		3 AM.	The gun at K20c60 was withdrawn. Fine day, occasional threatening of showers. During morning enemy shelled J27a and J27b. [initials]	
	10	3 AM.	Six of the ten barrage guns mentioned above were withdrawn, two returning to local reserve at J21d44 and four returning to Transport lines at O6a Central. The four guns at Nos 1, 2, 3 & 4	

(A7092). Wt. W12839/M1293. 750,000. 1/17. D. D. & L., Ltd. Forms/C.2118/14.

Instructions regarding War Diaries and Intelligence Summaries are contained in F. S. Regs., Part II. and the Staff Manual respectively. Title pages will be prepared in manuscript.

WAR DIARY
or
INTELLIGENCE SUMMARY.
(Erase heading not required.)

Army Form C. 2118.

45 Machine Gun Coy

Place	Date	Hour	Summary of Events and Information	Remarks and references to Appendices
HERMIES - DEMICOURT	June 6		Very quiet day. Hot with threatening thunderstorms. 2 days' rations were brought up in view of operations on night 8/9th June. [signature]	
	7		Very hot, thunderstorms in north and south. Very slight showers. Towards 6pm enemy shelled Factory in J9b and LOUVERVAL PARK in J4. Arrangements were made to assist 1st BUCKS BATTn in an attack to be made between K26a9235 and K26a9555. One gun was placed at the disposal of O.C. 1st BUCKS BATTn and reported to K26a06 at 11pm. The object of this gun was to protect the left flank of the assaulting platoons, in conjunction with one platoon forming a left flank guard at K26a68 against a possible counter attack. Zero hour was fixed for 12 midnight & artillery opened a steady barrage. At Zero + 5 the assaulting platoons made the attack, and the barrage lifted to trenches on E bank of Canal until Zero + 10 when it gradually subsided. The attack was a complete success, and a new post was made at K26a9235. No counter-attack was forthcoming and the MG which had been placed in position at K20a60 was not called upon for any action. [signature]	

(A7092). Wt. W12839/M1293. 750,000. 1/17. D. D. & L., Ltd. Forms/C.2118/14.

Instructions regarding War Diaries and Intelligence Summaries are contained in F. S. Regs., Part II. and the Staff Manual respectively. Title pages will be prepared in manuscript.

WAR DIARY
or
INTELLIGENCE SUMMARY.
(Erase heading not required.)

Army Form C. 2118.

145 Machine Gun Coy.

Place	Date	Hour	Summary of Events and Information	Remarks and references to Appendices
HERMIES -DEMICOURT	June 1		Preparations were made to cooperate with the R.A + special R.E's in an operation to be carried out on night 1/2nd June. This operation however was cancelled. Weather fine, very hot. LIEUT. GELDARD left for Grantham. 2/Lt CLUTTON slightly wounded on hand but remained at duty.	
	2		Preparations were again made as for 1st June, 5 guns being used in the operations. Steady fire was kept up from 12.30am – 12.50 am. and from 1.5 am to 1.15 am. Bursts of fire were maintained from 1.32 to 2.30 am at irregular intervals. Gas was discharged by R.E. from Stokes mortars and projectors, and a total of 12,500 rounds were expended by our M.G's. Weather Fine with occasional wind. 2/Lt MAYOR proceeded to England. Mined dug-out commenced at Coy H.Q. (J21 d+4)	
	3		Very fine & hot. Inter-section relief took place on night 3/4th June. Very quiet. Enemy aerial activity of hostile planes observed above the lines.	
	4		Weather very hot. Quiet day. Nothing to report.	
	5		Fine weather continues. Pte GEAR accidentally shot himself in right foot with revolver. Very quiet day.	

(A7092). Wt. W12839/M1293. 750,000. 1/17. D. D. & L., Ltd. Forms/C.2118/14.

CONFIDENTIAL

Vol 17

WAR DIARY

OF

145th MACHINE GUN COMPANY

FROM JUNE 1st 1917 TO JUNE 30th 1917

[illegible] Lieut. O/C 145 Machine Gun Coy

POSITION OF GUNS ON THE NIGHT MAY 15th/16th 1917
Boursies
Louverval
Doignies
Demicourt
Hermies
ANTI-AIRCRAFT POST (CELLAR)
No 9 POSITION.
No 8 POSITION
No 7 POSITION
LEFT S-SECTION HQ LEFT SECTION.
No 6 POSITION.
RIGHT S-SECTION HQ. LEFT SECTION
No 5 POSITION.
RIGHT SECTION HQ
No 4 POSITION.
No 3 POSITION.
No 2 POSITION.
No 1 POSITION.
Coy HQ.
Canal du Nord (Under construction)
5th Field Survey Coy R.E. (656) 7-4-17
SCALE 1:20,000

APPENDIX 'C'

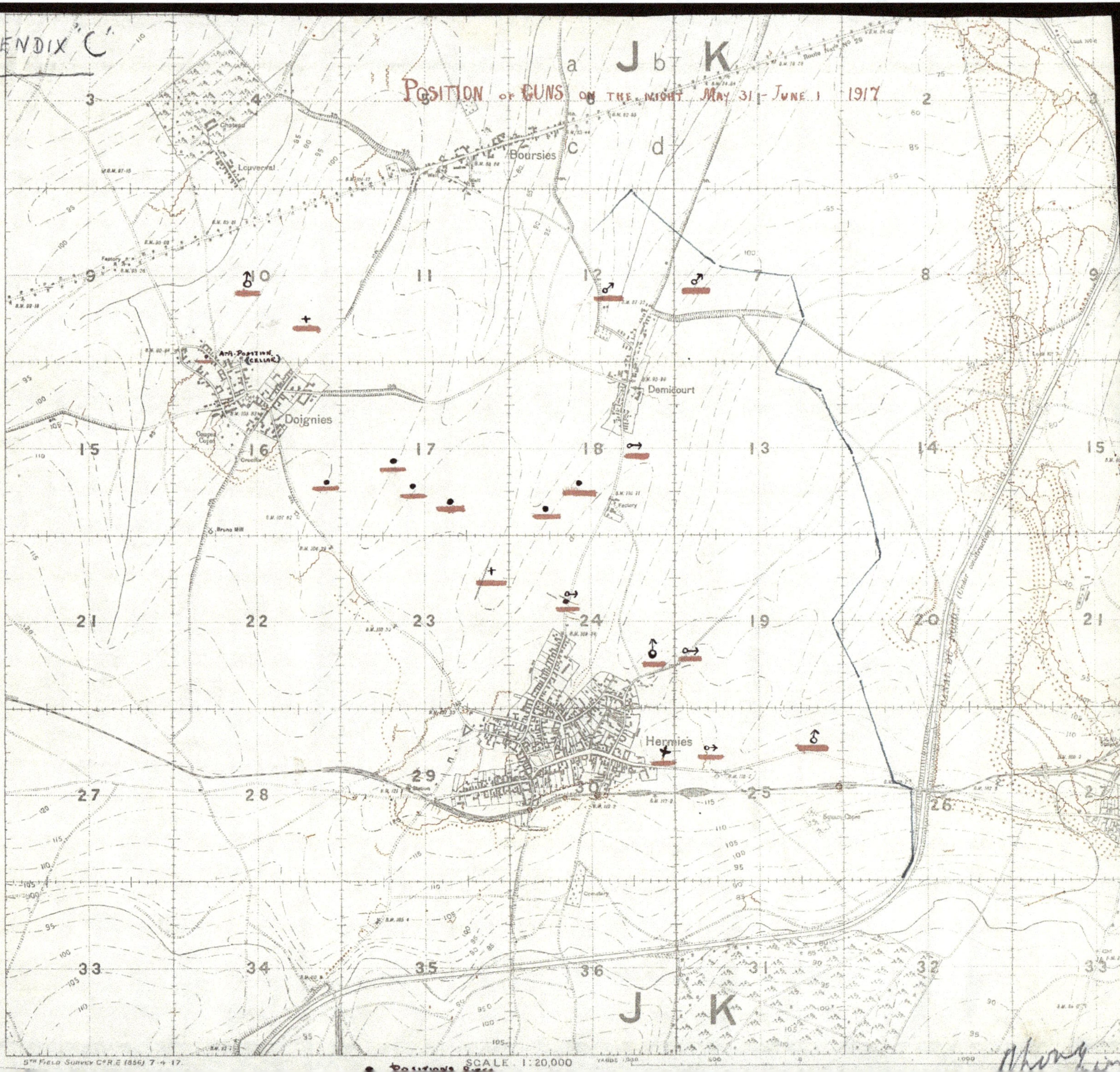

POSITION OF GUNS ON THE NIGHT MAY 31 - JUNE 1 1917
Louverval
Chateau
Boursies
Doignies
Anti-Position (Cellar)
Demicourt
Hermies
Bruno Mill
Factory
Cemetery
Canal du Nord (Under construction)
Route Nale No 29
5th Field Survey Coy R.E. (856) 7-4-17.
SCALE 1:20,000

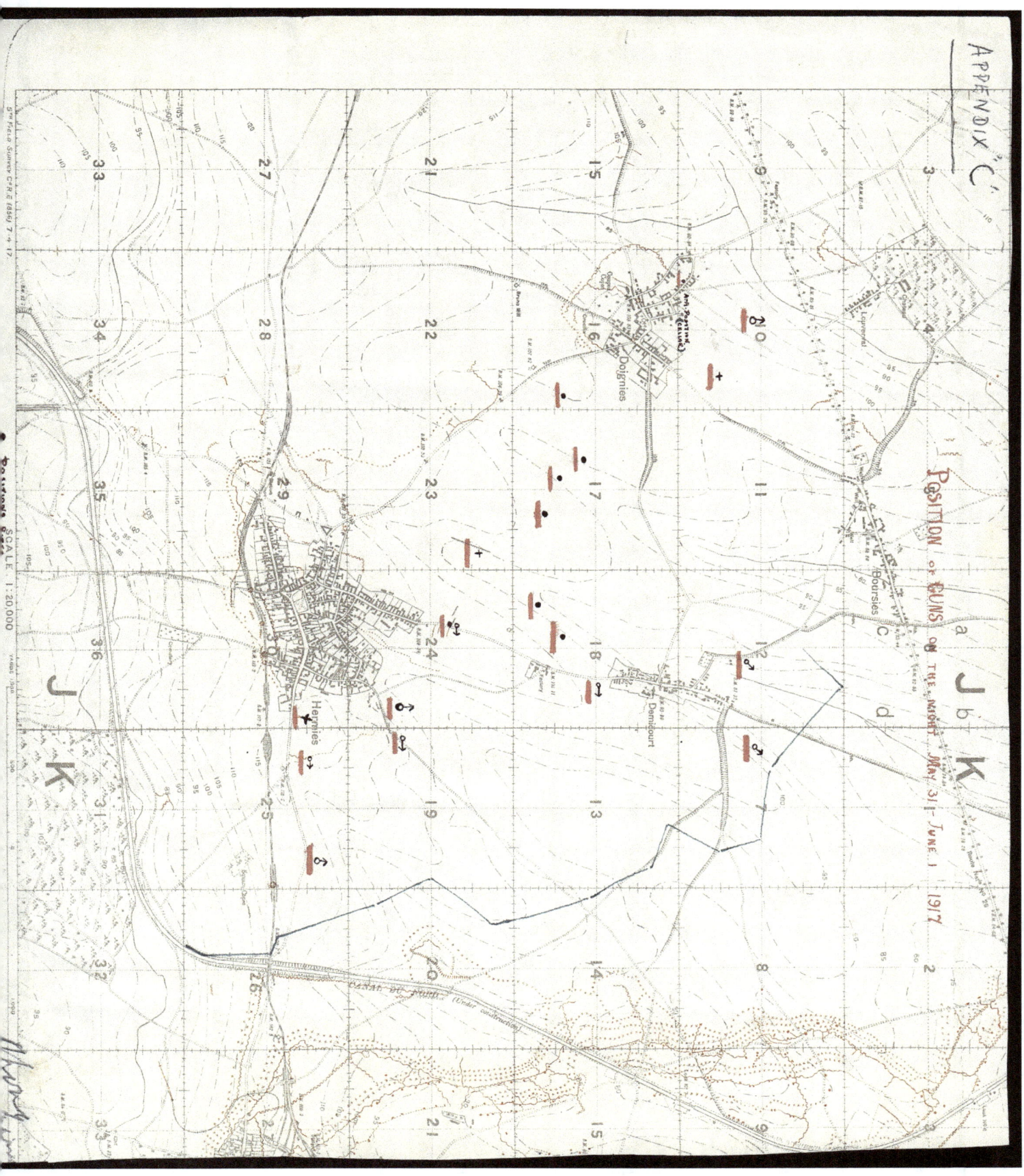

Instructions regarding War Diaries and Intelligence Summaries are contained in F. S. Regs., Part II. and the Staff Manual respectively. Title pages will be prepared in manuscript.

WAR DIARY
or
INTELLIGENCE SUMMARY.

(Erase heading not required.)

Army Form C. 2118.

145 Machine Gun Company

Place | Date | Hour | Summary of Events and Information | Remarks and references to Appendices

APPENDIX "A" Contd

Date 1917	Hour	Effective strength for previous day Off	Effective strength for previous day OR	Increase during day Off	Increase during day OR	Decrease during day Off	Decrease during day OR	To Hospital during day Off	To Hospital during day OR	Rejoined from Hospital Off	Rejoined from Hospital OR	Total in Hospital Off	Total in Hospital OR	Rejoined from Course Leave etc. Off	Rejoined from Course Leave etc. OR	Total on Course Leave etc. Off	Total on Course Leave etc. OR	Killed Off	Killed OR	Wounded Off	Wounded OR	Missing Off	Missing OR	Available for duty Off	Available for duty OR	Effective strength Off	Effective strength OR
May 17		11	175				5		1				8			1	4							10	157	11	170
18		11	170		1		1				1		6			1	4							10	159	11	170
19		11	170		1								6		1	2	5							9	157	11	171
20		11	171										6			2	5							9	159	11	171
21		11	171						1				7			2	6							9	158	11	171
22		11	171		1				2		3		6		1	2	4							9	161	11	172
23		11	172						1				7			2	5							9	159	11	172
24		11	172										7			2	5							9	159	11	172
25		11	172		2				1		1		7		2	2	3							9	162	11	174
26		11	174						1		1		7			2	3							9	162	11	174
27		11	174								1		6	1		1	3							10	163	11	174
28		11	174				1				1		5			1	3							10	163	11	173
29		11	173										5			1	3							10	163	11	173
30		11	173						2		1		6			1	3				1			10	162	11	173
31		11	173										6			1	3							10	162	11	173

[Signature] Major
O.C.
145 Machine Gun Company.

(A7092). Wt. W12839/M1293. 750,000. 1/17. D. D. & L., Ltd. Forms/C.2118/14.

Army Form C. 2118.

Instructions regarding War Diaries and Intelligence Summaries are contained in F. S. Regs., Part II. and the Staff Manual respectively. Title pages will be prepared in manuscript.

WAR DIARY
or
INTELLIGENCE SUMMARY.

(Erase heading not required.)

145 Machine Gun Company.

Place	Date	Hour	Summary of Events and Information	Remarks and references to Appendices

APPENDIX "A"

Date	Effective strength for previous day		Strength increase during day		Strength decrease during day		To Hospital during day		Rejoined from Hospital		Total in Hospital		Rejoined from Course, Leave etc		Total on Course, Leave etc		Killed		Wounded		Missing		Available for duty		Effective Strength	
1917 May	Off	OR	Off	OR	Off	OR	Off	OR	Off	OR	Off	OR	Off	OR	Off	OR	Off	OR	Off	OR	Off	OR	Off	OR	Off	OR
1	11	169				1		1			1	14				4				1			10	147	11	168
2	11	168				1		1		1	1	13		1		3							10	148	11	167
3	11	167		2		1		2		2	1	12				3							10	150	11	168
4	11	168		6				1	1	1		12				3							11	156	11	174
5	11	174						1		2		11				3							11	157	11	174
6	11	174						1		1		11				3							11	157	11	174
7	11	174						2		1		12				3							11	156	11	174
8	11	174		2		2				1		9				6							11	158	11	174
9	11	174										9				6							11	158	11	174
10	11	174								1		8		1	1	5							10	160	11	174
11	11	174		1				1				9		1	1	5							10	160	11	175
12	11	175										9		1	1	4							10	161	11	175
13	11	175								1		8			1	4							10	162	11	175
14	11	175						8		3		13			1	4							10	157	11	175
15	11	175						1				14			1	4							10	156	11	175
16	11	175								1		13			1	4							10	157	11	175

(A7092). Wt. W12839/M1293. 750,000. 1/17. D. D. & L., Ltd. Forms/C.2118/14.

Army Form C. 2118.

Instructions regarding War Diaries and Intelligence Summaries are contained in F. S. Regs., Part II. and the Staff Manual respectively. Title pages will be prepared in manuscript.

WAR DIARY
or
INTELLIGENCE SUMMARY.
(*Erase heading not required.*)

145 Machine Gun Coy

Place	Date	Hour	Summary of Events and Information	Remarks and references to Appendices
HERMIES -DEMICOURT	May 24		Extremely hot, nothing to report. [initials]	
	25		Hot weather continued, situation very quiet. [initials]	
	26		Nothing to report. [initials]	
	27		Discharge of gas again arranged for, & arrangements again fell through. [initials]	
	28/29		Gas eventually discharged 2 am night 28-29th machine guns co-operated with artillery in a prearranged scheme. [initials]	See appendix C
	29 Contd		Commenced alteration of dispositions (with a view to putting down barrage) as indicated in appendix C [initials]	
	30		Alteration of dispositions continued. Very quiet day. [initials]	
	31		Alteration of dispositions continued. Quiet day [initials]	

(A7092). Wt. W12839/M1293. 750,000. 1/17. D. D. & L., Ltd. Forms/C.2118/14.

Army Form C. 2118.

WAR DIARY
or
INTELLIGENCE SUMMARY.
(Erase heading not required.)

Instructions regarding War Diaries and Intelligence Summaries are contained in F. S. Regs., Part II. and the Staff Manual respectively. Title pages will be prepared in manuscript.

145 Machine Gun Coy

Place	Date	Hour	Summary of Events and Information	Remarks and references to Appendices
	May 15 (Contd)		The two detachments in local reserve at Coy HQ were however kept at mobile strength, to allow of reinforcing, if necessary. Fine clear day. M	v. Appendix B
	May 16		A quiet night (15-16th), practically no shelling, & only a few bursts of machine gun fire. Enemy machine guns did not appear to be traversing at all, but only firing in certain places, & then very high, this at any rate as far as HERMIES & ground in front was concerned. Rain set in during the early morning & continued most of the day and the following night. Visibility very low permitting of increased freedom of movement. M	
	May 17		Weather dull & overcast. Enemy extraordinarily quiet. M	
	18		Uneventful day. M	
	19		Quiet day, very hot. M	
	20		Very fine, hot day, during the night intermittent fire was kept up by 3 guns, by way of retaliation for hostile M.G. fire. M	
	May 21		Made preparations for firing on tracks, & centres of activity behind the enemy's line in view of a proposed discharge of gas which however did not take place. M	
	May 22		The same thing happened, the wind apparently not being favourable. M	
	23		Discharge of gas again failed to take place. M	

(A7092). Wt. W12839/M1293. 750,000. 1/17. D. D. & L., Ltd. Forms/C.2118/14.

Instructions regarding War Diaries and Intelligence Summaries are contained in F. S. Regs., Part II. and the Staff Manual respectively. Title pages will be prepared in manuscript.

WAR DIARY
or
INTELLIGENCE SUMMARY.
(Erase heading not required.)

Army Form C. 2118.

148 Machine Gun Coy

Place	Date	Hour	Summary of Events and Information	Remarks and references to Appendices
PERONNE – COMBLES	May 12		Left PERONNE with rest of Brigade about 8 am & marched to Bois de DOUAGE near COMBLES, to bivouacs, shelters & dug-outs. March was very trying, on account of the excessive heat. Camping ground rather foul, & stank, on account of number of corpses not properly interred.	
COMBLES – REINCOURT les BAPAUME	May 13		Moved off 6 am to RIENCOURT, near BAPAUME & CO went up same afternoon to see 33rd Company who were in the line between BOURSIES & the CANAL DU NORD, to the north of BOIS d'HAVRINCOURT. Reconnaissance forward said to be impossible during the day; not altogether correct. Very hot & exhausting weather.	
	14		Relieved 33rd M.G Coy in the line during the night 14-15th. Dispositions: 8 guns forward of a line HERMIES – DEMICOURT 1 gun in local reserve at DOIGNIES 2 " in local reserve at Coy HQ (J21 D44) 5 guns remaining with transport at RIENCOURT for the night, & moving with transport to neighbourhood of VELU early in morning of 15th.	
HERMIES – DEMICOURT	May 15		The relief was a long one, some of the outcoming detachments not passing Coy HQ till 4.30 am. As 9 gun positions were taken over, detachments were reduced to a strength of 4 men each; with a N.C.O. Officer, & batman per subsection	

(A7092). Wt. W12839/M1293. 750,000. 1/17. D. D. & L., Ltd. Forms/C.2118/14.

Instructions regarding War Diaries and Intelligence Summaries are contained in F. S. Regs., Part II. and the Staff Manual respectively. Title pages will be prepared in manuscript.

WAR DIARY
or
INTELLIGENCE SUMMARY.
(Erase heading not required.)

Army Form C. 2118.

145 Machine Gun Company

Place	Date	Hour	Summary of Events and Information	Remarks and references to Appendices
PERONNE	May 4 (Contd)		In the evening NCOs were lectured; + officers either gave or attended lectures or read under the direction of the 2nd in Command.	[illegible]
	May 5		Training continued. Inspection of Transport 9 am by G.O.C. Brigade. Wire cutting demonstration for C.O.s at Bde HQ 2 pm. Div. Conference 3 pm.	[illegible]
	May 6		Inspection of Company in fighting order by O.C. Coy, otherwise no parade.	[illegible]
	May 7		Training continued. G.O.C. Division conducted a staff ride in the afternoon.	[illegible]
	May 8		Training continued.	[illegible]
	May 9		Commenced re-inoculating Company; remainder training.	[illegible]
	May 10		Continued re-inoculating; remainder recovering from previous day's inoculation.	[illegible]
	May 11		Commenced rifle + revolver instruction and practices.	[illegible]

(A7092). Wt. W12839/M1293. 750,000. 1/17. D. D. & L., Ltd. Forms/C.2118/14.

Instructions regarding War Diaries and Intelligence Summaries are contained in F. S. Regs., Part II. and the Staff Manual respectively. Title pages will be prepared in manuscript.

WAR DIARY
or
INTELLIGENCE SUMMARY.
(Erase heading not required.)

Army Form C. 2118.

143 Machine Gun Company [illegible]

Place	Date	Hour	Summary of Events and Information	Remarks and references to Appendices
ALDER SPINNEY (ROISEL) - PERONNE	May 1		Company moved off 10.15 am to billets in PERONNE. Billets were in the main street & were practically the same as those occupied March [illegible] except that houses had been cleared by this time & so were occupied instead of cellars. Weather very fine & hot. MK	
	May 2		Day occupied with fatigues (constructing Bde HQ, cleaning up own billets & making proper sanitary accomodation) Weather continuing fine, & sudden warmth almost oppressive. PERONNE proved very dusty, while the continued heavy traffic made the billets very noisy. MK	
	May 3		Fatigues continued (Bde HQ, Town Major & own cleaning & sanitary fatigues) MK	
	May 4		Being free of fatigues, devoted day to examining kit & equipment, taking stock of shortages etc., all available men proceeding to train as follows:- 5.40 am Short Run & Physical Training ([illegible] only) 6.15 am Breakfast 7.30 Move off in fighting order to DOINGT HILLS Physical Training (Games etc) Squad Drill Arms Drill Mechanism 1-0 pm March back to PERONNE. MK	

(A7092). Wt. W12839/M1293. 750,000. 1/17. D. D. & L., Ltd. Forms/C.2118/14.

Vol 16

CONFIDENTIAL

WAR DIARY

OF

145th MACHINE GUN COMPANY.

FROM MAY 1st 1917 TO MAY 31st 1917.

[illegible] Major
O.C.
145th Machine Gun Coy.

Instructions regarding War Diaries and Intelligence Summaries are contained in F. S. Regs., Part II. and the Staff Manual respectively. Title Pages will be prepared in manuscript.

WAR DIARY
or
INTELLIGENCE SUMMARY
(Erase heading not required.)

Army Form C. 2118

145th Machine Gun Company

Place | Date | Hour | Summary of Events and Information | Remarks and references to Appendices

APPENDIX "A" Contd.

Date	Effective strength for previous day Off	Effective strength for previous day ORs	Strength increase during day Off	Strength increase during day ORs	Strength decrease during day Off	Strength decrease during day ORs	To Hospital during day Off	To Hospital during day ORs	Rejoined from Hospital Off	Rejoined from Hospital ORs	Total in Hospital Off	Total in Hospital ORs	Rejoined from Course, Leave etc. Off	Rejoined from Course, Leave etc. ORs	Total on Course, Leave etc. Off	Total on Course, Leave etc. ORs	Killed Off	Killed ORs	Wounded Off	Wounded ORs	Missing Off	Missing ORs	Available for duty Off	Available for duty ORs	Effective Strength Off	Effective Strength ORs	Remarks
April																											
16	10	174					1	2		1	2	9				3							8	162	10	174	
17	10	174									2	9				3							8	162	10	174	24 T.M.B. returned to units.
18	10	174									2	9				3							8	162	10	174	
19	10	174						1			2	10				3							8	161	10	174	
20	10	174				1					2	10				3				1			8	160	10	173	
21	10	173		3							2	10				3							8	163	10	176	
22	10	176									2	10				3							8	163	10	176	
23	10	176						1			2	11				3							8	162	10	176	
24	10	176				1				1	2	9				4							8	161	10	175	7 TMB returned to units
25	10	175									2	9				4							8	161	10	175	
26	10	175			1			1		1	1	9				4							8	161	9	175	
27	9	175						2			1	11				4							8	159	9	175	
28	9	175				6		1			1	12				4				5			8	151	9	169	
29	9	169	2								1	12				4							10	151	11	169	
30	11	169						2			1	14				4							10	149	11	169	

1875 Wt. W593/826 1,000,000 4/15 J.B.C. & A. A.D.S.S./Forms/C. 2118.

[illegible signature] Lt for Major

OC 145 Machine Gun Company

Instructions regarding War Diaries and Intelligence Summaries are contained in F. S. Regs., Part II. and the Staff Manual respectively. Title Pages will be prepared in manuscript.

WAR DIARY
or
INTELLIGENCE SUMMARY
(Erase heading not required.)

Army Form C. 2118

145 M. G. Coy

APPENDIX "A"

Place	Date	Hour	Effective Strength for previous day		Strength Increase during day		Strength Decrease during day		To Hospital during day		Rejoined from Hospital		Total in Hospital		Rejoined from Course Leave etc.		Total absent on Course Leave etc.		Killed		Wounded		Missing		Available for duty		Effective strength		Remarks and references to Appendices
	April		Off	OR	Off	OR	Off	OR	Off	OR	Off	OR	Off	OR	Off	OR	Off	OR	Off	OR	Off	OR	Off	OR	Off	OR	Off	OR	
	1		11	174									2	3				4							9	167	11	174	
	2		11	174									2	3				4							9	167	11	174	
	3		11	174						1			2	4				5							9	165	11	174	
	4		11	174									2	4		1		4							9	166	11	174	32 OR attached from 145 T.M. Battery
	5		11	174							1		1	4		1		3							10	167	11	174	
	6		11	174		1	1	5	1	1			1	4				3	1			4			9	163	10	170	
	7		10	170		1				1		2	1	3				3							9	165	10	171	
	8		10	171		2							1	3				3							9	167	10	173	
	9		10	173						1			1	4				3							9	166	10	173	
	10		10	173				1					1	3				3							9	166	10	172	
	11		10	172									1	3				3							9	166	10	172	
	12		10	172		2				3			1	6		1		2							9	166	10	174	
	13		10	174						1			1	7				2							9	165	10	174	
	14		10	174									1	7				2							9	165	10	174	
	15		10	174						1			1	8				2							9	164	10	174	

1875 Wt. W593/826 1,000,000 4/15 J.B.C. & A. A.D.S.S./Forms/C. 2118.

Instructions regarding War Diaries and Intelligence Summaries are contained in F. S. Regs., Part II. and the Staff Manual respectively. Title Pages will be prepared in manuscript.

WAR DIARY
or
INTELLIGENCE SUMMARY
(Erase heading not required.)

Army Form C. 2118

[illegible] M.G. Coy.

Place	Date	Hour	Summary of Events and Information	Remarks and references to Appendices
	28th continued		This subsection was made up to strength and placed in cellars [illegible] at the N. end of LEMPIRE. [illegible]	
	29th		Comparatively quiet time with exception of intermittent shelling of villages RONSSOY, BASSÉ-BOULOGNE, LEMPIRE. [illegible]	
			Weather continued excellent.	
			144 M.G. Coy relieved this Company. On relief the Company bivouacked in ALDER SPINNEY. [illegible]	
	30th		Company cleaned up in preparation of moving back [illegible]	

Instructions regarding War Diaries and Intelligence Summaries are contained in F. S. Regs., Part II. and the Staff Manual respectively. Title Pages will be prepared in manuscript.

WAR DIARY
or
INTELLIGENCE SUMMARY
(Erase heading not required.)

Army Form C. 2118

145 M.G. Coy.

Place	Date	Hour	Summary of Events and Information	Remarks and references to Appendices
	25th		Again "stood to". Rouse 12.45 am. Moved off 2.25 am to the valley running St EMILIE – RONSSOY. Arrived in position at 4.15 am.	S.H.G.
			144 Bde attacked GILLEMONT FARM with some measure of success.	S.H.G.
			This Company relieved 144 M.G. Coy in their new dispositions the same night remaining in the valley all the day.	S.H.G.
	26th		Dispositions as taken over from 144 M.G. Coy — Approx:— 1 Section forward on the left and in front of TOMBOIS FARM.	
			1 Section on the crest running due N. & S. from in front of BASSÉ - BOULOGNE almost to MALAKOFF FARM	
			1 Section in support on the BROWN LINE.	
			The remaining section & transport moved to ALDER SPINNEY.	
			H.Q. were established on the TEMPLEUX GUÉRARD — RONSSOY ROAD.	S.H.G.
	27th		Situation Normal — weather excellent.	S.H.G.
	28th		4 am, a outsection about 1000x E. of TOMBOIS FARM was withdrawn having suffered 6 Casualties	

Instructions regarding War Diaries and Intelligence Summaries are contained in F. S. Regs., Part II. and the Staff Manual respectively. Title Pages will be prepared in manuscript.

WAR DIARY
or
INTELLIGENCE SUMMARY
(Erase heading not required.)

Army Form C. 2118

145 M.G. Coy

Place	Date	Hour	Summary of Events and Information	Remarks and references to Appendices
	19th (continued)		The dispositions taken over by 144 M.G. Coy were the same as those handed over by them with the addition of 2 guns on the TOMBOIS FARM Road & S. of TOMBOIS FARM respectively. S.H.S.	
			On relief the Coy returned to TINCOURT WOOD S.H.S.	
	20th		Weather began to clear. Gun equipment was cleaned and kits dried etc. S.H.S.	
			A general move was made to the open ground rather than to villages for the purpose of rest billets, on account of the number of delayed mines which had blown. S.H.S.	
			The 144 M.G. Coy having relieved this unit in VILLERS-FAUCON had six casualties owing to delayed mine.	
	21st		Cleaning guns etc continued. Two A-A positions were occupied on the HAMEL - MARQUAIS ROAD. S.H.S.	
	22nd		Spring weather appeared to have started at last. S.H.S. CHURCH PARADES.	
	23rd		General sanitation in camp also mending road. S.H.S.	
	24th		"Stood to" as from 4.15 am - Rouse at 2.30 am. owing to 144 Bde attacking GILLEMONT FARM. Attack failed. This was Work continued on camp.	
			The Company bathed - This was the first bath for this unit for over 4 weeks S.H.S.	

1875 Wt. W593/826 1,000,000 4/15 J.B.C. & A. A.D.S.S./Forms/C. 2118.

Instructions regarding War Diaries and Intelligence Summaries are contained in F. S. Regs., Part II. and the Staff Manual respectively. Title Pages will be prepared in manuscript.

WAR DIARY
or
INTELLIGENCE SUMMARY
(Erase heading not required.)

Army Form C. 2118

M.G. Coy

Place	Date	Hour	Summary of Events and Information	Remarks and references to Appendices
	14th		Comparatively quiet – Some shelling of the three villages with particular attention to the S. of RONSSOY. S.H.G.	
	15th		Situation quiet – usual slight shelling. The right flank which ran almost due E. & W. due N. of HARGICOURT seemed to get more attention from the enemy than the LEMPIRE side which was comparatively quiet. Weather continued wet and inclement. S.H.G.	
	16th & 17th		At 11.30 pm the 1/1 Bn BUCKS on the left attacked TOMBOIS FARM and the 1/4 BERKS on the Right attacked GILLEMONT FARM. S.H.G.	
			A Sub-section was attached to each Battalion. The attack on the right failed. The attack on the left eventually succeeded, the two guns taking up positions as follows:– one in the sunken road immediately to the S. of TOMBOIS FARM. The other on the S. side of the BASSÉ-BOULOGNE – TOMBOIS FARM road about 500x clear of the village. The night was very dark with very heavy storms of hail & rain. S.H.G.	
	18th		Situation normal – shelling on TOMBOIS FARM. Weather continued bad. S.H.G.	
	19th		This unit was relieved by 144 M.G. Coy. On the right the 1/4th OXFORDS & BUCKS L.I. again attacked GILLEMONT FARM. The attack again failed. A Subsection attached to them for these operations did not come into action at all and returned at dawn. S.H.G.	

1875 Wt. W593/826 1,000,000 4/15 J.B.C. & A. A.D.S.S./Forms/C. 2118.

Instructions regarding War Diaries and Intelligence Summaries are contained in F. S. Regs., Part II. and the Staff Manual respectively. Title Pages will be prepared in manuscript.

WAR DIARY
or
INTELLIGENCE SUMMARY
(Erase heading not required.)

Army Form C. 2118

145 M.G. Coy

Place	Date	Hour	Summary of Events and Information	Remarks and references to Appendices
	5		~~Fonq g.~~ A sub-section at mobile strength in support at ST EMILIE	
	6		The remainder of Coy + Transport moved from VILLERS-FAUCON to ST EMILIE accommodation being found inadequate. The Coy immediately returned to VILLERS-FAUCON.	
	7.		144 M G Coy relieved this Coy in the line. On relief this Coy moved to bivouacs in TINCOURT WOOD. Weather during these few days was very cold, with snow, hail, + rain	
	8		Weather, Fine sunny day, day spent in cleaning up.	
	9		Exceedingly bad weather, very cold, little training possible	
	10		Bad weather continued stronger winds.	
	11		Alternate snow and rain. Cold winds	S.H.G.
	12		Same weather continued. The Coy during this time worked chiefly on cleaning guns equipment and general sanitation ~~S.H.G.~~	S.H.G.
	13		This Coy relieved the 144 M.G. Coy with two sections in the line. The remaining two sections and transport remained at VILLERS-FAUCON with a forward H.Q. and telephone station in front of the slag heaps to the S. of RONSSOY. Dispositions were 1 subsection N. of LEMPIRE 1 subsection S. of BASSÉ-BOULOGNE 1 section in line BASSÉ-BOULOGNE — HARGICOURT	S.H.G. S.H.G.

1875 Wt. W593/826 1,000,000 4/15 J.B.C. & A. A.D.S.S./Forms/C. 2118.

Instructions regarding War Diaries and Intelligence Summaries are contained in F. S. Regs., Part II. and the Staff Manual respectively. Title Pages will be prepared in manuscript.

WAR DIARY
or
INTELLIGENCE SUMMARY
(Erase heading not required.)

Army Form C. 2118

145 M. G. Coy

Place	Date	Hour	Summary of Events and Information	Remarks and references to Appendices
HAMEL	April 1		One section retained in MARQUAIX, for work on MG positions in main line of defence, to North and East of MARQUAIX.	
"	2		Weather stormy.	
	3		Two sections moved off to relieve 144 MG Coy in front of EPÉHY ST EMILIE + TEMPLEUX WOOD. Established forward HQ in VILLERS-FAUCON leaving remainder of Company + Transport in HAMEL.	
VILLERS-FAUCON	4		Remainder of Coy moved up to VILLERS-FAUCON. 143 MG Coy relieved ~~the~~ 4 guns in front of EPÉHY. 32 men arrived for attachment from T.M. Battery	
	5	4.45am	The Glosters on left, Oxfords in middle + R. Berks on right attacked + captured LEMPIRE + RONSSOY. A sub-section of this Coy was placed at the disposal of each Battalion Commander. The sub-section attached to the Oxfords, was unfortunate in having 4 men hit, early in the attack. Late in the afternoon 2/Lt G.H. BAILEY who was in command of this sub-section was mortally wounded, + another man, his batman, was wounded at same time. The dispositions of M.G.s at close of day were, approximately. 2 guns on outskirts of LEMPIRE, on LEMPIRE-EPÉHY Road. 4 guns to south + south east of RONSSOY covering ground between that + HARGICOURT.	

1875 Wt. W593/826 1,000,000 4/15 J.B.C. & A. A.D.S.S./Forms/C. 2118.

Vol 15

CONFIDENTIAL

WAR DIARY

OF

145th MACHINE GUN COMPANY

FROM APRIL 1st 17 TO APRIL 30th 17.

[illegible] Lt
for Major.
O.C.
145th Machine Gun Coy.

145 M.G. Coy supplies 4 guns in CRUCIFORM POST in DOLFUS TR at about [H 36 a 62]

1 gun firing on DUBOIS TR from I 32 c 3520 to junction at I 32 c 6020 & searching track from I 32 c 6020 to I 32 d 0510.

1 gun enfilading DUBOIS TR from I 32 c 6020 to trench junctions at O 2 a 9500.

2 guns enfilading BOSTON TR from I 32 c 1070 to corner of VERRIER TR at I 32 c 7040.

143 M.G. Coy supplies 4 guns.

2 guns to engage H.Q.rs dug-outs along bank from I 32 c 7050 to I 32 d 2023.

2 guns to enfilade BOSTON TR from I 32 c 1082 to I 32 c 7243.

OC 143 M.G. Coy also would undertake to barrage German front and support trenches contained by the following co-ordinates.

I 31 d 7080. I 31 d 8575 I 31 b 7200, and I 31 b 8200.

He would be firing from positions in his sector.

[signature] Lt
OC
145 M.G. Coy.

SECRET

APPENDIX 'A'

SCHEME
MACHINE GUN BARRAGE

144 M.G. Coy will fire with 7 guns.
145 M.G. Coy will supply a section to fire from the CRUCIFORM POST (DOLFUS TR) at about H36 a 62.
143 M.G. Coy will fire with 4 guns from positions to be selected later by O.C. and M.G. Coy's

REFERENCE 1/5,000 plan of MAISONETTE dated 22.2.17.

Dispositions & targets for M.G. Coy.

Position	Nº of guns	Targets.
Nº 11 Empt [N.6.b. 1545]	2	Trench running East & West from O1.b. 7513 to O2a 5910. [JEAN TR and continuations]
Nº 10 Empt [N.6.c 1560]	2	Target (i) HERVÉ TR from junction with JEAN TR at O2a 4013 to O2a 4843. Target (ii) ORGANISE TR from junction with JEAN TR at O2a 5809 to O2a 7339.
New CHEMINADE Position.	1	WILHELM TR from O1.b. 7028 to O2a 0555 & searching across to trench junctions at O2a 7590, I32c 8903, and I32c 9500.
Nº 1 Empt. [N12 b 2598]	1	HERVÉ TR from O2a 4445 to I32c 9500.
No 11(a) Empt [N.6.b. 6072]	1	(i) Dug-outs in bank from O2b 7062 to O2b 7095. (ii) Dug-outs in bank along road from O2b 8868 to O3a 1580.

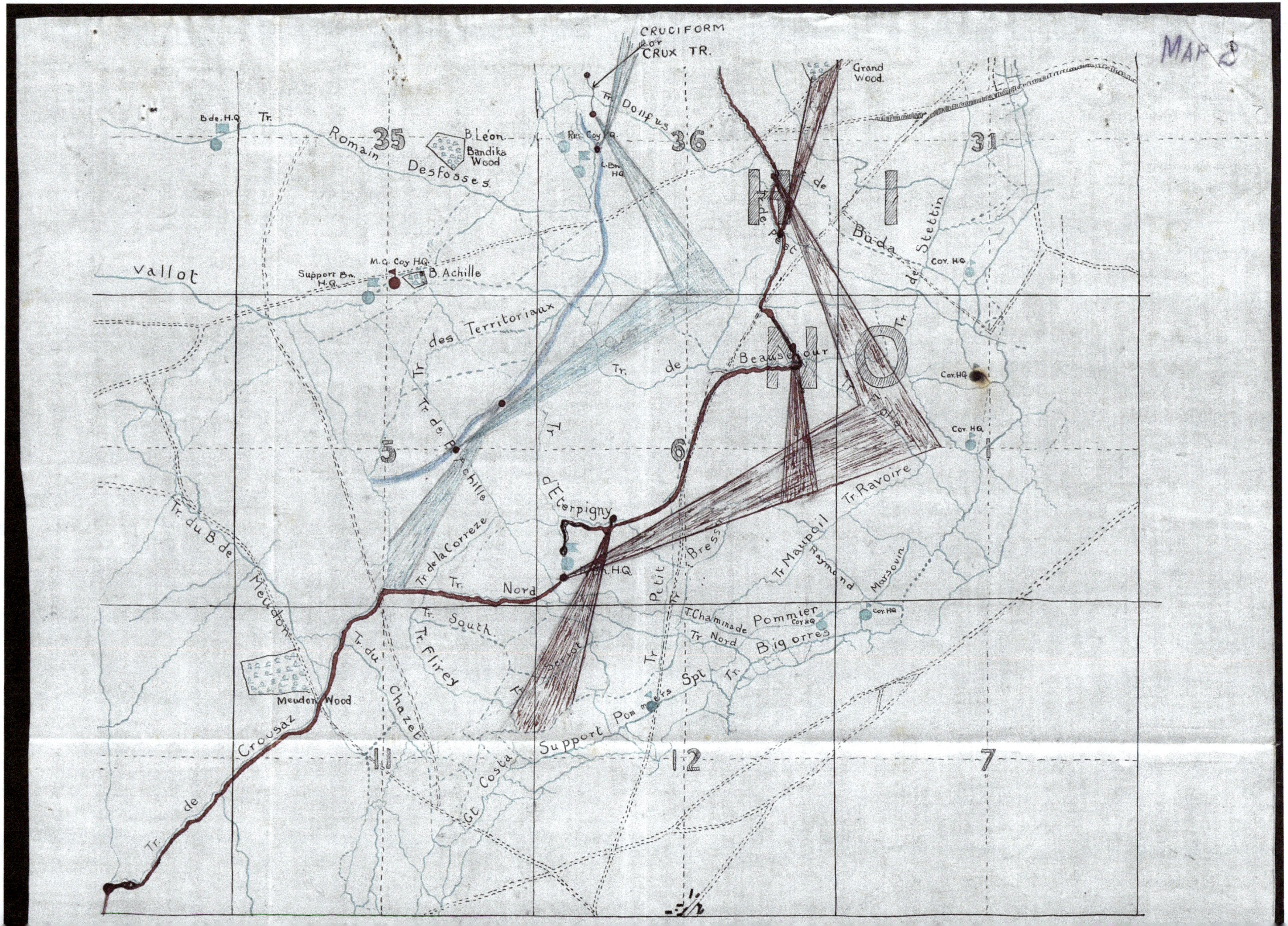

MAP 2
CRUCIFORM or CRUX TR.
Grand Wood.
Bde. H.Q. Tr.
Romain
35
B. Léon
Bandika Wood
Desfosses
Res. Coy H.Q.
L.Bn. H.Q.
Tr. Dollfus
36
31
Tr. de Pest
Tr. de Buda
de Stettin
Coy. H.Q.
Vallot
Support Bn. H.Q.
M.G. Coy H.Q.
B. Achille
Tr. des Territoriaux
Tr. de Beauséjour
Cov. H.Q.
Tr. de B. Achille
5
6
Tr. d'Eterpigny
Tr. de la Correze
Tr. Nord
Bn. H.Q.
Tr. Bresse
Tr. Maupoil
Raymond
Marsouin
Tr. Ravoire
Tr. du B. de Meudon
Meudon Wood
Tr. South
Tr. Flirey
Tr. du Chazet
Tr. Petit
T. Chaminade
Tr. Nord
Pommier
Coy H.Q.
Bigorres
Tr. Pommiers Spt
Support
Gt. Costa
Tr. de Crousaz
11
12
7

MAP
(Parts of Trench Map. Peronne. 62c N.W.4. 1/10.000 and
Barleux 62c S.W.2.)

SECRET.

MAP 1

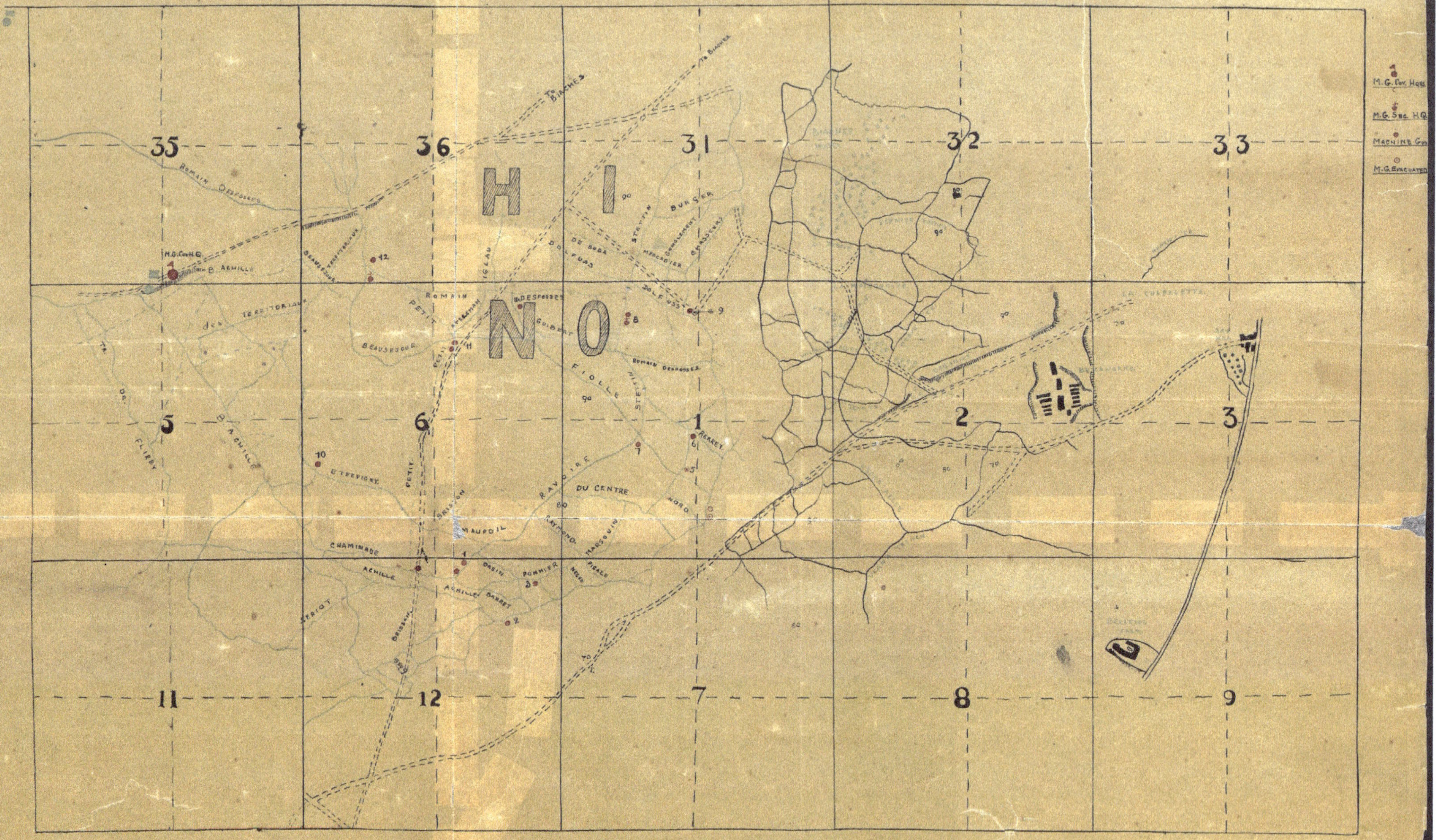

Instructions regarding War Diaries and Intelligence Summaries are contained in F. S. Regs., Part II. and the Staff Manual respectively. Title Pages will be prepared in manuscript.

WAR DIARY
or
~~INTELLIGENCE SUMMARY~~
(Erase heading not required.)

Army Form C. 2118

1 Section
145 M.G. Coy.

Place	Date	Hour	Summary of Events and Information	Remarks and references to Appendices
			position was built at K23a34 covering the right road to HERVILLY by night and the open country to the right of the road by day. The limber was moved up to HAMELET and the other team took up billets in ROISEL and was held in reserve. A Sub-section remained at BOUVINCOURT.	
	27		B. Sub section. Remained as before & Teams were changed round to provide a relief. An enemy post was observed at K23b70 and fired on road near gun in the evening. A few rounds were exchanged. A Sub section returned to the Company in the evening at BUIRE.	
	28		B Sub section Was relieved about 8 AM by a section of the 59th Division Returned to HAMELET & later in the day rejoined the Company	

[illegible signature]

Instructions regarding War Diaries and Intelligence Summaries are contained in F. S. Regs., Part II. and the Staff Manual respectively. Title Pages will be prepared in manuscript.

WAR DIARY
or
~~INTELLIGENCE SUMMARY~~
(Erase heading not required.)

Army Form C. 2118

1 Section
145 M.G. Coy

Place	Date	Hour	Summary of Events and Information	Remarks and references to Appendices
	Mar 25		B. Sub-Section. Moved up from CARTIGNY to BOUCLY during the afternoon. One team remained at BOUCLY in billets, the other team moved on to HAMELET & took up a defensive position at K21a22, covering ground on right of HAMELET-ROISEL road & acting in conjunction with a Lewis gun which covered the left of the road. Crossfire was found to be impossible owing to the formation of the ground.	
			A Sub-Section. Fired on 4 hostile aircraft and drove them off	
	26		B Sub-Section: Team from BOUCLY relieved team from HAMELET. The latter moved up at about 11.0 am to railway crossing K22a39 to give covering fire to infantry held up on embankment, who were engaged in attacking ROISEL. Covering fire was impossible as other attacking troops had already entered the village and their position was unknown. Later is was decided to make a move forward but no covering fire was carried out as the enemy had already left the village. The gun was therefore dismounted & moved forward with the infantry. Some delay was caused by the L/Cpl in charge of the team being wounded and the team entered the village after the infantry. A defensive	

Instructions regarding War Diaries and Intelligence Summaries are contained in F. S. Regs., Part II. and the Staff Manual respectively. Title Pages will be prepared in manuscript.

WAR DIARY
or
~~INTELLIGENCE SUMMARY~~
(Erase heading not required.)

Army Form C. 2118

1 Section
145 M.G. Coy

Place	Date	Hour	Summary of Events and Information	Remarks and references to Appendices
CARTIGNY	Mar 23		Enemy machine guns were reported by our aircraft in the arm of the wood running into K7a. Indirect fire was applied to this target at about 6.0 pm, one belt (250 rounds) being fired. Our patrols next day reported signs of enemy casualties presumably caused by our fire. A Sub Section was attached to 1/5 GLOSTER REGT & moved up during the afternoon to BOUVINCOURT. Built defensive positions in outpost line as follows:- (1) P24c19 firing on a true bearing of 92° across the valley along a depression in the ground. (2) P18a8085 covering ground from P18 Central to P12d44. An anti aircraft post was established at P24a18. These positions were only to be occupied in case of alarm. This sub-section remained in BOUVINCOURT during the rest of the tour of duty, & the positions were not altered	
	24		B Sub-Section. The right team moved up to MARQUAIX which had been occupied by the infantry & took up a position in a house at K14b31 firing along the left flank of ROISEL. This position was also an advantageous one for engaging any parties of enemy cavalry that might approach. The left team remained in the same position as before for night firing. About 6.0 pm orders were received to return to CARTIGNY. Moved off about 8.0 pm. A Sub Section remained at BOUVINCOURT.	

1875 Wt. W593/826 1,000,000 4/15 J.B.C. & A. A.D.S.S./Forms/C. 2118.

Army Form C. 2118

Instructions regarding War Diaries and Intelligence Summaries are contained in F. S. Regs., Part II. and the Staff Manual respectively. Title Pages will be prepared in manuscript.

WAR DIARY
or
INTELLIGENCE SUMMARY
(Erase heading not required.)

1 Section
145 M.G. Coy.

Place	Date	Hour	Summary of Events and Information	Remarks and references to Appendices
			APPENDIX "C" OPERATIONS OF No 1 SECTION ATTACHED WARDS' COLUMN.	
PERONNE	Mar 22		Joined WARDS COLUMN and marched from PERONNE to CARTIGNY. An anti-aircraft position was made and manned at P8 b 56 and defensive positions were constructed as follows:- (1) P8 b 56 covering open ground from P9 a 01 to P8 d 6575. (2) P3 c 8580 covering open ground from P3 c 80 to P3 d 00. (3) P3 b 50 covering main road in CARTIGNY. These positions were only to be manned in case of an enemy attack and were never actually used.	Map references 62 c NE and 62 c SE. 1/20,000.
CARTIGNY	23		B Sub-Section received orders to move with infantry company of 1/4 OXFORD & BUCKS L.I. and started off at 5 AM. Marched from CARTIGNY through BUIRE to TINCOURT with orders to co-operate with infantry to secure TINCOURT and BOUCLY. Both villages were found to be evacuated by the enemy and occupied by our cyclists and cavalry. HAMEL was also empty, but cavalry reported enemy in MARQUAIX. Defensive positions taken up as follows and occupied from dusk till dawn. (1) K19 a 41 firing across both HAMEL-MARQUAIX roads & along left flank of MARQUAIX. (2) Cross roads J18 c 61 covering road to TINCOURT WOOD	

Instructions regarding War Diaries and Intelligence Summaries are contained in F. S. Regs., Part II. and the Staff Manual respectively. Title Pages will be prepared in manuscript.

WAR DIARY
or
INTELLIGENCE SUMMARY
(Erase heading not required.)

Army Form C. 2118

145th Machine Gun Company.

Place	Date	Hour	Summary of Events and Information	Remarks and references to Appendices

APPENDIX "B"

March	Effective strength for previous day		Strength increase during day		Strength decrease during day		To Hospital during day		Rejoined from Hospital		Total in Hospital		Absent on Course, Leave, etc.		Rejoined from Course, Leave, etc.		Killed		Wounded		Missing		Available for duty		Effective Strength		Remarks
	Off	OR	Off	OR	Off	OR	Off	OR	Off	OR	Off	OR	Off	OR	Off	OR	Off	OR	Off	OR	Off	OR	Off	OR	Off	OR	
1	11	174	-	2	.	.	.	.	.	.	1	3	1	2	.	.	.	.	.	.	.	.	9	170	11	176	
2	11	176	.	.	.	1	.	.	.	.	1	3	1	2	.	.	.	.	.	.	.	.	9	169	11	175	
3	11	175	.	.	.	.	.	2	.	.	1	5	1	2	.	.	.	.	.	.	.	.	9	167	11	175	
4	11	175	.	.	.	.	.	.	.	1	1	4	1	2	.	.	.	.	.	.	.	.	9	168	11	175	
5	11	175	.	.	.	.	.	.	.	.	1	4	1	2	.	.	.	.	.	.	.	.	9	168	11	175	*
6	11	175	.	.	.	1	.	*2	.	.	1	5	1	2	.	.	.	.	.	.	.	.	9	166	11	174	1 OR to Hosp. Diphtheria. 1 OR to Hosp. Measles. Of the total available for duty 13 OR under Lt ALEXANDER were left at CAPPY, having been segregated as contacts, Diphtheria, Measles suspected. These men were left at CAPPY on 31st March.
7	11	174	.	.	.	.	.	.	.	.	1	5	1	2	.	.	.	.	.	.	.	.	9	166	11	174	
8	11	174	.	.	.	.	.	3	.	1	1	7	1	3	.	.	.	.	.	.	.	.	9	164	11	174	
9	11	174	.	.	.	2	.	.	.	.	1	6	1	3	.	.	.	.	.	1	.	.	9	162	11	172	
10	11	172	.	1	.	.	.	.	.	.	1	6	1	3	.	.	.	.	.	.	.	.	9	163	11	173	
11	11	173	.	.	.	.	.	.	.	.	1	6	1	3	.	.	.	.	.	.	.	.	9	163	11	173	
12	11	173	.	.	.	.	.	1	.	.	1	7	1	2	.	1	.	.	.	.	.	.	9	163	11	173	
13	11	173	.	.	.	.	.	1	.	.	1	8	1	2	.	.	.	.	.	.	.	.	9	162	11	173	
14	11	173	.	.	.	.	.	.	.	.	1	8	1	2	.	.	.	.	.	.	.	.	9	162	11	173	
15	11	173	.	.	.	.	.	1	.	.	1	9	.	2	1	.	.	.	.	.	.	.	10	161	11	173	
16	11	173	.	.	.	1	.	.	.	1	1	7	.	2	.	.	.	.	.	.	.	.	10	162	11	172	
17	11	172	.	.	.	1	.	.	.	.	1	6	.	2	.	.	.	.	.	.	.	.	10	162	11	171	
18	11	171	.	2	.	.	.	.	.	1	1	5	.	2	.	.	.	.	.	.	.	.	10	165	11	173	

1875 Wt. W593/826 1,000,000 4/15 J.B.C. & A. A.D.S.S./Forms/C. 2118.

Instructions regarding War Diaries and Intelligence Summaries are contained in F. S. Regs., Part II. and the Staff Manual respectively. Title Pages will be prepared in manuscript.

WAR DIARY

or

~~INTELLIGENCE SUMMARY~~

(Erase heading not required.)

Army Form C. 2118

145 M. G. Coy.

Place	Date	Hour	Summary of Events and Information	Remarks and references to Appendices
BUIRE.	29.		were cancelled by wire received in the evening, but the M.G. relief was allowed to proceed. [initials]	
	30		2/Lt INWOOD relieved the 3 guns of 144 M.G. Coy on the main line; relief was complete by noon. Weather during last few days wet, heavy rain, strong winds, some hail, occasional snow. Very cold at night. [initials] A fourth gun was placed in main line during the morning.	
HAMEL	31		Moved off from BUIRE 1.30 p.m. and proceeded via TINCOURT to HAMEL. Company billeted complete in large farm. [initials]	

[signature]
Major
Comdg 145 M.G. Coy

1375 Wt. W593/826 1,000,000 4/15 J.B.C. & A. A.D.S.S./Forms/C. 2118.

Instructions regarding War Diaries and Intelligence Summaries are contained in F. S. Regs., Part II. and the Staff Manual respectively. Title Pages will be prepared in manuscript.

WAR DIARY
or
~~INTELLIGENCE SUMMARY~~
(Erase heading not required.)

Army Form C. 2118

145 M.G. Coy.

Place	Date	Hour	Summary of Events and Information	Remarks and references to Appendices
BUIRE.			½ the reserve section under 2/Lt MOSS. moved off at 8.30 pm to positions North of MARQUAIX, on the outpost line then held by the Oxfords.	
	27		The section at DOINGT WOODS was withdrawn at dawn to BUIRE. This village had been completely wrecked, & accommodation was very limited. 2/Lt BAILEY relieved 2/Lt MOSS on the outpost line North of MARQUAIX, taking up 3 guns. ½ of No1 Section under 2/Lt MAYOR returned late in evening from WARDS Column. ½ Section under 2/Lt INWOOD moved up on to the reserve line, ie., HAMEL – TINCOURT WOOD.	M.
	28		Remainder of No1 Section rejoined from WARDS Column, under 2/Lt CLUTTON. ½ Section on reserve line was withdrawn to BUIRE. ½ section at full strength under 2/Lt MOSS reported to the Bucks, for duty with their outpost line East of VILLERS-FAUCON which place had been taken by 8th Hussars on the previous afternoon. M.	
	29		½ Section on outpost relieved by 144 M.G. Coy, & the 3 guns on the main line running North & South & to the East of MARQUAIX. The relief orders issued arranging for the relief of the entire Brigade	

1875 Wt. W593/826 1,000,000 4/15 J.B.C. & A. A.D.S.S./Forms/C. 2118.

Instructions regarding War Diaries and Intelligence Summaries are contained in F. S. Regs., Part II. and the Staff Manual respectively. Title Pages will be prepared in manuscript.

WAR DIARY
or
~~INTELLIGENCE SUMMARY~~
(Erase heading not required.)

Army Form C. 2118

145 M. G. Coy.

Place	Date	Hour	Summary of Events and Information	Remarks and references to Appendices
PERONNE	24		Section with WARDS Column was without rations, an emergency ration of sorts had to be raised & despatched in the early morning to find this section, half of which was reported to be at HAMEL & the other half at BOUVINCOURT. 2/LT BAILEY with 2 of the guns from the LEMESNIL sector moved to the Bucks outpost line, one gun being placed by the WOOD firing down the BOIS DE BUIRE - TINCOURT Road, the other at the East end of BUIRE itself watching the BUIRE - TINCOURT Road. M.	
	25		16 men arrived, 8 from Berks & 8 from Bucks for attachment. Dispositions of the Company then were, 1 section at full strength with WARDS Column, ½ section ~~on~~ the BOIS DE BUIRE - BUIRE outpost line. 1 section on the DOINGT WOODS line, ½ section on the continuation of the latter line South of the River COLOGNE. HQrs. M. Transport & 1 section in PERONNE.	
	26		HQrs, Section in reserve & Transport moved to BUIRE, arriving about 7.30 pm, ½ section ~~on~~ outpost line withdrawn to BUIRE as also ½ section, south of the river. M.	

1875 Wt. W593/826 1,000,000 4/15 J.B.C. & A. A.D.S.S./Forms/C. 2118.

Instructions regarding War Diaries and Intelligence Summaries are contained in F. S. Regs., Part II. and the Staff Manual respectively. Title Pages will be prepared in manuscript.

WAR DIARY
or
~~INTELLIGENCE SUMMARY~~
(Erase heading not required.)

Army Form C. 2118

145 M G Coy

Place	Date	Hour	Summary of Events and Information	Remarks and references to Appendices
CAPPY	March 20		Training in morning. In the afternoon received sudden orders to move to PERONNE. Left CAPPY 5pm marching via FRISE, FEUILLERES, thence along Canal bank to BAZINCORT FARM BRIDGE, HALLE, LA QUINCONCE, PERONNE, arriving about 11pm. A very trying march. Accomodation in PERONNE was limited to cellars, very dirty & full of rubbish. The town itself having been thoroughly wrecked by the Germans before leaving. The Transport moved separately via HERBECOURT, BIACHES, BAZINCORT FARM BRIDGE arriving shortly after midnight. 13 men under Lt ALEXANDER were left behind at CAPPY, having been segregated as contacts, Diptheria & Measles being suspected. M	
PERONNE	21		Engaged in clearing up billets. M	
	22		No 1 Section, made up to full strength, under 2/Lt CLUTTON & 2/Lt MAYOR, moved off at 9AM with WARDS Column. M	see Appendix C
	23		1 Section under 2/Lt BAILEY moved off to take up positions, East & N East of MESNIL. 1 Section ~~under~~ 2/Lt INWOOD moved off to take up positions in front of DOINGT WOODS M	
	24		It having been discovered late the night before that the	

1875 Wt. W593/826 1,000,000 4/15 J.B.C. & A. A.D.S.S./Forms/C. 2118.

Instructions regarding War Diaries and Intelligence Summaries are contained in F. S. Regs., Part II. and the Staff Manual respectively. Title Pages will be prepared in manuscript.

WAR DIARY
or
INTELLIGENCE SUMMARY
(Erase heading not required.)

Army Form C. 2118

145 M.G. Coy

Place	Date	Hour	Summary of Events and Information	Remarks and references to Appendices
CAPPY	Mar 15		No 56 Camp. Training. Weather fine. M	
	16		No 1 Section under 2/Lt MOSS & 2/Lt CLUTTON proceeded to line to take up positions at CRUCIFORM POST opposite LA MAISONETTE, & act in co-operation with the 143 & 144 M.G. Coys. This Coy being out of the line at the time was allotted the role given in the original scheme to the 144 M.G. Coy. A composite section under 2/Lt BAILEY & 2/Lt LAWRENCE moved up to line at 6.45 pm, half the section under 2/Lt G.H. BAILEY reported to OC 1/4 Oxfords, the remaining half under 2/Lt LAWRENCE to OC 1/5 Glosters to take part in the scheme against LA MAISONETTE. M	
	17		2.30 am Oxfords & Glosters raided the enemy trenches in the neighbourhood of LA MAISONETTE & found them practically empty. The evacuation to the EAST of the SOMME having begun. No 1 Section returned to CAPPY during the morning & later that evening the composite section also returned. The whole Brigade was pulled out that night. M	
	18		CAPPY Weather fine. No training. M	
	19		CAPPY Training. M	

1875 Wt. W593/826 1,000,000 4/15 J.B.C. & A. A.D.S.S./Forms/C. 2118.

Instructions regarding War Diaries and Intelligence Summaries are contained in F. S. Regs., Part II. and the Staff Manual respectively. Title Pages will be prepared in manuscript.

WAR DIARY
or
~~INTELLIGENCE SUMMARY~~
(Erase heading not required.)

Army Form C. 2118

145 M.G. Coy.

Place	Date	Hour	Summary of Events and Information	Remarks and references to Appendices
	March 11th (continued)		forward slope of the contour during a fairly light period of the morning was unsound, this scheme was cancelled. S.H.G.	
	12th		4 new indirect fire positions were sited in N.5.b & N.6.a by resection and targets arranged for them on the following scheme. S.H.G.	See MAP 1
			1 gun on HENRIOT TR; 2 guns on HERVÉ TR; 2 guns on ORGANISE ALLEY; 1 gun on JEAN TR; 1 gun on WILHELM ALLEY — These seven guns were ordered to fire at 2.0 am on 13th. This was done - the aim being to catch ration parties coming up, which had been heard the night before at about that hour. S.H.G.	See MAP. 1
	13th		144 M.G. Coy relieved this unit in the line. Relief complete 11.30 pm. Some showers during the day. S.H.G.	
	14th		Heavy showers - Cleaning guns and Equipment. Major LONG returned to the Company from leave and resumed command. S.H.G.	
			G.O.C. 145 Inf Bde required a M.G. defence scheme for Reserve and intermediate lines - Duplicate attached. S.H.G.	See MAP 2

1875 Wt. W593/826 1,000,000 4/15 J.B.C. & A. A.D.S.S./Forms/C. 2118.

Army Form C. 2118

Instructions regarding War Diaries and Intelligence Summaries are contained in F. S. Regs., Part II. and the Staff Manual respectively. Title Pages will be prepared in manuscript.

WAR DIARY
or
~~INTELLIGENCE SUMMARY~~
(Erase heading not required.)

145 M. G. Coy.

Place	Date	Hour	Summary of Events and Information	Remarks and references to Appendices
BOIS d' ACHILLE	March 9th		Aerial activity – 2nd i C visited left and support sectors.	S.H.G.
	10th		In view of intended operation m/night 10/11th – all preparation for barrage scheme were completed – All guns were ready laid by 6.30 pm. Zero was ordered for 11.0 pm. At 8.30 pm operation were cancelled. All guns were brought back to respective positions by 9.15 p.m. At 9.25 pm phone message was received from Bde ordering M.G. fire to be carried out at original ZERO hour. The difficulty of this was pointed out to 145 Inf Bde and half an hours extra time was given.	See Appendix A
			Barrage started at 11.30 pm and ceased at Midnight. A certain amount of retaliation occured otherwise all operations were successful.	S.H.G.
	11th		2nd i C collected reports from all firing guns early in the morning & forwarded to Bde	
			Operations as for the 10th were again arranged – These were again cancelled at about 6.30 pm. Inter section relief was hurriedly arranged – Later M.G. Barrage was again ordered at 5.0 am. This was to be done together with an artillery barrage. After representations had been made to the G.O.C. 145 Inf Bde that the firing of guns from the	S.H.G.

Instructions regarding War Diaries and Intelligence Summaries are contained in F. S. Regs., Part II. and the Staff Manual respectively. Title Pages will be prepared in manuscript.

WAR DIARY
or
~~INTELLIGENCE SUMMARY~~
(Erase heading not required.)

Army Form C. 2118

145 M.G. Coy

Place	Date	Hour	Summary of Events and Information	Remarks and references to Appendices
BOIS d'ACHILLE	March 1st		Quiet day – misty in the morning – 2nd-in-C went round right sector, trenches very bad S.H.G.	
	2nd		Misty early in the morning – later cleared up and hostile aircraft was active. This unit fired on enemy planes no hits were obtained apparently. 2nd in C went round supports and left sector. Kite Balloon of No14 Coy (Kite Balloons) was brought down in evening – hostile plane was engaged by 4 guns of this unit S.H.G.	
	3rd		144 M.G. Coy relieved 145 M.G. Coy and this unit returned to billets at the KLOOF near 35th October Wood. S.H.G.	
	4th		2nd in C attended M.G. Conference at HERBECOURT. Sunshine – Training started. S.H.G.	
	5th		2 inches of snow fell in the early morning – Day devoted to cleaning guns & Equipment. 1 case of Measles and 1 case of suspected Diphtheria – contacts were isolated and all precautions were taken. S.H.G.	See appen. B
	6th		Training continued – Cold weather and strong wind. S.H.G.	
	7th		145 M.G. Coy relieved 144 M.G. Coy in the line. Relief complete by 10.30 pm. In consequence of depleted sections owing to infection, this unit took over only 8 gun positions. 2nd in C visited the whole BOS sector. S.H.G.	
	8th		Very cold – 2nd in C submitted a barrage scheme to G.O.C. 105 Inf Bde – Manned another position with 2 guns and prepared fire orders for Barrage scheme. Gun at No 2 position hit by "grey pigeon" [GRANATENWERFER] one O.R. wounded S.H.G.	See Appen. A

1875 Wt. W593/826 1,000,000 4/15 J.B.C. & A. A.D.S.S./Forms/C. 2118.

CONFIDENTIAL

Vol 14

WAR DIARY

OF

145 MACHINE GUN COMPANY

FROM MARCH 1st 1917 TO MARCH 31st 1917.

[signature] Major
O.C.
145 Machine Gun Coy.

Instructions regarding War Diaries and Intelligence Summaries are contained in F. S. Regs., Part II. and the Staff Manual respectively. Title Pages will be prepared in manuscript.

WAR DIARY
or
INTELLIGENCE SUMMARY
(Erase heading not required.)

Army Form C. 2118

145 Machine Gun Company.

Place	Date	Hour	Summary of Events and Information	Remarks and references to Appendices

APPENDIX "B" Contd.

March	Effective strength for previous day Off	Effective strength for previous day ORs	Strength increase during day Off	Strength increase during day ORs	Strength decrease during day Off	Strength decrease during day ORs	To Hospital during day Off	To Hospital during day ORs	Rejoined from Hospital Off	Rejoined from Hospital ORs	Total in Hospital Off	Total in Hospital ORs	Absent on Course, Leave, etc. Off	Absent on Course, Leave, etc. ORs	Rejoined from Course Leave etc. Off	Rejoined from Course Leave etc. ORs	Killed Off	Killed ORs	Wounded Off	Wounded ORs	Missing Off	Missing ORs	Available for duty Off	Available for duty ORs	Effective Strength Off	Effective Strength ORs
19	11	173	.	1	.	.	.	.	.	1	1	4	1	4	.	.	.	.	.	.	.	.	9	165	11	174
20	11	174	.	.	.	.	.	2	.	.	1	6	1	4	.	.	.	.	.	.	.	.	9	163	11	174
21	11	174	.	.	.	2	.	1	.	.	1	5	1	5	.	.	.	.	.	.	.	.	9	161	11	172
22	11	172	.	.	.	.	.	.	.	1	1	4	1	5	.	.	.	.	.	.	.	.	9	162	11	172
23	11	172	.	.	.	.	.	.	.	.	1	4	1	5	.	.	.	.	.	.	.	.	9	162	11	172
24	11	172	.	3	.	.	.	.	.	.	1	4	1	4	.	1	.	.	.	.	.	.	9	166	11	175
25	11	175	.	.	.	.	1	1	.	.	2	5	.	3	.	1	.	.	.	.	.	.	9	166	11	175
26	11	175	.	.	.	.	.	.	.	1	2	4	.	3	.	.	.	.	.	.	.	.	9	167	11	175
27	11	175	.	.	.	1	.	.	.	.	2	3	.	3	.	.	.	.	.	.	.	.	9	167	11	174
28	11	174	.	.	.	1	.	.	.	.	2	3	.	3	.	.	.	.	.	1	.	.	9	167	11	173
29	11	173	.	.	.	.	.	.	.	.	2	3	.	3	.	.	.	.	.	.	.	.	9	167	11	173
30	11	173	.	1	.	.	.	1	.	.	2	4	.	3	.	.	.	.	.	.	.	.	9	166	11	174
31	11	174	.	.	.	.	.	.	.	1	2	3	.	3	.	.	.	.	.	.	.	.	9	167	11	174

[signature]
O.C.
145 Machine Gun Coy.

1875 Wt. W593/826 1,000,000 4/15 J.B.C. & A. A.D.S.S./Forms/C. 2118.

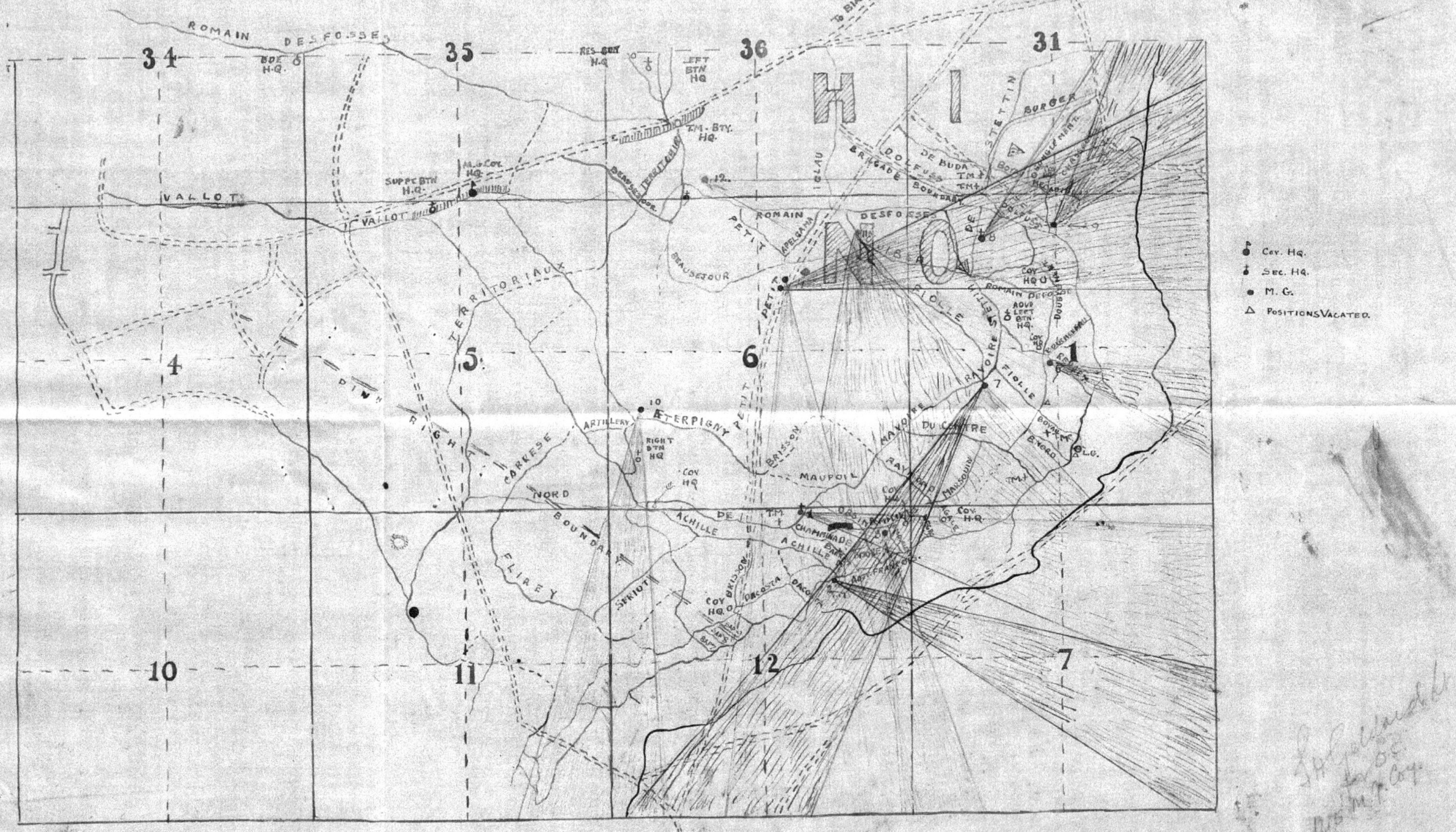
ROMAIN DESFOSSE
BDE H.Q.
RES. BTN H.Q.
LEFT BTN HQ
T.M. BTY. HQ
TERRITORIAUX
SUPPt BTN H.Q.
M.G.COY. HQ.
VALLOT
PETIT ROMAIN DESFOSSE
BEAUSEJOUR
APELGAMA
GLAU
BRIGADE BOUNDARY
DE BUDA
DOLFUSS
STETTIN
BURGER
H
I
N
O
PIMH
RIGHT
CARKESE
ARTILLERY
ÆTERPIGNY
PETIT
RIGHT BTN HQ
COY HQ
NORD
BOUNDARY
FLIREY
SERIOT
BRISSON
MAUPOIL
MAYOIRE
DU CENTRE
RAYOIRE
FIOLLE
ACHILLE
CHAMPADE
COY HQ
TM
10
12
7
34
35
36
31
4
5
6
1
10
11
12
7
Coy. HQ.
Sec. HQ.
M. G.
Positions Vacated.

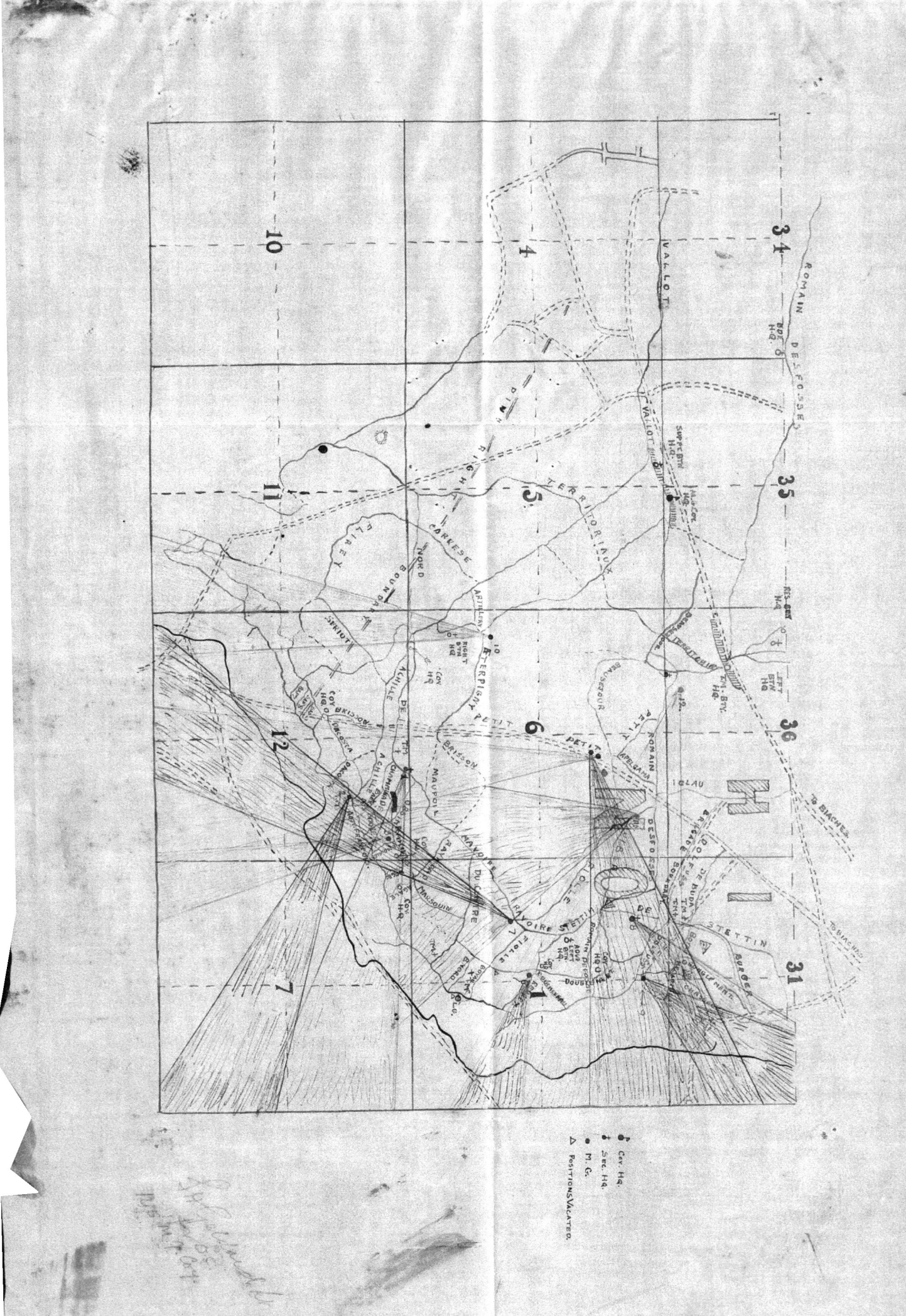

Relief Orders.

To Lt BAILEY.

I Reliefs will take place within the Coy on the night 14/15th

II No I Section (now at Hd Qrs) will take over Nos 1, 2, 3 & 10 positions

No II Section will take over Nos 8, 12 & (two guns) 11 positions.

No III Section will take over Nos 5, 6, 7 & 9 positions.

No IV Section will return to Coy Hd Qrs.

[Position No 4 is being relieved by a LEWIS gun]

III On ~~the~~ relief ~~of~~ [the] team at No 4 ~~Section~~ position, ~~they~~ will be guided to No 11 position carrying all their gun equipment, with exception of S.A.A. [Guide provided by Coy Hd Qrs]

Cpl ABBOTT and team from No 10 position will return to Hd Qrs on relief. From there they will be guided to No 9 position. Lt Bailey will detail a guide from No 9 position to be at Coy Hd Qrs not later than 8.0p.m.

The team then relieved from No 9 position will proceed to Section Hd Qrs and be guided to No 7 position, which they will take over. [Guide provided by Lt BAILEY]

APPENDIX. C.

Relief Orders.

To Lt INWOOD.

I Reliefs will take place within the Coy on the night 14/15th

II No I Section (now at Hd Qrs) will take over positions Nos 1, 2, 3, & 10

No II Section will take over positions Nos 8, 12, and (two guns) 11

No III Section will take over positions Nos 5, 6, 7, 9.

No IV Section will return to Hd Qrs

[Position No 4 is being relieved by a LEWIS gun

III No I Section under Lt Clutton will start at 8 pm. and will relieve positions Nos 1, 2, 3, & 10.

Lt INWOOD will detail guides from Nos 1, 2, & 3 positions to be at Coy Hd Qrs not later than 7.0 pm

Cpl ABBOTT will detail a guide from No 10 position to be at Coy Hd Qrs not later than 7.0 pm.

On relief all teams will return to Hd Qrs

Lt INWOOD will hand over Section Hd Qrs to Lt Clutton, and will then return to Coy Hd Qrs

All guns, tripods, equipment, periscopes & stores will be handed over.

[illegible signature]

Continued. 3

III ✗ On relief the team from No 7 position will proceed to Section Hd Qrs and will relieve the (No 4 Section) team there at No 8 position.

The (No 4 Section) team relieved from No 8 position will then return to Coy Hd Qrs.

On the arrival of team from No 4 position at No 11 position, the (No 3 Section) team at No 11 position starts off ~~and~~ picking up the team at No 12 position. These two teams (from Nos 11 & 12 position) will be guided down to positions Nos 5 & 6, and will relieve the teams there.

On relief the teams at Nos 5 & 6 position will be guided back to Nos 11 & 12 positions.

[Guide down to Nos 5 & 6 positions and back to Nos 11 & 12 positions will be provided by Coy Hd Qrs]

Lt ALEXANDER will relieve Lt BAILEY in the line.

Lt BAILEY will return to the transport and Lt Mayer will return to Coy Hd Qrs.

All guns, tripods, and equipment will be handed over [Periscopes included]

14 – 2 – 17

S H Goddard Lt for Major
OZ. [illegible]

Note.

Ref Appendix "B"

Originally when the 145 M.G. Coy took over the line, two positions marked by red Δ were occupied.
One position at about O 1 d 1530 was moved to No 11 position where there are now 2 guns.
This position was relieved by a LEWIS gun
The other position at about O 1 c 9565 was vacated and moved to 11(a) by 144 M.G. Coy

[signature] Lt
for O.C. 145 M.G. Coy

Instructions regarding War Diaries and Intelligence Summaries are contained in F. S. Regs., Part II. and the Staff Manual respectively. Title Pages will be prepared in manuscript.

WAR DIARY
or
INTELLIGENCE SUMMARY

(Erase heading not required.)

Army Form C. 2118

145th Machine Gun Company.

Place	Date	Hour	Summary of Events and Information	Remarks and references to Appendices

APPENDIX "A" (Contd)

Date	Effective strength for previous day		Strength increase during day		Strength decrease during day		To Hospital during day		Rejoined from Hospital		Total in Hospital		Absent on Course, leave, etc.		Rejoined from Course, Leave, etc.		Killed		Wounded		Missing		Available for duty		Effective Strength	
Feby 1917	Off	OR	Off	OR	Off	OR	Off	OR	Off	OR	Off	OR	Off	OR	Off	OR	Off	OR	Off	OR	Off	OR	Off	OR	Off	OR
23	11	173	.	3	.	.	.	1	.	.	1	4	1	4	.	.	.	.	.	.	.	.	9	167	11	176
24	11	176	.	.	.	.	.	.	.	1	1	3	1	4	.	.	.	.	.	.	.	.	9	168	11	176
25	11	176	.	.	.	.	.	.	.	.	1	3	1	4	.	.	.	.	.	.	.	.	9	168	11	176
26	11	176	.	.	.	3	.	1	.	.	1	4	.	1	1	3	.	.	.	.	.	.	10	167	11	173
27	11	173	.	.	.	.	.	.	.	1	1	3	1	1	.	.	.	.	.	.	.	.	9	168	11	173
28	11	173	.	1	.	.	.	.	.	.	1	3	1	2	.	.	.	.	.	.	.	.	9	168	11	174

S.H. Calclough Lt
for O.C.
145 M.G. Coy.

Instructions regarding War Diaries and Intelligence Summaries are contained in F. S. Regs., Part II. and the Staff Manual respectively. Title Pages will be prepared in manuscript.

WAR DIARY
or
INTELLIGENCE SUMMARY
(Erase heading not required.)

Army Form C. 2118

145th Machine Gun Company

Place	Date	Hour	Summary of Events and Information	Remarks and references to Appendices

APPENDIX "A"

Date	Effective strength for previous day. Off	OR	Strength increase during day. Off	OR	Strength decrease during day. Off	OR	To Hospital during day. Off	OR	Rejoined from Hospital. Off	OR	Total in Hospital. Off	OR	Absent on Course, Leave, etc. Off	OR	Rejoined from Course Leave, etc. Off	OR	Killed Off	OR	Wounded Off	OR	Missing Off	OR	Available for duty. Off	OR	Effective Strength. Off	OR
Feby 1917																										
1	12	172	.	.	.	.	.	3	–	-	1	4	4	20	-	.	.	.	.	.	.	-	7	148	12	172
2	12	172	.	.	.	1	.	3	.	.	1	6	4	20	.	.	.	.	.	.	.	.	7	145	12	171
3	12	171	.	.	.	.	.	1	.	3	1	4	3	20	1	.	.	.	.	.	.	.	8	147	12	171
4	12	171	.	.	.	.	.	.	.	.	1	4	3	20	.	.	.	.	.	.	.	.	8	147	12	171
5	12	171	.	.	.	.	.	.	.	.	1	4	3	20	.	.	.	.	.	.	.	.	8	147	12	171
6	12	171	.	.	.	.	.	.	.	.	1	4	4	21	.	2	.	.	.	.	.	.	7	146	12	171
7	12	171	.	.	.	2	.	.	.	.	1	4	4	21	.	.	.	.	.	.	.	.	7	144	12	169
8	12	169	.	.	.	.	.	.	.	.	1	4	4	20	.	1	.	.	.	.	.	.	7	145	12	169
9	12	169	.	.	.	.	.	1	.	.	1	5	4	20	.	.	.	.	.	.	.	.	7	144	12	169
10	12	169	.	.	.	.	.	.	.	2	1	3	4	11	.	8	.	.	.	.	.	.	7	154	12	169
11	12	169	.	.	.	.	.	.	.	.	1	3	3	8	1	3	.	.	.	.	.	.	8	157	12	169
12	12	169	.	.	1	2	.	2	.	.	1	3	1	7	1	1	.	.	.	.	.	.	9	156	11	167
13	11	167	.	.	.	.	.	.	.	.	1	3	1	7	.	.	.	.	.	.	.	-	9	156	11	167
14	11	167	.	.	.	.	.	.	.	.	1	3	1	8	.	.	.	.	.	.	.	.	9	155	11	167
15	11	167	.	6	.	.	.	.	.	2	1	1	1	8	.	.	.	.	.	.	.	.	9	163	11	173
16	11	173	.	.	.	.	.	.	.	.	1	1	1	4	.	4	.	.	.	.	-	.	9	167	11	173
17	11	173	.	.	.	.	.	.	.	1	1	.	1	5	.	.	.	.	.	.	.	.	9	167	11	173
18	11	173	.	.	.	.	.	.	.	.	1	.	1	5	.	.	.	.	.	.	.	.	9	167	11	173
19	11	173	.	.	.	.	.	1	.	.	1	1	1	5	.	.	.	.	.	.	.	.	9	166	11	173
20	11	173	.	.	.	.	.	1	.	.	1	2	1	5	.	.	.	.	.	.	.	.	9	165	11	173
21	11	173	.	.	.	.	.	1	.	.	1	3	1	5	.	.	.	.	.	.	.	.	9	164	11	173
22	11	173	.	.	.	.	.	.	.	.	1	3	1	4	.	1	.	.	.	.	.	.	9	165	11	173

1875 Wt. W593/826 1,000,000 4/15 J.B.C. & A. A.D.S.S./Forms/C. 2118.

Army Form C. 2118

WAR DIARY
or
~~INTELLIGENCE SUMMARY~~
(Erase heading not required.)

Instructions regarding War Diaries and Intelligence Summaries are contained in F. S. Regs., Part II. and the Staff Manual respectively. Title Pages will be prepared in manuscript.

145th Machine Gun Company.

Place	Date	Hour	Summary of Events and Information	Remarks and references to Appendices
	Feb 18th		Relief of this unit by 144 M.G. Coy takes place. Relief complete by midnight. A-A gun of 144 M.G. Coy relieved by this unit. S.H.G.	
CAPPY	19th		Cleaning of personnel & guns &c. S.H.G.	
	20th till 25th		Training continued during this period. Rather hindered by rain and continued thaw. S.H.G.	
			On 25th Feb. No 2 & 4 sections went in to take over the front line from 144 M.G. Coy. Relief complete at 4.a.m. Condition of trenches apalling. No 5 Gun to new position in FIOLLE T.R. S.H.G.	see Appendix "B"
	26th		A-A gun relieved by 144 M.G. Coy. Nos 1, & 3 sections and HQ Qrs of this unit relieved the support reserve section & HQ Qrs of 144 M.G. Coy. Major LONG went on leave. 2/c went round right section of guns S.H.G.	
	27th		2/Lt BAILEY went round left section of guns by day – bad journey 2nd i/c went round support section of guns. Nos 4 & 2 section relieved (inter teams) No 7 team relieved No 9 and No 1 team relieved No 2. S.H.G.	
	28th		2nd i/c went round right section of guns by day – bad journey and also Nos 10, & 11 positions. S.H.G.	

1875 Wt. W593/826 1,000,000 4/15 J.B.C. & A. A.D.S.S./Forms/C. 2118.

Instructions regarding War Diaries and Intelligence Summaries are contained in F. S. Regs., Part II. and the Staff Manual respectively. Title Pages will be prepared in manuscript.

Army Form C. 2118

WAR DIARY
or
~~INTELLIGENCE SUMMARY~~
(Erase heading not required.)

145th Machine Gun Company.

Place	Date	Hour	Summary of Events and Information	Remarks and references to Appendices
	Feb. 11		Lt Alexander returned to duty from [illegible] school - C.O & 2nd i/c visited the left sector and inspected all the positions there in detail. Cold continues. S.H.G.	
	Feb 12		No 1 Section returned from 143 Bde and came into Coy H.Q.rs in Reserve. Lt OLDACRE struck off the strength on ~~[illegible]~~ having a Medical board in England. C.O & 2nd i/c visited the gun positions in the right sector in detail. Cold continues. S.H.G.	
	Feb 13th		Misty day - cold weather starting to break up. Gun at No 11 position did some firing by day onto the BRICK FIELDS. S.H.G.	
	Feb 14th		Inter section relief - very complicated affair (see Appendix "C") Cold at night - slight thaw by day. Disposition changed. S.H.G.	see Appendices "B" & "C"
	Feb 15th		Enemy aerial activity - Anti-aircraft gun at H.Q.rs (Coy) did their best to prevent this - Several belts were fired at enemy aircraft. This activity was followed by severe shelling on 115th battery R.F.A (1st D.A) at about 4.35 c a d, also on Support Bn H.Q.rs and on Coy H.Q.rs Fortunately no casualties to this unit. This unit had three other guns beyond that Coy H.Q.rs firing at hostile aircraft. Nos 12, ~~and~~ 11, and 10 S.H.G.	see Appendix "B."
	Feb 16th		Hostile and friendly aerial activity, thaw very slow, still very cold at night. 2nd i/c met representative of No 3 Coy M.G.C at Rt Bn H.Q.rs and arranged mutual support S.H.G.	
	Feb 17th		Ground getting softer - still frozen hard beneath the surface O.C. 144 M.G. Coy arrived to arrange inter-Company relief S.H.G.	

1875 Wt. W593/826 1.000.000 4/15 J.B.C. & A. A.D.S.S./Forms/C. 2118.

Instructions regarding War Diaries and Intelligence Summaries are contained in F. S. Regs., Part II. and the Staff Manual respectively. Title Pages will be prepared in manuscript.

WAR DIARY
or
~~INTELLIGENCE SUMMARY~~
(Erase heading not required.)

Army Form C. 2118

145th Machine Gun Company.

Place	Date	Hour	Summary of Events and Information	Remarks and references to Appendices
CAPPY			forward men and approaches. MB	
	Feb 7		Intense cold continues MB	
	Feb 8		No 1 section sent to 143 Bde, their M.G. Coy having had two teams knocked out during relief: to be returned by this unit. This section went into the line immediately in front of LA MAISONNETTE MB	
	Feb 9		Training continued: still intensely cold, particularly at night MB	
	Feb 10		145 M.G. Coy relieved 144 M.G. Coy in line with 3 sections: right Bde Sector. Dispositions 9 guns in front system 3 guns in support H.Q. at BOIS ACHILLE.	
			2/Lt MAYOR returned to duty from M.G. school. MB C.O. & 2nd i/c went round all sector, starting from the right – Intensely cold. LHG	

1875 Wt. W593/826 1,000,000 4/15 J.B.C. & A. A.D.S.S./Forms/C. 2118.

Instructions regarding War Diaries and Intelligence Summaries are contained in F. S. Regs., Part II. and the Staff Manual respectively. Title Pages will be prepared in manuscript.

WAR DIARY
or
~~INTELLIGENCE SUMMARY~~
(Erase heading not required.)

Army Form C. 2118

145th Machine Gun Company.

Place	Date	Hour	Summary of Events and Information	Remarks and references to Appendices
HAMEL	Feb 1		Training continued. Weather still very cold. Lieut GELDARD rejoined for duty from 30 days leave. R.L.	
CAPPY (No 56 Camp)	Feb 2		Moved off at 12 noon to huts (camp 56) on CAPPY–ÉCLUSIER road, arriving there about 4.45 p.m. Accommodation for men, Adrian huts (capacity 100 each); officers in smaller wooden huts. On extremely cold march no one fell out. The intense cold continues. R.L.	
	Feb 3		One team & gun relieved A.A. position E of ÉCLUSIER on ÉCLUSIER–HERBECOURT road, taking over from a team of 144 M.G. Coy. R.L.	
	Feb 4		C.O. and 2nd i/c reconnoitred approaches to forward area in view of approaching relief of 143 & 144 M.G. Coys, who had relieved the French in this area (viz. in front of PERONNE). A raid was made by the Germans the same night on the 143 and 144 Bdes, after almost continuous shelling from 5.30 a.m. in the morning. R.L.	
	Feb 5		Further reconnaissance of forward area by C.O. and 2Lt BAILEY, it being as yet uncertain which company would be relieved by this. The going was good, owing to the intense frost. The Coy continued such training as was possible. R.L.	
	Feb 6		Training continued: officers sent, two at a time, to reconnoitre	

CONFIDENTIAL

Vol XIII

WAR DIARY

OF

145th MACHINE GUN COMPANY.

FROM FEBRUARY 1st 1917 TO. FEBRUARY 28th 1917.

S H Geldard. Lt
OC
145 M.G. Coy.

Army Form C. 2118

Instructions regarding War Diaries and Intelligence Summaries are contained in F. S. Regs., Part II. and the Staff Manual respectively. Title Pages will be prepared in manuscript.

WAR DIARY
or
INTELLIGENCE SUMMARY
(Erase heading not required.)

145 Machine Gun Coy.

Place	Date	Hour	Summary of Events and Information	Remarks and references to Appendices
FRUCOURT	1917 Jan 17		1 OR. To Field Ambulance; Strength Increase 4 OR. Reinforcements.	
	18		1 Off: 2/Lt F.W. MOSS + 2 OR. to III Corps M.M.G. Battery for Anti-Aircraft instruction	
			LIEUT. J.S. ALEXANDER to 48th Divisional School. Strength Increase 1 OR.	
	20		2/Lt. F.G. LAWRENCE rejoined for duty; ~~1~~ 1 OR. Rejoined from Field Amb.	
	21		1 OR. To Field Ambulance.	
	22		1 OR. " " "	
	23		1 OR To Field Ambulance Strength Decrease 2 OR.	
	24		Strength Decrease 2/Lt. W.M. SANGSTER. + 2 OR. Strength Increase 1 O.R.	
	25		" Increase 1 OR.	
	26		" ditto 1 OR	
	27		" Decrease 1 OR. 2 OR. Rejoined from Field Amb. 1 OR. To Field Amb.	
	28		1 Officer 2/Lt F.W. MOSS + 2 OR. Rejoined for duty.	
HAMEL.	29		3 OR. To Field Ambulance.	
	30		Strength Decrease. 1 OR.	
	31		3 OR. To Field Ambulance.	
			[signature] Major	

1875 Wt. W593/826 1,000,000 4/15 J.B.C. & A. A.D.S.S./Forms/C. 2118.

Army Form C. 2118

Instructions regarding War Diaries and Intelligence Summaries are contained in F. S. Regs., Part II. and the Staff Manual respectively. Title Pages will be prepared in manuscript.

WAR DIARY
or
INTELLIGENCE SUMMARY
(Erase heading not required.)

145 Machine Gun Coy.

Place	Date	Hour	Summary of Events and Information	Remarks and references to Appendices
			APPENDIX A Casualties etc.,	
	1917.			
BRESLE	Jan 2		1 OR. To Field Ambulance. Strength Decrease 2 OR. Strength Increase 1 Off. 2/Lt H. H MAYOR.	
	3		1 OR To Course. Strength Increase 1 OR. Strength Decrease 1 OR. to C.C.S.	
	4		1 OR. Rejoined for duty. Strength Decrease 2/Lt. L LEATHLEY {Auth. III Corps List 624 d/. 26.12.16.	
	5		1 OR To Field Amb: 1 OR. Rejoined for duty. Strength Decrease 1 OR. {Base under age.	
	6		1 OR. Rejoined for duty.	
	7		2 OR Rejoined for duty.	
	8		2 OR To Field Amb:	
	9.		Strength Decrease 1 OR. to C.C.S.	
FRUCOURT	10		1 OR To Field Amb:	
	12		2 OR. Rejoined from Field Amb:	
	13		1 OR " " "	
	14		1 OR To Field Ambulance.	
	15		1 Off 2/Lt H. H. MAYOR to M.G. School CAMIERS for Course. 3 OR. Course. 1 OR. Rejoined from Field Ambulance.	
	16		Strength Decrease 1 OR to C.C.S.	[illegible signature]

Instructions regarding War Diaries and Intelligence Summaries are contained in F. S. Regs., Part II. and the Staff Manual respectively. Title Pages will be prepared in manuscript.

WAR DIARY
or
INTELLIGENCE SUMMARY
(Erase heading not required.)

Army Form C. 2118

145 Machine Gun Coy.

Place	Date	Hour	Summary of Events and Information	Remarks and references to Appendices
	29		under cover. Baggage conveyed as follows:– (a) 1 Lorry shared with T.M Battery for conveyance of Blankets etc. to AIRAINES Station. (b) Part of one lorry for conveyance of Officers Mess etc direct to HAMEL. As much baggage & stores as possible were sent on the transport. The transport took 3 days on the journey one horse, a rider, slipped down bank & broke its neck.	
HAMEL.	30		Through lorry from FRUCOURT to HAMEL direct did not arrive until 2.30 AM. Training, Route March only; Cleaning & overhauling guns. Very cold, some snow. Billets here consisted mostly of stables. Condition of stables good.	
	31		Training: [illegible], squad drill, gun mounting. Rest of time devoted to cleaning & overhauling guns, ammunition, Equipment &c. Weather extremely cold. Conference Bde H.Q. (HAMEL) 6 p.m.	

N.L.

1875 Wt. W593/826 1,000,000 4/15 J.B.C. & A. A.D.S.S./Forms/C. 2118.

Instructions regarding War Diaries and Intelligence Summaries are contained in F. S. Regs., Part II. and the Staff Manual respectively. Title Pages will be prepared in manuscript.

WAR DIARY
or
INTELLIGENCE SUMMARY
(Erase heading not required.)

Army Form C. 2118

145 Machine Gun Coy.

Place	Date	Hour	Summary of Events and Information	Remarks and references to Appendices
			and Nonconformists (6 p.m.).	
			Party of officers walked over to neighbourhood of HALLENCOURT in afternoon to look over ground taped out for practice of Drill Attack on following day. M.	
	22nd	2	Coy. moved off 8.45 a.m. for HALLENCOURT, returning about 3 p.m. Very cold day: heavy frost continued: making riding almost impossible. M.	
	23rd		Staff tour with G.O.C. Division, meeting at X roads near HAMEL: advance guard scheme without troops: idea being eventual capture of enemy line and bridge head near LONGPRÉ. A bitterly cold day. M.	
	24th		Contact aeroplane practice on ground between HALLENCOURT and GRAND SART. M.	
	25th		Conference Div HQ 2.30 p.m. M.	
	26th		Training in morning: afternoon devoted to packing, limbers for move next day. M.	
	27th		Transport under 2/Lt HUGMAN moved off 8 AM to proceed to new area by road. M.	
			2/Lt G H BAILEY & 2 NCOs proceeded by train from AIRAINES to HAMEL for billetting	
	28		Parade. Non-Conformists only 5.45 P.M. M.	
	29		Company paraded 4.20 AM & proceeded to AIRAINES entraining at 8 AM for CERISY arriving there about 2.15 PM & marching thence to HAMEL into billets. Accommodation good; Horses	

Instructions regarding War Diaries and Intelligence Summaries are contained in F. S. Regs., Part II. and the Staff Manual respectively. Title Pages will be prepared in manuscript.

WAR DIARY
or
INTELLIGENCE SUMMARY
(Erase heading not required.)

Army Form C. 2118

145 Machine Gun Corp.

Place	Date	Hour	Summary of Events and Information	Remarks and references to Appendices
	Jan 15/17		Training continued, consisting of 7AM Run 8.30 Physical; Rest of day devoted to Elementary Training & Squad Drill. Inspection of transport 2 PM. Weather: Frosty & Bright. 2nd/Lt G.H.H. MAYOR to CAMIERS for Course.	M
	Jan 16/17		Afternoon parades done away with except instruction for backward men	M
	Jan 17/17		Weather: Cold & Bright. Obtained permission to use village school-room as a reading & writing room from 5 to 8.45 nightly.	M
	Jan 18		Weather extremely cold, heavy frost, but dry & bright. 2/Lt F.W. MOSS proceeded to LAVIEVILLE with 1 N.C.O. for attachment to 3rd Corps MMG Battery for instruction in Anti-Aircraft work. Lt J.S. ALEXANDER proceeded to Divisional School, ST GRATIEN for Course on instruction.	M
	19.		Training consisted of Run 7AM Route March 9AM.	M
	20		2/Lt LAWRENCE rejoined for duty from the Base. Brigade Boxing Contests continued at OISEMONT 5.30 pm.	M
	21		Inspection of Coy. 10.30 a.m. Only church parade for Roman Catholics (10.20 a.m.)	

1875 Wt. W593/826 1,000,000 4/15 J.B.C. & A. A.D.S.S./Forms/C. 2118.

Instructions regarding War Diaries and Intelligence Summaries are contained in F. S. Regs., Part II. and the Staff Manual respectively. Title Pages will be prepared in manuscript.

WAR DIARY
or
INTELLIGENCE SUMMARY
(Erase heading not required.)

Army Form C. 2118

145 Machine Gun Coy.

Place	Date	Hour	Summary of Events and Information	Remarks and references to Appendices
			and 145 T.M. Battery were billetted in same village. Weather cold. some snow.	
FRUCOURT.	Jan 10/17.		No morning parades by order from Brigade. Day devoted to cleaning & overhauling guns & equipment etc. Conference of C.O.s Bde H.Q. 4 p.m.	
	Jan 11/17		Training continued. Rise 7 AM : P.T. 8.20 a.m.: squad drill and Elementary gun drill for rest of day. In the afternoon the Coy played the T.M. Batty & Bde H.Q. at football.	
	Jan 12/17		Training cld. V. wet, some snow: weather very cold.	
	Jan 13/17		Training continued, though hampered by bad weather. Divisional Conference (on Training) 2.30 p.m. at Div H.Q. (HALLENCOURT)	
	Jan 14/17		No Training. Inspection of Coy. at 10.30 a.m. Church parades 9 a.m. (C of E) 10.30 a.m. (R.C.) 6 p.m (Nonconformists) Weather very wet. Some sleet.	

Instructions regarding War Diaries and Intelligence Summaries are contained in F. S. Regs., Part II. and the Staff Manual respectively. Title Pages will be prepared in manuscript.

WAR DIARY
or
INTELLIGENCE SUMMARY
(Erase heading not required.)

Army Form C. 2118

145 M.G. Company.

Place	Date	Hour	Summary of Events and Information	Remarks and references to Appendices
BRESLE	Jan 6/17	9.30am	Inspection by Gen. Pulteney, commanding III Corps, of the whole Brigade: a wet day, & very cold.	[illegible]
	Jan 7/17		Paraded for church 10.45 a.m.: no service, as no chaplain arrived. Route march.	[illegible]
	Jan 8/17		2Lt G. H. DAILEY and 2 NCO's left for FRUCOURT to arrange billets, travelling by bus via AIRAINES. Lecture for all officers & NCO's in canteen 4.0 p.m. on "Contact Patrols" by Capt PAGET R.F.C. Transport moved by road to new area, moving off at 8 a.m. (2 days march) [illegible]	
	Jan 9/17		Company moved off at 3.45 am from BRESLE and entrained at HEILLY at 5 AM. arriving at OISEMONT at 12 noon, marching thence about 4 miles to FRUCOURT. Blankets were conveyed by lorry to HEILLY & taken on the train & were again conveyed from OISEMONT to FRUCOURT by lorry. All bulky baggage, (e.g. Officers valises, QM Stores etc.,) was conveyed by through lorry to FRUCOURT. Accommodation at FRUCOURT was ample & good. Stabling was found for all horses. The 2nd SM Field Ambulance	

1875 Wt. W593/826 1,000,000 4/15 J.B.C. & A. A.D.S.S./Forms/C. 2118.

Army Form C. 2118

Instructions regarding War Diaries and Intelligence Summaries are contained in F. S. Regs., Part II. and the Staff Manual respectively. Title Pages will be prepared in manuscript.

WAR DIARY
or
INTELLIGENCE SUMMARY
(Erase heading not required.)

145 Machine Gun Coy.

Place	Date	Hour	Summary of Events and Information	Remarks and references to Appendices
BRESLE	Jan 1/17		Training including the firing of Table C PART I A.h.	
	Jan 2/17		Training: continued Table C PART I Conference at Div. H.Q. (BAISIEUX) 3 p.m. 2Lt H H MAYOR joined for duty A.h.	
	Jan 3/17		Training continued Staff Tour for commanding officers without troops by G.O.C. Division, starting from MILL on BAISIEUX – HENENCOURT ROAD 10 a.m. Nature of scheme – an advanced guard, moving in direction of AMIENS via the neighbourhood of BEHENCOURT. A.h.	
	Jan 4/17		Training somewhat restricted by wet weather: route march in the morning. Cinema in the Canteen in the evening. A.h.	
	Jan 5/17		Training continued: Conference at Div HQ 3 p.m. Brigade boxing contests, first round, 5.30 p.m.: two entries only from the Company: one retired, the other was beaten on points. A.h.	

1875 Wt. W593/826 1,000,000 4/15 J.B.C. & A. A.D.S.S./Forms/C. 2118.

CONFIDENTIAL.

Vol 12

War Diary

of

145th Machine Gun Company.

From Jan 1st 1917 To Jan 31st 1917.

Major

APPENDIX 'A'

GUE
1:10,000
M
Pys
Warlencourt
Eaucourt
Little Wood
Grundy Road
Quarry
Le Sars
(In Ruins)
Cemetery
Butte de Warlencourt
Destremont Farm
Eaucourt L'A
(In Ruins)
Courcelette
(In Ruins)
Twenty Road
Martinpuich
(In Ruins)
Prue Trench
Pys Copse

Instructions regarding War Diaries and Intelligence Summaries are contained in F. S. Regs., Part II. and the Staff Manual respectively. Title Pages will be prepared in manuscript.

or

INTELLIGENCE SUMMARY

(Erase heading not required.)

145 Machine Gun Coy

Place	Date	Hour	Summary of Events and Information	Remarks and references to Appendices
	Dec 28		70639 Pte Campbell C.S, 70630 Pte Price J., 43121 Pte Lamb J. to C.C.S.	
	30		60815 Pte Mackern K, Rejoined for duty. 15441 Pte Williams Y, to Hospital; Strength Decrease:- 70639 Pte Campbell C.S, 70630 Pte Price J, 43121 Pte Lamb J. Struck off.	
	31		Strength Increase:- 2nd LIEUT R.W. HUGMAN. MGC Posted for duty.	[signature] Major

WAR DIARY
or
INTELLIGENCE SUMMARY
(Erase heading not required.)

Instructions regarding War Diaries and Intelligence Summaries are contained in F. S. Regs., Part II. and the Staff Manual respectively. Title Pages will be prepared in manuscript.

145 Machine Gun Coy.

Place	Date	Hour	Summary of Events and Information	Remarks and references to Appendices
	Dec 18		Strength Increase:- 28216 Pte Miller T, 43792 Pte Hills A.W. joined for duty; Strength Decrease:- 23942 Pte Brindley A.E. To C.C.S. struck off;	
	19		Strength Decrease:- 21729 Pte Martin J.T. to C.C.S. Struck off. 21726 Sgt Bruce A.E. to Hospital;	
	20		21115 L/Cpl Atkinson J.E. To Hospital; 21726 Sgt Bruce A.E. To C.C.S.	
	21		21720 Pte Harris G, 60815 Pte Macken K. To Hospital. 2nd LIEUT W.H. GREEN 1st R. Lancs: to Hospital;	
	22		Strength Increase:- 36501 Cpl O'Neill C. joined for duty. 21122 Sgt Glover A, 8944 Pte Newham H, To Hospital.	
	23		21115 L/Cpl Atkinson, Rejoined for duty;	
	24		70081. Pte Hartley R.H, To Hospital.	
	25		19053 Pte Holmes W.J. To Course G.H.Q. School. Strength Increase:- LIEUT. J.S. ALEXANDER 6th Seaforths; 2nd LIEUT F.W. MOSS, MGC joined for duty; 21726 Sgt Bruce A.E. Struck off;	
	27.		Strength Increase:- 53902 Pte Maloney P, 21728 Pte Large W.J., 27057. Pte Batten J. 30978 Pte Hobson A.J. 13612 Pte Nash W. 20879. Pte Vallance S, joined for duty. 70639. Pte Campbell C.S 70630 Pte Price J. 63121 Pte Lamb J. To Hospital.	[illegible]

1875 Wt. W593/826 1,000,000 4/15 J.B.C. & A. A.D.S.S./Forms/C. 2118.

Instructions regarding War Diaries and Intelligence Summaries are contained in F. S. Regs., Part II. and the Staff Manual respectively. Title Pages will be prepared in manuscript.

WAR DIARY
or
INTELLIGENCE SUMMARY

(Erase heading not required.)

Army Form C. 2118

145 Machine Gun Coy.

Place	Date	Hour	Summary of Events and Information	Remarks and references to Appendices
	Dec 6		63121 Pte Lamb A.E., 63098 Pte May J. 60813 Pte Mackern J. 60815 Pte Mackern R., 60557 " McQuaker D, Joined for duty;	
	7		~~22917~~ Pte Stanners G, To Hospital; 22122 Sgt Glover H, To Hospital; 70640 (2652 1st Bucks) Pte Whitty E, To C.C.S;	
	9		Strength Increase:- 70632 (5118 1/4 Oxf & Bucks L.I.) Pte Collins W. joined for duty;	
	11		Strength Increase:- 44494 Pte Button C, 35063 Pte Willett R.J. 37047 Pte Fletcher J, 8499 Pte Simpson J.L. 70639 Pte Campbell C.S, Joined for duty;	
	12		Strength Increase:- 12354 Pte ~~Fenton G~~. 57069 Pte Forte H, 54867 Pte Fox F.E, Joined for duty;	
	13		21122 Sgt Glover H. Rejoined for duty;	
	15		Strength Decrease:- 70633 Pte Newman W. To C.C.S; 70640 Pte Whitty E. Struck off 16.12.16; 2nd LIEUT INWOOD. C.H; 21107 Pte Lines W, 21735 Pte Lansome W, 22918 Pte Lacey J, Rejoined from M.G School. G.H.Q.; 70654 (5998 1/4 R. Berks) Pte Blewitt K. M.G.C. To Hospital;	
	17		Strength Decrease:- 15532 Pte Downing A. To M.G. Corps Base underage; 2nd LIEUT. F.W. LAWRENCE. M.G.C. To Hospital;	[signature] Maj.
	18		2nd LIEUT W.M. SANGSTER. M.G.C. 2nd LIEUT L. LEATHLEY. 11th K.R.R. To Hospital;	

Instructions regarding War Diaries and Intelligence Summaries are contained in F. S. Regs., Part II. and the Staff Manual respectively. Title Pages will be prepared in manuscript.

WAR DIARY or **INTELLIGENCE SUMMARY**

(Erase heading not required.)

145 Machine Gun Coy.

Place	Date	Hour	Summary of Events and Information	Remarks and references to Appendices
			APPENDIX "B"	
			Casualties.	
	Dec 1		1824. Pte Howell WH. 1/5 Gloster To Hospital; Strength Decrease:- 5118 Pte Collins W. 1/4 Oxf Bucks L.I. To C.C.S; 3268 Pte Stacey A.F. 1/4 R. Berks. To C.C.S; 6051 Pte Tegg H. 1/4 R. Berks to C.C.S.; 21737 L/Sgt Parrott J. M.G.C. C.C.S; 21114 Pte Bricknell H. M.G.C. C.C.S; 21717 Pte Wheatley P. to C.C.S; 36501 Cpl O'Neill C. to C.C.S; 15943 Pte Druse H. to C.C.S;	
	2		23905 Pte Rowbotham G. Killed in action; 21118 L/Cpl Randall L.J. wounded; 21716 Pte Downham F. wounded; 4652 Pte Whitty E. 1st Bucks, To Hospital;	
	3		70627 (1824 1/5 Glosters) Pte Howell W.H. M.G.C. Rejoined for duty;	
	4		36889 Pte Morrisey, M, To Hospital, To C.C.S; 22902 Pte Wilsdon H, To Hospital; 70653 Pte Millard W.J. M.G.C. to Hospital;	
	5		21729 Pte Martin J. To Hospital; Strength Decrease:- 36889 Pte Morrisey, M, to C.C.S; 22902 Pte Wilsdon H. To C.C.S;	
	6		Strength Increase:- 60131 Pte Atkins O.L, 59884 Pte Bradley F, 10528 Pte Butcher F, 42360 Pte Board D.C, 63102 Pte Decort A, 60366 Pte Jepson J.H, 60363 Pte Kirk W.R, 60253 Pte Kershaw R, 60548 Pte. Kane R, 60570 Pte Keating O, 63052 Pte Lowe A.V, 60600 Pte Littlewood A, 60542 Pte Lawson E.P, 60229 Pte Lewis H.A,	[signature] Major

1875 Wt. W593/826 1,000,000 4/15 J.B.C. & A. A.D.S.S./Forms/C. 2118.

Instructions regarding War Diaries and Intelligence Summaries are contained in F. S. Regs., Part II. and the Staff Manual respectively. Title Pages will be prepared in manuscript.

or

INTELLIGENCE SUMMARY

(Erase heading not required.)

145 Machine Gun Coy.

Place	Date	Hour	Summary of Events and Information	Remarks and references to Appendices

APPENDIX "A"

Reference to Map.

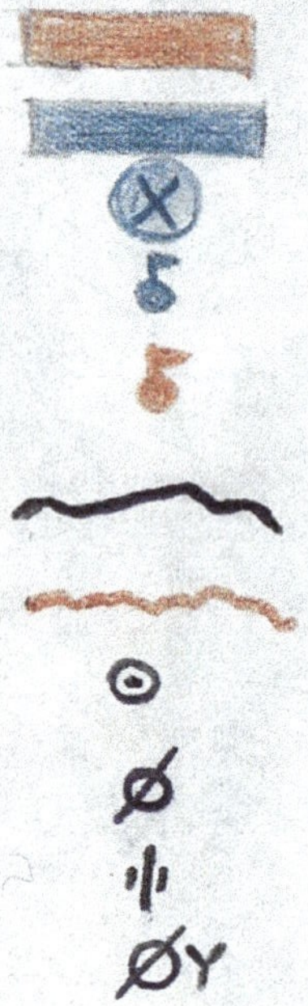

Belts of Cross Fire
Zones of Fire
Targets engaged by indirect + searching fire.
Forward H.Q. + ammunition reserve.
H.Q. + ammunition reserve
Front line system (British)
Enemy system
Machine Guns, Corps Line.
Machine Guns, forward system.
Alternative + other M.G. emplacements.
Left flank gun of right Brigade.

[illegible]

Instructions regarding War Diaries and Intelligence Summaries are contained in F. S. Regs., Part II. and the Staff Manual respectively. Title Pages will be prepared in manuscript.

or

INTELLIGENCE SUMMARY

(Erase heading not required.)

145 Machine Gun Coy.

Place	Date	Hour	Summary of Events and Information	Remarks and references to Appendices
			had rather failed as such.	
BÉCOURT	Dec 15th to 28th		At BECOURT CAMP during all this period over Christmas, the time being spent mostly on the camp or roads with a little training. *4 Officers to Hospital during this period with Trench Fever, while +2 Reinforcement Officers joined for duty.	* See Appendix "B" under 17, 18 & 21.12.16.
	Dec 28th		On Thursday 28th the whole Brigade moved to BRESLE where	+ See Appendix B under 25.12.16.
BRESLE			this company went into billets, finding no fatigues other than its own, so able to devote time to training, a very necessary proceeding, owing to the fact that it received during the month 27 reinforcements. An improvement in many ways on the earlier reinforcements received by the Company, & yet varying a great deal, the knowledge of some men being good, while others being very sketchy.	
	Dec 30th		Another reinforcement Officer ‡ joined for duty.	‡ See Appendix B under 31.12.16.

[signature] Major, OC. 145 M. G. Coy.

1875 Wt. W593/826 1,000,000 4/15 J.B.C. & A. A.D.S.S./Forms/C. 2118.

WAR DIARY

or

INTELLIGENCE SUMMARY

(Erase heading not required.)

Instructions regarding *War Diaries* and *Intelligence Summaries* are contained in F. S. Regs., Part II. and the Staff Manual respectively. Title Pages will be prepared in manuscript.

145 Machine Gun Coy.

Place	Date	Hour	Summary of Events and Information	Remarks and references to Appendices
CONTALMAISON MARTINPUICH LE SARS	Dec 14th		in Factory Lines, were ordered to occupy positions at M15A 5.2 approx: but eventually moved a little further forward. No news of this shifting of the guns arrived until the night of 14-15th + in the meantime arrangements for relief by the 45th M.G. Coy on the night 14-15th had been made. The despatch took from 10.35 on Wednesday night till about 6.30 on the Thursday night to get from MARTINPUICH to CONTALMAISON, and, as there had been several wires received in amplification of the despatch, which had not been received, which were consequently unintelligible some confusion resulted: ~~which~~ this was not cleared by another fact, that the code call of the relieving Company, the 45th, differed hardly at all from the 143rd of this Division so that messages commonly had JV ? U JU ? V. Howbeit the relief went off alright on the night of the 14-15th, + that part of the Company, which was at ACID DROP CAMP moved on the	
	Dec 15th		morning of 14th to BECOURT CAMP, where the transport joined them from CHAPES SPUR on the 15th + the rest of the Company that was in the line also on the 15th moving straight down without a halt. ACID DROP CAMP had been for many of the men the only rest place, + as it was intermittently shelled	[signature]

Instructions regarding War Diaries and Intelligence Summaries are contained in F. S. Regs., Part II. and the Staff Manual respectively. Title Pages will be prepared in manuscript.

Army Form C. 2118

WAR DIARY or INTELLIGENCE SUMMARY

(Erase heading not required.)

145 Machine Gun Coy.

Place	Date	Hour	Summary of Events and Information	Remarks and references to Appendices
CONTALMAISON MARTINPUICH LE SARS	Dec 1 to 13th		At the beginning of the month & up to the 13th the dispositions of this Company were as follows. Two guns in front system at M15c 95-75 and M15D 8.8. Two guns in Corps nest at about M21 Central, 1 gun at M21D 8.7. 2 guns in local reserve at Factory Lines. MARTINPUICH. (For gun positions see appendix "A".) The remainder of the Company was at ACID DROP CAMP SOUTH CONTALMAISON with Transport at CHAPES SPUR. BECOURT. Nothing of any importance happened during this period. ACID DROP CAMP proved to be very wet, very cold, and muddy. It was not possible to have a complete relief of the men in the line; we relieved about 35 a time every 4 days.	
	13th		During this period it should be stated that the forward guns & guns in local reserve were under the control of the 143 & 144 Brigades respectively during their tours in the line. The 145 Brigade had one Battn in turn in always on the left, while the 143 & 144 relieved each other on the right. Eventually the guns in the Corps nests came under the control of the Brigade in MARTINPUICH for tactical purposes. On the night of the 13th some person or persons started a rumour that the Germans were going to attack from the direction of M8D. The two guns in local reserve in	

ORIGINAL

CONFIDENTIAL

Vol XI

WAR DIARY

OF

145 MACHINE GUN COMPANY

FOR

DECEMBER 1916.

31.12.16.

[signature] Major

Cmdg. 145 M. G. Coy.

145th Brigade

48th Division.

145th BRIGADE MACHINE GUN COMPANY

DECEMBER 1 9 1 6

165 M. G. Coy.

Appendix to War Diary

for

Nov. 1916.

Appendix A

Contours corrected from latest information SECRET

LE SARS TO LOUPART WOOD AND LE BARQUE

TRENCHES CORRECTED TO 21-11-16 2ND EDITION

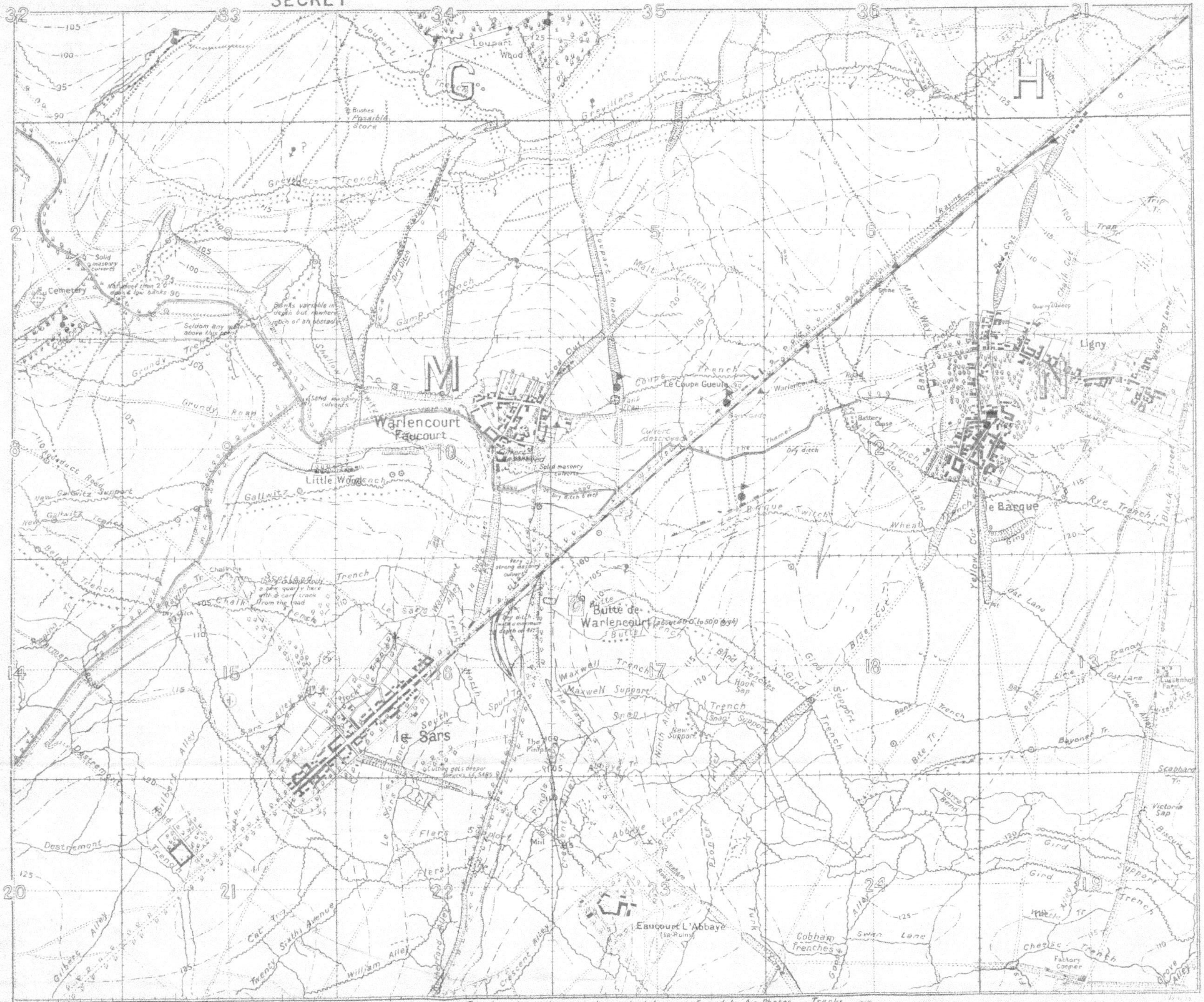

1st Printing Coy. R.E. 10 Army Sect. (899)

Dugouts ... M.G. ... O.P. H.Q. Batt. Regt. Trenches shown thus ..... have not yet been confirmed by Air Photos. Dump ▲ Buried Cable or Pipe Line ——— Tracks Gap in wire

Army Form C. 2118

WAR DIARY
or
INTELLIGENCE SUMMARY

(Erase heading not required.)

Instructions regarding War Diaries and Intelligence Summaries are contained in F. S. Regs., Part II. and the Staff Manual respectively. Title Pages will be prepared in manuscript.

145 M.G. Coy

Place	Date	Hour	Summary of Events and Information	Remarks and references to Appendices
MARTINPUICH LE-SARS CONTALMAISON	20th 30th Continued		These conditions continued ~~with~~ the 30th and still continue with the exception that on the night of the 30th in accordance with orders 1 of the guns from the "Nest" was withdrawn and we were able to bring 4 men out. This will almost enable us to work reliefs of 4 days up and 4 days right back at CONTALMAISON (ACID DROP COPSE) During this month we were fortunate in having comparatively few casualties; guns were buried, positions blown in, but very few men hurt. We relieved always in the early hours of the morning and thus avoided casualties during relief which other units, relieving at early hours in the evening, suffered. Despite the extremely bad conditions we had comparatively little sickness and only ~~two~~ cases, very slight, of Trench Feet, and even these were attributed to the poor quality of the boot they were wearing at the time, which shrank and rubbed their feet, rather than to any other causes. On the whole a most unpleasant month, though it might have been worse	5632 Pte Gordon, W.A. wounded 28/11/16; 3976 Pte Campbell, C.S., 21428 Pte Large, J., 20890 Pte Watson, K.B. to C.C.S., struck off 25/11/16; 21723 Cpl MAY, W.E., wounded 23/11/16; 22903 Sgt JEFFERY, A.S. Rejoin for duty 24/11/16; 2nd Lt L. LEATHLEY; 21108 Pte Flack, J., 22906 " Gibbs, W., 21720 " Nuccoll, J. to duty 25/11/16; 2nd Lt INWOOD, E.H.; 21107 Pte Sims, W; Hd 21735 Samson, W to course 22/11/16; 21117 Sgt Gale, F.A.; 21734 Cpl Underwood, F.A., to Cadet School 29.11.16

[signature]

1875 Wt. W593/826 1,000,000 4/15 J.B.C. & A. A.D.S.S./Forms/C. 2118.

WAR DIARY
or
INTELLIGENCE SUMMARY
(Erase heading not required.)

Army Form C. 2118

Instructions regarding War Diaries and Intelligence Summaries are contained in F. S. Regs., Part II. and the Staff Manual respectively. Title Pages will be prepared in manuscript.

145 M.G. Coy.

Place	Date	Hour	Summary of Events and Information	Remarks and references to Appendices
MARTINPUICH LE-SARS	15th–20th		On the night 15/16th we had entertained hopes of being relieved but — "DIS ALITER VISUM" —. Instead we took over a more extended front than before. We relieved the 143 M.G. Coy in the front system with 8 guns recalling our 19 men from BECOURT (TRANSPORT LINES) to do so. 144 M.G. Coy relieved us in the "Nests". On the night of 18th/19th still retaining the 8 guns in the front line, we were ordered to take over the 2 Left "Nests" with 4 guns; we did so. [see Appendix. A]	1965 Pte GIBBS, W.E to leave 16-26/11/16. 4937 Pte KING, J., to duty 17/11/16; 23939 Pte GRINNEL, T.J. To duty 17/11/16, 21112 Corpl Jones, F.W., 21729 Pte Wright, F.G., 46327 Pte Booth, F., struck off 18/11/16.
" " and CONTALMAISON	20th–30th		On the night 20/21st we were relieved on the S of the LE-SARS — BAPAUME road by the 144 M.G. Coy and were thus left with 2 guns in the front system – 4 guns in CORPS "NESTS" and 2 guns in local reserve at MARTINPUICH (We had been permitted to withdraw one of the guns N. of the LE-SARS — BAPAUME Road), the idea being that we should thus be able to rest our men, a section at a time. In point of fact we now managed to get a few extra men out by thinning down the teams in the CORPS "Nests". The Coy had thus averaged per man from Nov. 2nd to Nov 20th half the time in the front system, the remaining half being spent more or less evenly in the CORPS "Nests" or MARTINPUICH, with the exception that 19 men had spent 3 nights out at BECOURT	4186 Pte BURKE, J slightly wounded at duty 18/11/16. 43889 Pte O'BRIEN, J killed in action 20/11/16

Instructions regarding War Diaries and Intelligence Summaries are contained in F. S. Regs., Part II. and the Staff Manual respectively. Title Pages will be prepared in manuscript.

WAR DIARY
or
INTELLIGENCE SUMMARY
(Erase heading not required.)

Army Form C. 2118

143 M.G. Coy.

Place	Date	Hour	Summary of Events and Information	Remarks and references to Appendices
MARTINPUICH LE-SARS	8th-11th	continued	It existed at that time, on a tracing at HÉNENCOURT with red circles round various co-ordinates, on the ground these red circles took the shape of pieces of much dilapidated trench or shell holes, distinguished from other like pieces and holes by the presence of sundry guns and teams. Shelters of sorts were constructed as soon as possible. These "snuggeries" were officially known as "Nests". Each "Nest" had a pair of guns and we held 4 "Nests"	21717 Pte Wheatley, P to duty 9/11/16 5006 Pte Newman, W accidentally wounded 10/11/16
	11th-15th	inclus.	On the night of the 11th 143 M.G. Coy relieved our forward guns. We were thus left with 8 guns in the CORPS LINE and 8 in MARTINPUICH. As occupants of the CORPS LINE we were nobody's children, nothing was being done to improve the conditions except that little which we could do ourselves. From various orders and memoranda we had gathered that a tunnelling section was devoting its energies to the construction of dug-outs at these "Nests", which however still remained "in statu quo ante" as far as the vagaries of nature and the pressing attentions of an occasional 5.9" permitted. During this period we managed to send 19 men back to the transport lines. On the 12th Nov in response to many appeals, an officer from the Corps appeared to see what work had or had not been done on the nests. He came; He saw; He sighted 6 fresh "Nests"; He went away, carrying with him spiritual impressions and bodily traces of having spent some inspiring moments in shell holes. The GERMANS 4.2" is extraordinarily accurate; their observation is very thorough	22932 Pte Young, E. G., 2744 Pte Lewis, E struck off 11/11/16. 23939 Pte Grinnell, J. J. wounded 11/11/16 2nd Lieut C.H. INWOOD, 2nd Lieut F G LAWRENCE, 43145 Pte ALLEN, E., joined for duty 12/11/16

G.H.Howarth Lt

1875 Wt. W593/826 1,000,000 4/15 J.B.C. & A. A.D.S.S./Forms/C. 2118.

Instructions regarding War Diaries and Intelligence Summaries are contained in F. S. Regs., Part II. and the Staff Manual respectively. Title Pages will be prepared in manuscript.

WAR DIARY
or
INTELLIGENCE SUMMARY
(Erase heading not required.)

Army Form C. 2118

145 M.G. Coy.

Place	Date	Hour	Summary of Events and Information	Remarks and references to Appendices
MARTINPUICH LE-SARS	Nov. 5th		Very cold & windy day – Div's on our right attacked the BUTTE-de-WARLENCOURT and the GIRD trench – The hostile & vigorous reply made LE-SARS even more unpleasant than usual 2/Lt T. H. MITCHELL was fatally wounded in the afternoon, being shot through the throat by a GERMAN Sniper whilst sighting a new position. It took over 4 hrs to carry this officer as far as MARTINPUICH and from there eventually a party of 8 men had to be detailed to carry him to CONTALMAISON, that being the opseediest method of conveyance, this latter part of the journey taking 2½ hours. He died the same night.	2nd Lieut T.H. MITCHELL killed in action. 22902 Pte Wilsdon, H, to duty. 2744 Pte Earis E to C.C.S.
" "	6th – 8th inclusive		Carried on with the same dispositions. No 2 Section rejoined the Coy on the 6th The weather continued very cold and very wet. 24 hr reliefs were aimed at, but as the period out included the journeys to & from the trenches and ration parties, it proved rather trying though it did keep the men exercised to a certain extent – Some record times were made between LE-SARS and MARTINPUICH, this is attributed to the stimulating influence of 5.9"s in and about	4934 Pte KING, J wounded 7/11/16 20892 Pte HORST, W to duty 8/11/16
" "	8th – 11th inclusive		DESTREMONT FARM. On Nov. 8th the Corps line was ordered to be occupied in addition to the DEFENCE line – Twelve guns and teams were employed reliefs then only being possible in the proportion of 3 days in and one day out. As the Corps M.G. line ran roughly from DESTREMONT to EAUCOURT L'ABBAYE, it did not afford much chance of repose	2nd Lt W.H. GREEN to duty 9/11/16

1875 Wt. W593/826 1,000,000 4/15 J.B.C. & A. A.D.S.S./Forms/C. 2118.

Instructions regarding War Diaries and Intelligence Summaries are contained in F. S. Regs., Part II. and the Staff Manual respectively. Title Pages will be prepared in manuscript.

WAR DIARY
or
INTELLIGENCE SUMMARY
(Erase heading not required.)

Army Form C. 2118

145 M.G. Coy

Place	Date	Hour	Summary of Events and Information	Remarks and references to Appendices
MILLENCOURT	Nov. 1st 1916		O.C Coy visited MARTINPUICH to see O.C 45th Coy with a view to relieving him in the near future probably two or three days time. At 5.45 pm orders arrived that the Coy should relieve the Coy in Reserve of 15th Div at LOZENGE WOOD with a view to relieving Coy in line the following night. This Coy was still minus one section with 3 limbers who were attached to M.M.G. battery for instruction. Five limbers were out on Bde fatigue thus leaving only 4 limbers available to move 12 guns and their equipment & blankets &c of three sections. Eventually by dumping for the time being the S.A.A. two sections were enabled to move off to LOZENGE WOOD	20892 Pte HORST. A.W. to 21 C.C.S.
MILLENCOURT } LOZENGE WOOD } MARTINPUICH }	2nd		The limbers not having returned till 5. am in the morning Section No 1 was not able to move off to join the others at LOZENGE WOOD till noon, in the meantime orders had arrived definitely to relieve the 45th Coy in the line on the N. of the ALBERT BAPAUME Rd in the neighbourhood of LE-SARS with the whole Coy. Messengers were sent to recall the section in BAZENTIN-LE-PETIT who were promptly withdrawn to LAVIÉVILLE; they were found to be quite unfit to move into the line and were left back for a few days. Section I in the meantime picked up Sections 3, & 4 at LOZENGE WOOD and these three sections relieved 45th Coy in the line that night. Dispositions:— 5 guns in the front system, 2 in support & 5 in Local Reserve S.W of MARTINPUICH (FACTORY LINES). Relief complete at about midnight. Weather conditions very bad and a very dark night. Took over as H.Q. old GERMAN dug-outs at the MILL MARTINPUICH with forward H.Q. in the sunken road leading N.W. from LE-SARS.	2nd Lt. L. LEATHLEY 21108 Pte Fluck, J.T. 22906 " Gibbs, W. 31720 " Nuccoll J. to M.G. Course G.H.Q.
MARTINPUICH } LE-SARS }	3rd & 4th		Nothing of interest occured – Weather misty but mild – O.C. Coy in common with other officers of Bde lost a great quantity of kit, the more or less permanent denizens of MARTINPUICH strongly suspected. Ration and carrying parties very arduous, owing to bad roads, depth of the mud and the scoriated condition of the ground.	13301 Pte BERRIMAN, C joins for duty 4/11/16 [signature]

1875 Wt. W593/826 1,000,000 4/15 J.B.C. & A. A.D.S.S./Forms/C. 2118.

CONFIDENTIAL

Vol 10

ORIGINAL

WAR DIARY

OF.

145 MACHINE GUN COMPANY.

from 1st NOV. 1916 to 30th NOV. 1916.

[signature] MAJOR.

O.C. 145 M.G. Coy.

145th Brigade.

48th Division.

145th BRIGADE MACHINE GUN COMPANY

NOVEMBER 1 9 1 6

Instructions regarding War Diaries and Intelligence Summaries are contained in F. S. Regs., Part II. and the Staff Manual respectively. Title Pages will be prepared in manuscript.

[WAR DIARY] or

INTELLIGENCE SUMMARY

(Erase heading not required.)

Place	Date	Hour	Summary of Events and Information	Remarks and references to Appendices
	24th-31st		instructed, seemed very sanguine as to the results attained or indeed attainable, perhaps owing to the fact that on account of the inclement weather, birds were scarce.	
			At the time of writing, teachers & pupils alike were sitting in the mud somewhere to the N. of BAZENTIN-LE-PETIT.	
			General situation might be described as obscure.	
			On the 31st Moved to MILLENCOURT – Billets very indifferent, the outgoing troops seem to have had an indeed elementary idea of cleanliness & sanitation and the efforts of the party sent in advance 3 days before to guard & clean billets would appear to have disclosed rather than removed much that was unpleasant.	S H Fildes? Lt.

1875 Wt. W593/826 1,000,000 4/15 J.B.C. & A. A.D.S.S./Forms/C. 2118.

WAR DIARY
or
INTELLIGENCE SUMMARY
(Erase heading not required.)

Instructions regarding War Diaries and Intelligence Summaries are contained in F. S. Regs., Part II. and the Staff Manual respectively. Title Pages will be prepared in manuscript.

Place	Date	Hour	Summary of Events and Information	Remarks and references to Appendices
LES ANNELLES	21st		Lt WILLIAMSON left to go to GRANTHAM. Exceedingly cold weather during this period.	
	22nd		Moved to BEUVAL. Practically same billets as before, very good.	
	23rd		Moved to TALMAS. Billets exceedingly bad. Dry weather broke	24.10.16
	24th–31st		Moved to BÉHENCOURT and remained there. During these marches, every man was marched in full pack & none fell out. This improvement in March Discipline is attributed to the practise of making men who previously fell out, repeatedly do extra marching in full packs.	46690 Pte Goby R.G. 23941 Pte Higgins J.E.A. Struck off strength
			On the 30th, party of officers from the Bde including C.O & 2nd in Command paid a visit to CONTALMAISON and MARTINPUICH with a view to taking over from respective units of 15th Div.	
			During this period one section was detailed to be attached to M.M.Gunners for instruction in firing at aeroplanes. Nature of instruction seemed obscure when investigated by O.C. Coy. Neither the instructors nor the	S.H. Fielden Lt

WAR DIARY

or

INTELLIGENCE SUMMARY

(Erase heading not required.)

Army Form C. 2118.

Instructions regarding War Diaries and Intelligence Summaries are contained in F. S. Regs., Part II. and the Staff Manual respectively. Title Pages will be prepared in manuscript.

Vol 9

145 MG Coy.

Place	Date 1916	Hour	Summary of Events and Information	Remarks and references to Appendices
WARLINCOURT.	Oct. 1.		Bde left billets in neighbourhood of HUMBERCOURT & marched to WARLINCOURT reaching there about 2 P.M. 146th MG Coy took over billets vacated at HUMBERCOURT.	2. 10. 16 17648 Pte Dolan, J
	2.		Physical training, arms drill, & route march.	46002 Lcpl Phipps, F.H.
	3.		Rain & route march.	4186 Pte
	4 5		Physical training, arms drill & mechanism	Burke, J
	6		No 1 section left at 8.30 AM to take over positions East of HEBUTERNE from 143rd MG Coy. HQ's & other 3 sections remained at WARLINCOURT.	Joins for duty.
	7-14		During this period we held K Sector & found many changes since the 48 Div left. The trenches are greatly improved & well revetted. Wire cutting by our Artillery was in progress & our work consisted in keeping open the gaps through the enemy's wire during the night. On the night of the 9th about 3000 gas shells were fired on to the Plain between Hebuterne & Sailly resulting in a few colds in the head through walking about in night attire. On the night of the 14th we were relieved by the 144th M.G. Coy. N.B.W.	10. 10. 16 45638 Pte Geles, F.E. 45351 Pte Gillam, J joins for duty. 13. 10. 16 3976 Pte Campbell, C.S. wounded at duty.
	14-20		Remained at WARLINCOURT. 13th Lt S.H. GELDARD arrived to take over 2nd in command vice Lt GREEN to GRANTHAM. Moved off on Friday 20th to go to HUMBERCOURT. On the march destination changed to LES ANNELLES FARM near COUTURELLES	17. 10. 16 Cpl Bartlett to Cadet School

S H Geldard Lt.

1875 Wt. W593/826 1,000,000 4/15 I.R.C. & A. A.D.S.S./Forms/C. 2118.

145th Brigade.

48th Division.

145th BRIGADE MACHINE GUN COMPANY

OCTOBER 1 9 1 6

Instructions regarding War Diaries and Intelligence Summaries are contained in F. S. Regs., Part II. and the Staff Manual respectively. Title Pages will be prepared in manuscript.

WAR DIARY
or
INTELLIGENCE SUMMARY
(Erase heading not required.)

Army Form C. 2118

145 MG Coy

Place	Date 1916	Hour	Summary of Events and Information	Remarks and references to Appendices
BUS-LES-ARTOIS BEAUVAL	Sept 11.		Company marched with rest of brigade to BEAUVAL arriving at 7 P.M & going into billets in RUE NEUVE BG	12.9.16. No 22931 Sgt PEARSON struck off strength to No 2 Training Camp, ETAPLES preparatory to CADET SCHOOL
	12		Resting & cleaning up. BG	
	13		6 hours training under company arrangements. BG	
	14		ditto	
	15		ditto	
			Three officers & 5 NCO's reconnoitred AMIENS DEFENCE line from HERISSART to BEAUQUESNE (both exclusive) & chose positions for 12 MG's. Three of these were made emplacements with head cover. BG	13.9.16. 5632 Pte PLOWDEN W 43889 - O'BRIEN J joined from Base Depot
	16		Same as for 15.9.16 above. BG Cpl J. PARROTT No 21731. awarded Russian Cross of St George (2nd Class)	
	17.		Sunday. No Church Parade. BG	17.9.16. 6737 Pte SIRMAN J 36413 - ROUSE, H joined from Base Depot
FIENVILLERS	18.		Bde moved. Coy marched to FIENVILLERS Paraded at 10-15 AM, in billets by 1 P.M. BG A terrible day, everyone soaked through by incessant & heavy rain. 90th MG Coy occupied billets vacated at BEAUVAL. BG	
	19.		Intermittent heavy showers. Route march, arms drill & running during morning. BG 2nd LIEUTS BAILEY, G.H (MG Corps) & LEATHLEY, L (11th KOYLI) joined for duty from Base, bringing coy up to full strength in officers.. BG	29.9.16. No. 2275 Pte JOHNSTON, V.B 2nd Fd Amb. 48th Div. taken on strength vice 2380 Pte THACKER, C to CCS.
	20		Routine training much interfered with by rain. BG	
	21. 22 23 24 25		Routine training especially physical training & arms drill BG	
	26 27 28		Field training. BG	
HUMBERCOURT.	29		Bde marched via DOULLENS to HUMBERCOURT Left at 10 AM, in billets at HUMBERCOURT by 5.15 P.M. BG	BG
	30		Resting in billets BG	

WAR DIARY
or
~~INTELLIGENCE SUMMARY~~

(Erase heading not required.)

Instructions regarding War Diaries and Intelligence Summaries are contained in F. S. Regs., Part II. and the Staff Manual respectively. Title Pages will be prepared in manuscript.

Vol 8 Army Form C. 2118

145 M G Coy.

Place	Date	Hour	Summary of Events and Information	Remarks and references to Appendices
BUS-LES-ARTOIS	Sept. 1		In huts. B.G. Received 6 reinforcements from MG Corps base depot. (all ptes)	Rejoined, No 20892 Pte HURST. Struck off strength 2780 S/c LANE to Cadet School 21132 Pte HONOUR to base 21120 Pte ALEXANDER & 8262 Pte HEWERDINE to CCS (all 2/9/16)
"	2		Inspected by MAJ. GEN. FANSHAWE, G.O.C. 48 DIV. at 9 A.M. in same field as 1/4 OBLI & 145 ~~MG Coy~~ TMB. B.G. He mentioned fact that the division had captured over 700 prisoners during their last tour in firing line & surmised that warfare would be more open in nature when division next went in. Received 3 men from 1/5 Gloucesters & 2 men from 1/4 OBLI to make up casualties amongst men attached from battalions. B.G.	
"	3		} In huts at BUS. B.G.	
"	4		}	
BUS-LES-ARTOIS & MAILLY-MAILLET.	5.		Sections 2 & 4 relieved two sections of the 144 MG Coy in the trenches East of AUCHONVILLERS. Relief completed about 8 p.m. Dispositions as follows; Front line system, 4 guns at Q 4 a. 9.3, Q 4 c 85.60, Q 10 a. 80.25 & Q 10 b. 10.45. In support, 2 guns at Q 3 D. 95.40 & Q 3. a. 4.1. Local reserve, 2 guns at Q 9. a. 4.3. (Map. 57D SE 1&2 (parts of) 1/10,000) Coy H.Q's. No 10 billet MAILLY-MAILLET. Transport of two sections in line at Q. 17 c. Balance of company remaining at BUS. B.G.	3/9/16. 2/LIEUT. T.H. MITCHELL (DCLI) joined Coy from base.
"	6			
"	7		} Ordinary trench routine. Nothing to report. Very quiet sector. [illegible]	
"	8		}	
"	9		}	
BUS-LES-ARTOIS	10		Two sections in trenches relieved by 116th MG Coy beginning at 9 AM & joined other two sections at BUS by 1 P.M. B.G.	

1875 Wt. W593/826 1,000,000 4/15 J.B.C. & A. A.D.S.S./Forms/C. 2118.

145th Brigade.

48th Division.

145th BRIGADE MACHINE GUN COMPANY

SEPTEMBER 1 9 1 6

Instructions regarding War Diaries and Intelligence Summaries are contained in F. S. Regs., Part II. and the Staff Manual respectively. Title Pages will be prepared in manuscript.

WAR DIARY
or
INTELLIGENCE SUMMARY
(Erase heading not required.)

Army Form C. 2118

145 MG Coy

Place	Date	Hour	Summary of Events and Information	Remarks and references to Appendices
LAKE VIEW	Aug 25		but [illegible] much shaken & bruised & a few cuts they were not seriously hurt. The guns at Point 11 report good work on communication trenches SE of THIEPVAL. Several Germans were hit.	No. 8944 Pte NEWHAM No 46220 Pte WARD No 46237 Pte BOOTH (returned to duty 24/8/16)
	26.		Prospect of relief brighter - men in need of it. With 10 guns in the line & a shortage of men, complete reliefs are not possible. Difficulty is always experienced in getting rations to Point 44, owing to guides losing their way. 2/LT CLUTTON reported finding 2 x 5.9 in guns near point 44. He proceeded with a party of 6 men to dig them out.	
	27		2/LIEUT. CLUTTON found on investigation that supposed gun was a MINENWERFER. A German helmet & plenty of ammunition for the mortar were also dug up. A claim for this mortar for a war trophy for the company was sent in to BDE. Covering fire on communication trenches was carried out by Coy for successful attack by the Division at 7 PM. B.G.	Struck off strength (29/8/16) LIEUT M.C.COOPER & 20893 S/c SANSOME to 25th MG Coy 2787 S/c LANE to Cadet School.
	28		Relieved by 74th MG Coy, relief commencing at 7 A.M. One of their guns opened fire on a German stretcher party almost as soon as they had taken over. This stretcher was heavily laden & was being carried towards the German front line. This Coy marched to billets at BOUZINCOURT B.G.	
BOUZINCOURT			LIEUT. M.C. COOPER left to become Second-in-command of 25th MG Coy	
BUS-LES-ARTOIS.	29.		Marched to huts at BUS-LES-ARTOIS. B.G.	
	30. 31 }		Resting in huts at BUS-LES-ARTOIS. B.G.	
	~~[illegible]~~ ~~[illegible]~~			

B. Green Lieut

Army Form C. 2118

Instructions regarding War Diaries and Intelligence Summaries are contained in F. S. Regs., Part II. and the Staff Manual respectively. Title Pages will be prepared in manuscript.

WAR DIARY
or
INTELLIGENCE SUMMARY
(Erase heading not required.)

145 M G Coy

Place	Date	Hour	Summary of Events and Information	Remarks and references to Appendices
BOUZINCOURT	Aug 19.		Heavy shelling on Ovillers. Relieved by 144 Machine Gun Coy & marched to billets at BOUZINCOURT	
	20.		In billets. Baths for the men.	
	21 } 22 }		Standing by in billets. A number of Prisoners taken by the 48th DIV passed through the village	
	23		Breakfast at 6.0 AM & Sect 2 moved off at 7.0 AM & the remaining 3 Sections at 8.0 AM to relieve the 144 Machine Gun Coy in the trenches N.W. of POZIERES. 2 Guns were placed at point 44 (X.2.b) 2 at 11 (X.2.c) 2 at X.8.a.4.6. 2 in old German Front line just South of LEIPZIG SALIENT & 2 in local reserve at X.8.c.2.6. Forward H.Q. at X.8.a.4.6. H.Q. at LAKE VIEW	Killed No 21110 L/Cpl COOPER F M.G.C. [illegible]
LAKE VIEW (W.17.d.7.0)			Wire received from C in C to the effect that No 21731 Cpl PARROTT J had been awarded the D.C.M for his gallant conduct on the night of Aug 14th. Army, Corps, & Divisional congratulations enclosed.	Wounded No 3158 Pte LEWIS. E.L. 1/5 Glos
	24.		Very heavy shelling. Attack made by 25 DIV on our left on a line of trench N. of LEIPZIG SALIENT which was successful. All machine guns gave covering fire & on communication trenches. Position of guns slightly altered. 4 guns at X.2.c.1.1 & 1 at HOY TRENCH. 2 in local reserve at 05. 1 at Point 22. & 2 at X.2.b.4.4. A Sap behind HOY TRENCH was dug during the night for machine gun position & also a sap from 22.	No 2766 Pte MILNE 1/5 Glos No 11555 Pte BRERETON. 1/5 Glos CAPT LONG E 1/4 Ox & Bucks att- 145 M.G.C. Wounded (Slightly at duty)
	25.		Officers Mess blown in by a 5.9 shell, Capt LONG & CAPT GUTERBOCK were inside	

A B Green Lieut

1875 Wt. W593/826 1,000,000 4/15 J.B.C. & A. A.D.S.S./Forms/C. 2118.

Army Form C. 2118

Instructions regarding War Diaries and Intelligence Summaries are contained in F. S. Regs., Part II. and the Staff Manual respectively. Title Pages will be prepared in manuscript.

WAR DIARY
or
INTELLIGENCE SUMMARY
(Erase heading not required.)

145 MG Coy

Place	Date	Hour	Summary of Events and Information	Remarks and references to Appendices
USNA REDOUBT	Aug 16		The guns in the front situated about 5th Avenue increased to five, & all were shelled continually. Several attempts were made to get a gun to Point 81 but unsuccessful. If it had been successful, the gun would have knocked out in a very short time, as there was practically no trench available. An attack by the Bucks & Glosters in cooperation with the 144 Bde was not successful. There were a great number of casualties in 6th Avenue & communication trench leading to it.	WOUNDED No 1923 Pte COX H E; No 20885 Pte MILLARD W. J.; No 15835 Pte WAINWRIGHT T.
	17		A gun was put at the N E end of 5th Avenue. Was not possible to proceed further, but it was most useful there, as it covered the front of 6th Avenue. Men getting very tired & reliefs are made most difficult owing to the shortage of men.	MISSING No 5084 Pte [illegible]
			2nd Lt Green, & 2nd Lt Clutton joined the Unit for duty from the 144 M.G. Coy 143	
	18		2nd Lt Sangster	
			The 143 Bde attacked the German position at 78.62 & 44. & the R Berks cooperated with them in bombing from Point 89. They went over at 5 PM under cover of a smoke cloud from the trench opp. [illegible]. All objectives were taken, with comparatively slight casualties & they took 400 Prisoners.	

[illegible signature]

1875 Wt. W593/826 1,000,000 4/15 J.B.C. & A. A.D.S.S./Forms/C. 2118.

Instructions regarding War Diaries and Intelligence Summaries are contained in F. S. Regs., Part II. and the Staff Manual respectively. Title Pages will be prepared in manuscript.

WAR DIARY
or
INTELLIGENCE SUMMARY
(Erase heading not required.)

Army Form C. 2118

145 M G Coy

Place	Date	Hour	Summary of Events and Information	Remarks and references to Appendices
USNA REDOUBT	Aug 14		The enemy attacked their old front line & succeeded in reoccupying it. The right gun at ~~point~~ 81 was well handled by Cpl Parrott & his team & did a great deal of damage. Two of his men were knocked out, one being killed & one wounded. The No 1 of the team continued firing the gun, while Cpl Parrott picked off those not stopped by machine gun, with his rifle. They were forced back, but brought their gun with them. Cpl Clapman's team on his left was also forced back before bringing their gun into action. Two of the wounded men brought the gun back. All teams that had been in front & second lines were relieved. Very heavy shelling all day, chiefly on the Western portion of the front	Aug 14. Killed No 1413 Pte HARRIS E. No 31745 Pte PENNINGTON A. WOUNDED No 1679 Pte THATCHER W. No 2319 Pte KING A.J. No 8944 Pte NEWHAM H.B. No 21727 Pte FOULKES C.T. No 7651 Pte LEWIS W. No 20555 Pte MILLARD W.J (at duty)
	15		During the night of 14/15, the 6th Avenue was retaken by the Bucks & Glosters by bombing up the trench. The Australians on our right & the 144 Bde on our left did not succeed in reaching their objective. Two teams who had been in position on the left of 5th Avenue could not be found for 24 hours, as geography of trench had so much altered. An extra gun was sent up to the front line during the early evening to reinforce the right. Three guns were pushed forward on the right in order to cover the front of 6th Avenue with enfilade fire, should the enemy counter attack.	No 3480 Pte TUBB T.C 1st Bucks (returned to duty)

B Green Lieut

WAR DIARY
or
INTELLIGENCE SUMMARY
(Erase heading not required.)

Army Form C. 2118

Instructions regarding War Diaries and Intelligence Summaries are contained in F. S. Regs., Part II. and the Staff Manual respectively. Title Pages will be prepared in manuscript.

145 MG Coy.

Place	Date	Hour	Summary of Events and Information	Remarks and references to Appendices
CRAMONT. (LE MÉNAGE).	Aug 1st – 8th		Routine work, including early morning run, & physical drill. Eight men sent on to ABBEVILLE each day, starting at 7.0 AM & returning to Billets by 9.0 PM. All men [illegible] in orchard & [illegible] the whole time.	
BEAUVAL	9		The Brigade moved to BEAUVAL, starting at 5.15 AM, – weight & many men in the Bde fell out. The Machine Gun Coy arrived in Billets at 2.15 PM, 3 fell out; There was a cinematograph show in the square at 9.30 PM	
VARENNES	10		Bde moved to VARENNES via the lower road to BEAUQUESNE, & [redacted] RAINCHEVAL	
BOUZINCOURT.	11		Bde marched from VARENNES to BOUZINCOURT occupying billets, but in the case of the Machine Gun Coy moved to Bivouacs on the BOUZINCOURT – MILLENCOURT Road in consequence of enemy shelling.	
	12.		Remained in bivouacs;	
USNA REDOUBT.	13		First Section (6 guns) paraded at 2.0 AM & reported at 123.2 at 5.0 AM. Second Section (6 guns) reported at same place at 6.0 AM & Reserve guns were kept at Labourers W.17 d.7.d (approx) A new trench had been taken during the night by the 12th Div & 3 guns were sent up to garrison this, Two only were able to reach this, the third remaining in the 2nd line with 3 other guns. Five guns were placed in position neighbouring on 123.2 for indirect fire & 1 gun kept in local reserve at 123.2. No casualties	13 Green [illegible]

1875 Wt. W593/826 1,000,000 4/15 J.B.C. & A. A.D.S.S./Forms/C. 2118.

145th Brigade.

48th Division.

<u>145th BRIGADE MACHINE GUN COMPANY</u>

<u>AUGUST 1 9 1 6</u> ::P

48th Division.
G.x.1363.

145th Inf. Bde.

The Major General recognises how very gallant and determined the attacks were which the Bns made in the last few days and how very nearly they succeeded completely.

Those who took part in them may well be proud of their effort to break the German line here.

Those in the Brigades who were not engaged may well be equally proud of their comrades and the Brigade and Battalion commanders and staffs of having trained and directed such efforts.

Great successes have indeed already been gained by us. We must make one more effort and take advantage of all we have learnt about the position and show the Germans that in spite of all the difficulties and dangers we are going to beat them.

A victory gained after great efforts will be more really decisive as showing we are better fighting men than if we had gained it at our first attempt.

The decisive fights which lead to final victory are not those easily gained but those which like the first battle of YPRES are gained by the determination to win no matter what the odds in number and difficulties against us.

Here we are up against a strong position, the best German troops, machine guns and artillery fire.

Let our determination to win carry us through.

21-7-16. (Sd) R.FANSHAWE. M.G.

O.C.
All Units.
Please communicate the above remarks to all ranks.

Captain.B.M.
145th Infantry Brigade.

22-7-16.

48th Division. G.x.1363.
145th Inf. Bde. No. A.17.

O.C.

Battalions.
Bde. M.G.Coy.
<u>145th T.M.Battery.</u>

The Army Commander desires that the following message which has been received shall be communicated to the troops.

"The Commander-in-Chief warmly congratulates the troops of the Reserve Army on the complete success of their operations in and round OVILLERS.

The conditions were most difficult and the operations constituted a very high test of the endurance of the troops - a test to which they have proved themselves fully equal.

The steady, patient, untiring pressure maintained on the enemy was exactly what the situation required. The results gained are very satisfactory and have taken us another step forward on the way to final victory ".

Captain,
Brigade Major,
145th Infantry Brigade.

21.7.16.

MESSAGE.

From

Lieut.-General SIR AYLMER HUNTER-WESTON, K.C.B., D.S.O.

To

All OFFICERS, N.C.O.'s and MEN of the VIII. Army Corps

In so big a command as an Army Corps of four Divisions (about eighty thousand men) it is impossible for me to come round all front line trenches and all billets to see every man as I wish to do. You must take the will for the deed, and accept this printed message in place of the spoken word.

It is difficult for me to express my admiration for the splendid courage, determination and discipline displayed by every Officer, N.C.O. and Man of the Battalions that took part in the great attack on the BEAUMONT-HAMEL-SERRE position on the 1st July. All observers agree in stating that the various waves of men issued from their trenches and moved forward at the appointed time in perfect order, undismayed by the heavy artillery fire and deadly machine gun fire. There were no cowards nor waverers, and not a man fell out. It was a magnificent display of disciplined courage worthy of the best traditions of the British race.

Very few are left of my old comrades, the original "Contemptibles," but their successors in the 4th Division have shewn that they are worthy to bear the honours gained by the 4th Division at their first great fight at Fontaine-au-Pire and Ligny, during the great Retreat and greater Advance across the Marne and Aisne, and in all the hard fighting at Ploegsteert and at Ypres.

Though but few of my old comrades, the heroes of the historic landing at Cape Helles, are still with us, the 29th Division of to-day has shown itself capable of maintaining its high traditions, and has proved itself worthy of its hard earned title of "The Incomparable 29th."

The 31st New Army Division, and the 48th Territorial Division, by the heroism and discipline of the units engaged in this their first big battle, have proved themselves worthy to fight by the side of such magnificent regular Divisions as the 4th and 29th. There can be no higher praise.

We had the most difficult part of the line to attack. The Germans had fortified it with skill and immense labour for many months, they had kept their best troops here, and had assembled North, East, and South-East of it a formidable collection of artillery and many machine guns.

By your splendid attack you held these enemy forces here in the North and so enabled our friends in the South, both British and French, to achieve the brilliant success that they have. Therefore, though we did not do all we hoped to do you have more than pulled your weight, and you and our even more glorious comrades who have preceded us across the Great Divide have nobly done your Duty.

We have got to stick it out and go on hammering. Next time we attack, if it please God, we will not only pull our weight but will pull off a big thing. With such troops as you, who are determined to stick it out and do your duty, we are certain of winning through to a glorious victory.

I salute each Officer, N.C.O. and Man of the 4th, 29th, 31st, and 48th Divisions as a comrade-in-arms and I rejoice to have the privilege of commanding such a band of heroes as the VIII. Corps have proved themselves to be.

H.Q., VIII. CORPS,
4th July, 1916.

AYLMER HUNTER-WESTON,
Lieut.-General.

ARMY PRINTING AND STATIONERY SERVICES A. 7/16 80,000.

SPECIAL ORDER OF THE DAY

BY

GENERAL SIR DOUGLAS HAIG,

G.C.B., K.C.I.E., K.C.V.O., A.D.C.

Commander-in-Chief, British Armies in France.

The following telegrams, sent on the occasion of the celebration of the French National Fête on July 14th, are published for the information of all ranks:—

I. MONSIEUR POINCARÉ, PRESIDENT OF THE FRENCH REPUBLIC.

14th July.

The British Army, fighting by the side of the brave soldiers of France in the bitter struggle now proceeding, expresses on the occasion of this great anniversary its admiration for the results achieved by the French Army and its unshakeable confidence in the speedy realization of our common hopes.

SIR DOUGLAS HAIG.

II. GENERAL SIR D. HAIG, COMMANDER-IN-CHIEF, BRITISH ARMIES IN FRANCE.

14th July.

I thank you, my dear General, for the good wishes which you have expressed towards France, and beg you to convey to the brave British Army my lively admiration of the fine successes which it has just achieved and which only this morning have been so brilliantly extended. They have produced a deep impression on the hearts of all Frenchmen. Those of your magnificent troops who have to-day paraded in the streets of Paris, in company with those of our Allies, received throughout their march a striking proof of the public sentiment. I am glad to have this opportunity of sending you—to you personally and to your troops—my warm congratulations.

POINCARÉ.

D. Haig. Genl.

Commanding-in-Chief,
British Armies in France

General Headquarters,
18th July, 1916.

ARMY PRINTING AND STATIONERY SERVICES—7/16

V. GENERAL SIR D. HAIG, COMMANDER-IN-CHIEF, BRITISH ARMIES IN FRANCE.

(*Translation.*)

14th July.

The unbroken success of the offensive of the British Armies under your command confirms our unshakeable faith in the power and genius of the British people.

All honour to England in her greatness, to her King, her Armies and her Fleet! They have won immortality in a heroic contest.

PRESIDENT OF THE ASSEMBLY OF ZEMSTVOS
OF THE GOVERNMENT OF SAMARA.

VI. PRESIDENT OF THE ASSEMBLY OF ZEMSTVOS, SAMARA, RUSSIA.

14th July.

I beg you to convey to the Zemstvos of Samara on behalf of the British Army under my command our warm appreciation of your inspiriting message. On our side we have watched with admiration the great feats of the Russian Armies and Navy and the heroic determination of the Russian Emperor and his people. United in a great cause we shall march together with unshakeable confidence to the final triumph.

SIR DOUGLAS HAIG.

D. Haig. Genl.

General Headquarters,
17th July, 1916.

Commanding-in-Chief,
British Armies in France.

ARMY PRINTING AND STATIONERY SERVICES A—7/16

SPECIAL ORDER OF THE DAY

BY

GENERAL SIR DOUGLAS HAIG,

G.C.B., K.C.I.E., K.C.V.O., A.D.C.

Commander-in-Chief, British Armies in France.

The following telegrams are published for the information of all ranks :—

I. GENERAL SIR DOUGLAS HAIG, COMMANDER-IN-CHIEF, BRITISH ARMIES IN FRANCE.

16th July.

The continued successful advance of my troops fills me with admiration, and I send my best wishes to all ranks. The Emperor of Russia has asked me to convey his warm congratulations to the troops upon the great success they have achieved.

GEORGE, R.I.

II. HIS MAJESTY THE KING,
BUCKINGHAM PALACE, LONDON.

17th July.

The British Armies in France offer most respectful and grateful thanks for this further mark of your Majesty's gracious appreciation of what they have achieved.

They also respectfully beg that their grateful acknowledgment may be conveyed to the Emperor of Russia for His Majesty's congratulations.

SIR DOUGLAS HAIG.

III. GENERAL SIR D. HAIG, COMMANDER-IN-CHIEF, BRITISH ARMIES IN FRANCE.

14th July, 1916.

I have heard with great joy of the new successes just won by the British Army. The French Armies applaud the progress which is effected every day by our gallant comrades. I am glad to voice their feelings in offering to the Commanders and soldiers of your armies, and in particular to you, my dear General, my very cordial felicitations.

GENERAL JOFFRE.

IV. GENERAL JOFFRE, COMMANDER-IN-CHIEF OF THE FRENCH ARMIES.

15th July.

Sincere thanks from myself and all ranks under my command for your very kind telegram.

We cordially appreciate the felicitations of our brave Allies whose steadfast courage and endurance in the long struggle at Verdun gave us time to prepare for the combined offensive which has begun so well on both sides of the Somme. Your splendid artillery continues to give us valuable assistance.

GENERAL HAIG.

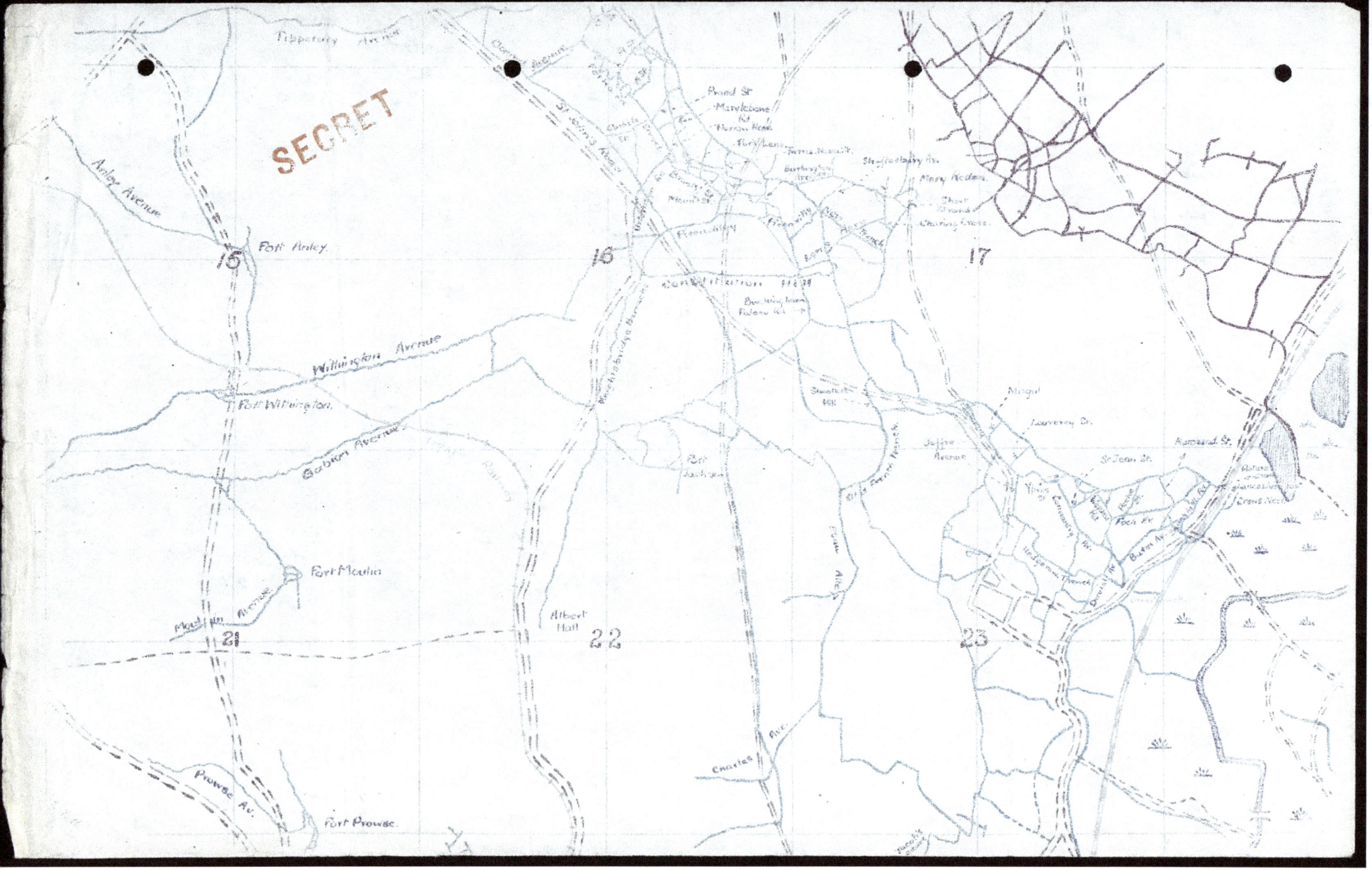
SECRET
Tipperary Avenue
Anley Avenue
Fort Anley
15
16
17
21
22
23
Prince St
Marylebone Rd
Harrow Road
Park Lane
Stafford Av.
Mary Redan
Charing Cross
Piccadilly
Willington Avenue
Fort Willington
Gabion Avenue
Fort Moulin
Moulin Avenue
Albert Hall
Laurency St.
St Jean St.
Butler Av.
Foch Av.
Charles Ave.
Prowse Av.
Fort Prowse

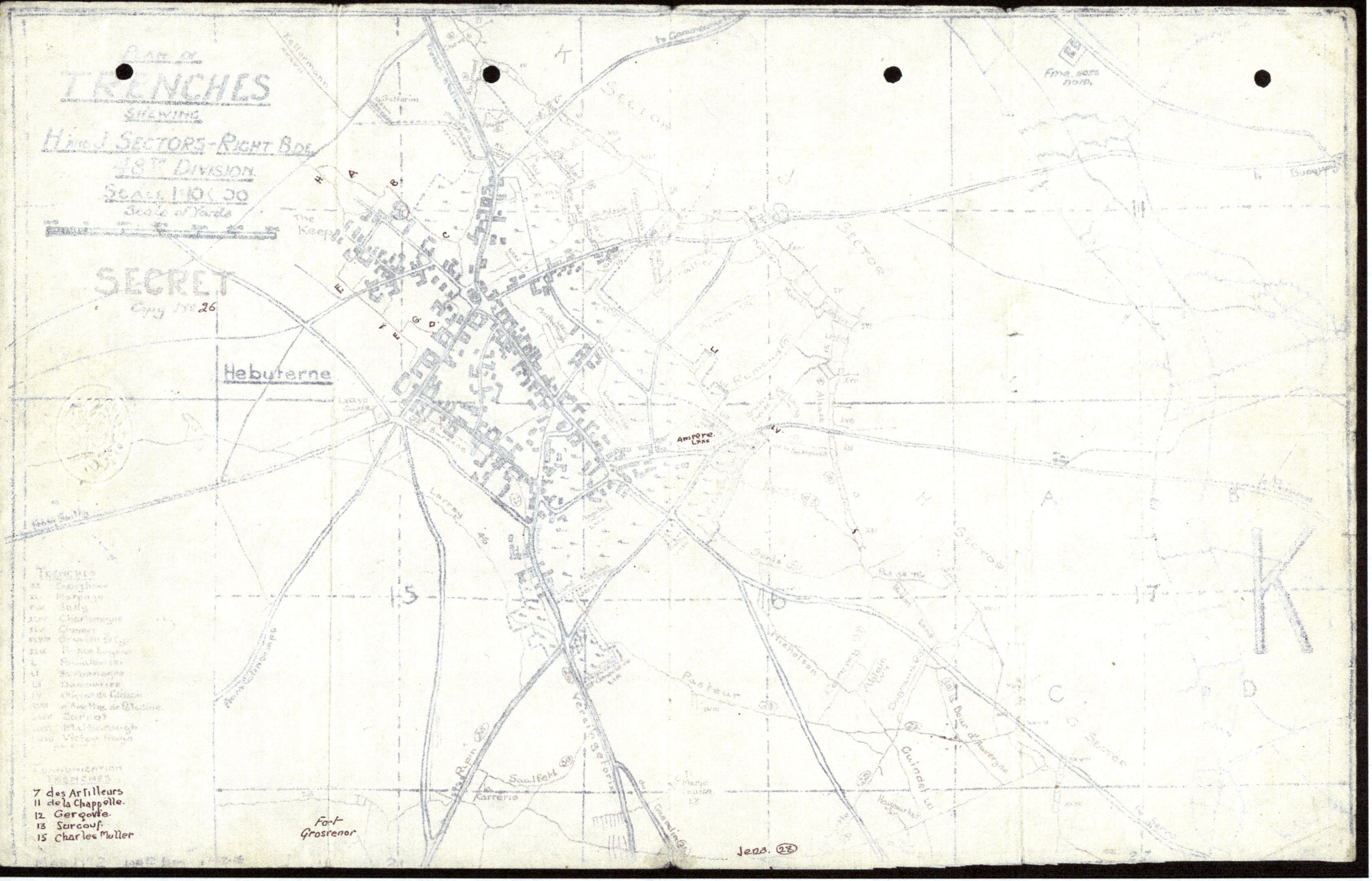

Plan of
TRENCHES
SHEWING
H and J SECTORS - RIGHT BDE
48TH DIVISION
SCALE 1/10,000
Scale of Yards
SECRET
Copy No 26
Hebuterne
The Keep
Ampere LXXX
K Sector
J Sector
H Sector
G Sector
Fme. sans nom
Fort Grosvenor
Jena 28
Pasteur
Saalfeld
Carreria
TRENCHES
COMMUNICATION TRENCHES
7 des Artilleurs
11 de la Chappelle.
12 Gergovie.
13 Surcouf.
15 Charles Muller

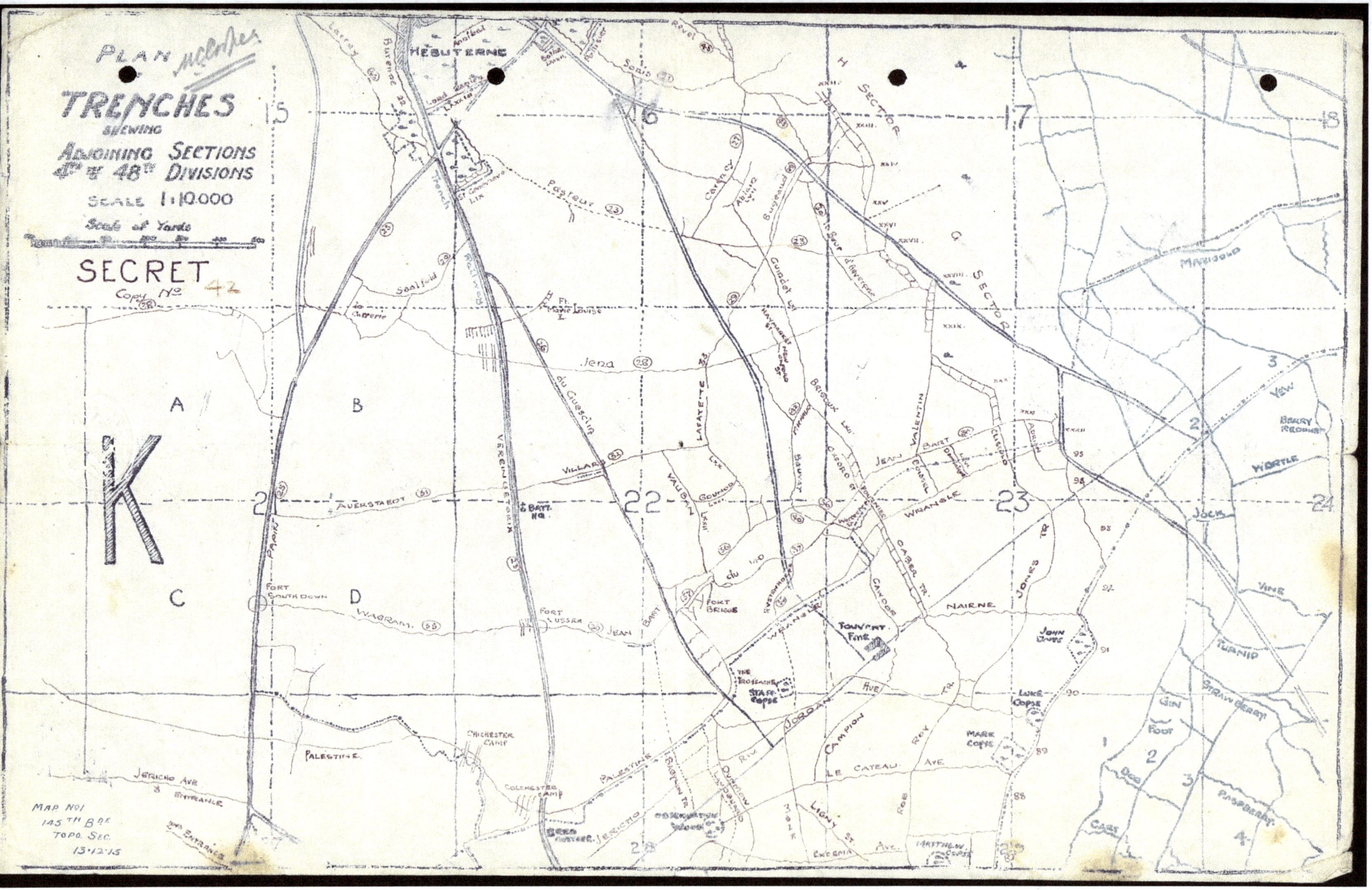
PLAN
TRENCHES
SHEWING
ADJOINING SECTIONS
4TH & 48TH DIVISIONS
SCALE 1:10,000
Scale of Yards
SECRET
Copy No 42
MAP No 1
145TH BDE
TOPO. SEC.
13.12.15
HEBUTERNE
K
A
B
C
D
15
16
17
18
22
23
24
28
H SECTOR
G SECTOR
Pasteur
Jena
Lafayette
Villars
Auerstaedt
Papin
Wagram
Vercingetorix
du Guesclin
Vauban
Gounod
Saalfeld
Caverly
Bugeaud
Guindet
Brisoux
Sauvat
Cafford
Valentin
Jean Bart
Wrangle
Cabber Tr.
Cancor
Nairne
Jones Tr.
Adrian
Clisbird
Jordan
Campion
Le Cateau Ave
Rob Roy Ave
Fort Southdown
Fort Briggs
Fort Lussier
Touvent Fme
The Rossignol
Star Copse
John Copse
Luke Copse
Mark Copse
Palestine
Jericho Ave
Chichester Camp
Colchester Camp
Ligny St.
Eczema Ave
Marigold
Yew
Berry Redoubt
Wortle
Jock
Vine
Turnip
Strawberry
Gin
Foot
Cars
Raspberry
Revel
Lavrey
Hebuterne

A P P E N D I C E S .

145 M. G. Coy

Instructions regarding War Diaries and Intelligence Summaries are contained in F. S. Regs., Part II. and the Staff Manual respectively. Title Pages will be prepared in manuscript.

WAR DIARY
or
INTELLIGENCE SUMMARY
(Erase heading not required.)

Army Form C. 2118

Place	Date	Hour	Summary of Events and Information	Remarks and references to Appendices
CRAMONT	JULY	29.	One of the most trying marches the men have had since they came to France. Breakfast was at 6.0 AM & the next meal was at 4. PM. Owing to the Company not having a cooker, it is impossible to give the men anything on the way, & it takes an hour to get tea after arrival. The Billets very good especially for the men.	
		30	Resting.	
		31.	"	

Capt.
O.C. 145 M. G. Coy
31.7.16.

1875 Wt. W593/826 1,000,000 4/15 J.R.C. & A. A.D.S.S./Forms/C. 2118.

145 M G Coy

Army Form C. 2118

Instructions regarding War Diaries and Intelligence Summaries are contained in F. S. Regs., Part II. and the Staff Manual respectively. Title Pages will be prepared in manuscript.

WAR DIARY
or
INTELLIGENCE SUMMARY
(Erase heading not required.)

Place	Date	Hour	Summary of Events and Information	Remarks and references to Appendices
USNA REDOUBT	Aug 24		machine guns in that Sector were relieved. The whole of the day there was continual heavy shelling on the front & support lines, & our teams were fortunate in leaving without serious casualty. Two teams of the 143rd Bde were knocked out & 1 officer killed on their way up to relieve us. The situation in the forward trenches was almost chaotic. The garrison & the relieving troops, intermingled with R.A.M.C. & Stretcher Bearers, fatigue parties & carrying parties in addition the trench being very narrow, none could move one way or the other.	
			On our new sector N & NE of OVILLERS, 4 guns were placed in position for overhead fire & 2 kept in local reserve at Batt H.Q.	Casualties wounded Pte DREDGE Shell, Pte PAGE Shell, Cpl CHAPMAN Shell, Sgt ROSSER Shell, Pte WILTON Shell-shock
		25	Company relieved by 144th Bde M.G. Coy & bivouaced at USNA REDOUBT	
BOUZINCOURT		26.	Moved from Bivouacs at USNA REDOUBT to Bivouacs near BOUZINCOURT at 6.0AM. Orders received to proceed to ~~[illegible]~~ LEALVILLERS. Arrived 4.15 PM.	
LEALVILLERS		27	All in Billets at LEALVILLERS	
BEAUVAL		28	Marched from LEALVILLERS to BEAUVAL as a Brigade, leaving at 7.15 & arriving at 11.0 AM.	
CRAMONT		29	Marched from BEAUVAL to LEMÉNAGE N of CRAMONT a distance of 16 miles. Moved at 7.45 from Billets & arrived 3.0PM. This was	

145 M.G. Coy

Instructions regarding War Diaries and Intelligence Summaries are contained in F. S. Regs., Part II. and the Staff Manual respectively. Title Pages will be prepared in manuscript.

WAR DIARY
or
INTELLIGENCE SUMMARY
(Erase heading not required.)

Army Form C. 2118

Place	Date	Hour	Summary of Events and Information	Remarks and references to Appendices
USNA REDOUBT	July 22		perform – Bring direct fire from right flank on possible counter attack; to bring indirect fire on points behind the enemy lines; to reinforce front line if attack successful. 3 guns under Lt OLDACRE were detailed to cover the right flank East of POZIERES, 6 guns to bring indirect fire on area N of POZIERES, 5 more guns to barrage trenches & points in rear of line to be assaulted, all these under Lt GREEN and 2 guns were kept in reserve at USNA REDOUBT to go forward under CAPT LONG if required. Wind NE by N. Weather fine. Special order of the day, copies attached, were circulated.	M.
	23		The attack started at 12.30 AM. On the right the OXFORDS obtained a footing in the trench after vigorous fighting & maintained it. On the left the 1/5 Glosters were held up for some time, but with the help of 2 companies of the BUCKS, they eventually gained the points required. The 2 guns in reserve were despatched at 8.30 AM under CAPT LONG to resist counter-attack if any. Several Prisoners were taken by the Bde, only a few being wounded. The Australian Division on our right gained more ground. The bombardment by the Germans on the points captured & on the SICKLE trench was very intense, causing a number of casualties.	
	24.		The right portion of the Sunrise line was taken over by the 143rd Bde, & the	

1875 Wt. W593/826 1,000,000 4/15 J.R.C. & A. A.D.S.S./Forms/C. 2118.

145 M. G. Coy

Instructions regarding War Diaries and Intelligence Summaries are contained in F. S. Regs., Part II. and the Staff Manual respectively. Title Pages will be prepared in manuscript.

WAR DIARY
or
INTELLIGENCE SUMMARY
(Erase heading not required.)

Army Form C. 2118

Place	Date	Hour	Summary of Events and Information	Remarks and references to Appendices
USNA REDOUBT	July 20		the German line of trench from X 2 b 2 0 to X 3 d 2 9. The Glosters on left & Berks on right of 145 Bde. These were the extreme limits of attack, the dividing line between the two Bdes being point 40. Three guns of Section 3 under Lt KAVENHOVEN were detailed to bring direct fire on right flank of attack from about X.9 b.8.6. & 3 guns under Lt GREEN & Lt OLDACRE to bring indirect fire on cemetery N of POZIERES, Point 7886 X.3.B.7.9. & to Chateau. These were placed, one at 82. (X.9.c.8.2), 2 at X.14.b.7.5 & 2 at X.9.c.4.6. Range not to be below 2000 yds. Eight guns were left in reserve at USNA REDOUBT. Fine day with wind N.E. Intermittent shelling throughout the day with several bursts of intense fire by the enemy on selected points. BOISSELLE Road received a great deal of this. 2nd Lt R MADDER killed instantaneously by shell at point 82, just as relieved	2nd Lt MADDER killed
	21		At 2.15 AM intense bombardment of enemy's line to be assaulted was commenced. At 2.45 AM assault began. 1/5 Glosters & 1st Bucks went forward, but were stopped by severe machine gun fire & shell barrage. Many casualties among officers & men. Wind blowing NE by E.	No 2805 Pte BENNETT 1/4 R. [illegible] (wounded)
	22.		Assault by 1/5 Glosters on point 79 after previous bombardment of same by trench mortars. This was driven back by machine gun fire. Orders were received about 3.30 PM for the 145 Bde M G Coy to attack. The Machine gun had three duties to	Lt KAVENHOVEN to Hospital with delirium

M. [illegible]

1875 Wt. W593/826 1,000,000 4/15 J.B.C. & A. A.D.S.S./Forms/C. 2118.

145 M.G. Coy

Instructions regarding War Diaries and Intelligence Summaries are contained in F. S. Regs., Part II. and the Staff Manual respectively. Title Pages will be prepared in manuscript.

WAR DIARY
or
INTELLIGENCE SUMMARY
(Erase heading not required.)

Army Form C. 2118

Place	Date	Hour	Summary of Events and Information	Remarks and references to Appendices
SENLIS	July 14		One & a half sections were brought by Motor Lorry to SENLIS. A few batches of prisoners were seen on the way.	
	July 16		Visited the old German trenches at BOISELLE. 48th DIV relieved by 38th DIV in trenches at HEBUTERNE	
	17		Remainder of company joined up at SENLIS. Heavy bombardment during the night. The Bucks Battalion went up to the front line on reconnaissance work. Weather still bad.	
BOUZINCOURT	18		Company moved to BOUZINCOURT, parading at 6.45 AM. Heavy bombardment continuing all day	
	19.		Orders received to take over line of trenches from 143 Bde. Paraded 2.0PM & marched through ALBERT to Bivouacs on right of ALBERT-BOISSELLE Road. Sections 1 & 4 relieved the machine gun Coy of the 143, 3 guns being sent to forward position S.W. by W. of POZIERES & 3 in 2nd line S.E. of OVILLERS, 2 being left at Forward HQ point 123.2. ~~[illegible]~~ 8 guns left in reserve at Bivouacs. Very heavy shelling during the night on ALBERT-BOISSELLE Road near Bivouacs. All men put into trench close by.	
	20.		All men in Bivouacs moved to USNA REDOUBT. Relief of Section in trenches by Sections 2 & 3. Orders received to the effect that the 144th & 148th Bde would	

1875 Wt. W593/826 1,000,000 4/15 J.B.C. & A. A.D.S.S./Forms/C. 2118.

145 M. G. Coy

Instructions regarding War Diaries and Intelligence Summaries are contained in F. S. Regs., Part II. and the Staff Manual respectively. Title Pages will be prepared in manuscript.

WAR DIARY
or
INTELLIGENCE SUMMARY
(Erase heading not required.)

Army Form C. 2118

Place	Date	Hour	Summary of Events and Information	Remarks and references to Appendices
SAILLY	July 13.		Intense Bombardment of THE POINT & along the front, including that of the 4th & 29th Divisions, during the night of 13-14. Machine guns fired bursts of 50 at frequent intervals throughout the night & following day. T. Mortars also fired & smoke clouds were sent over soon after dawn of 14th. The Germans sent up flares repeatedly throughout the night all along the front. Good news from the South, it is reported that BAZENTIN LE-PETIT & BAZENTIN LE GRAND have been taken. Heavy signs of an early move on our part. The WARWICKS left COUIN [illegible] by motor lorries.	M.
	14.		Machine gun programme carried out. Bursts of 25 rounds every 5 hours. Raid by 1/5 Glosters on German line N of Point at about K17 b.11. During raid, feint barrage on Points, but main barrage at point of entry. This lifted & Glosters went on to attack but the enemy stood on own parapet & repulsed the attack. Glosters retired & rang up the Artillery to put barrage on front line again. This was done & after barrage lifting again, Glosters again went forward, but met with strong opposition. Retired for the night.	
	15.		Anniversary of [illegible] of taking over HEBUTERNE & General Gethin 48th Div from the French. This was [illegible] commemorated in the renowned Dreamy Slater.	

No 145. Machine Gun Coy

Instructions regarding War Diaries and Intelligence Summaries are contained in F. S. Regs., Part II. and the Staff Manual respectively. Title Pages will be prepared in manuscript.

WAR DIARY
or
INTELLIGENCE SUMMARY
(Erase heading not required.)

Army Form C. 2118

Place	Date	Hour	Summary of Events and Information	Remarks and references to Appendices
SAILLY	JULY 5		withdrawn from HEBUTERNE to SAILLY, only 4 being left with each gun.	
BIVOUACS in the DELL	6		H.Q. withdrawn from SAILLY to the DELL & teams in reserve, all in Bivouacs.	
	7.		Very heavy shelling a little to the South of COLINCAMPS from 7.0 AM to 9.0 AM	[illegible]
	8		Relief of Sections in HEBUTERNE. Reports again that the shelling in HEBUTERNE has again become normal the last two days. Very heavy rain. A German aeroplane flew over BAYENCOURT at a great height, but was driven back by our anti-aircraft guns. The following morning shells fell near the [illegible] of the 5th SUSSEX. These were evidently spotted by the aeroplane.	
	9.		Work on mined dug-out at VERCINGETORIX, consisting of ~~and~~ making another dug-out running out of passage way completed. This was designed & completed by our own men under Sgt COLLIER. The entrance to dug-out behind Billet No 16 was blown in by a 5.9 - No casualties. The team manning BOTHA position are accommodated in a cellar under Billet 7.	
	10		Weather improving; Little rain with high wind from West. The Bantam Battalion bivouaced near us early this morning, & moved off again at 2.45 PM. in a Southerly direction	
	11 } 12 }		Nothing to report. Very quiet on front	

1875 Wt. W593/826 1,000,000 4/15 J.B.C. & A. A.D.S.S./Forms/C. 2118.

Instructions regarding War Diaries and Intelligence Summaries are contained in F. S. Regs., Part II. and the Staff Manual respectively. Title Pages will be prepared in manuscript.

WAR DIARY
or
~~INTELLIGENCE SUMMARY~~
(Erase heading not required.)

Army Form C. 2118

Place	Date	Hour	Summary of Events and Information	Remarks and references to Appendices
MAILLY MAILLET	July 2nd		attack the Germans 1st, 2nd & 3rd lines the following morning at 3.20AM after a very heavy bombardment by guns of all calibres. The 4 R Berks were to attack on the right & ~~left~~ the 5th Glos on the left on a front from Point 83 to the R ANCRE. The 4th OXF in Bde Reserve on road (sunken) in Q.22 a & Q.22.c, & the 1st Bucks in Divisional Reserve. The latter remained in bivouacs at MAILLY MAILLET. All Transport was left at MARTINSART. At 11.0PM orders cancelling operation was received & the Bde arrived at MAILLY MAILLET at 3.30AM. Orders	
	July 3rd		were received to return to COUIN starting at 6.20PM. Bivouaced at COUIN on COUIN-St LEGER road at 11.35PM	
COUIN	July 4th		Intelligence reports that attack by Germans on front about HEBUTERNE is to be expected. Ready to move at once. Very heavy rain. Ordered to take over trenches at HEBUTERNE & relieve the 143rd Bde M.G. Coy. Moved in one hour. Ten guns were sent up to the trenches, & 6 left in reserve at SAILLY. HEBUTERNE is shelled continuously & all men sleep in cellars or in the trenches.	
	" 5th		SAILLY intermittently shelled throughout the day & night. All surplus teamsmen	

Instructions regarding War Diaries and Intelligence Summaries are contained in F. S. Regs., Part II. and the Staff Manual respectively. Title pages will be prepared in manuscript.

WAR DIARY
or
INTELLIGENCE SUMMARY.
(*Erase heading not required.*)

Army Form C. 2118.

Place	Date	Hour	Summary of Events and Information	Remarks and references to Appendices
MAILLY MAILLET	July 1st		Marched as a Brigade to Bivouacs behind MAILLY MAILLET. There was considerable shelling along the whole front of the 8th Corps & many ambulances were met returning with wounded who had taken part in the attack on our front which started at 7.30 AM. Arrived at Bivouacs at 2.30 PM & had dinner, the orders being to be ready to move at a moments notice.	
	2nd		Received orders to march to MESNIL at 7. PM & the Brigade would	

145th Inf.Bde.
48th Div.

WAR
DIARY

145th MACHINE GUN COMPANY.

J U L Y

1 9 1 6

Attached:

Appendices.

Instructions regarding War Diaries and Intelligence Summaries are contained in F. S. Regs., Part II. and the Staff Manual respectively. Title Pages will be prepared in manuscript.

WAR DIARY

or

~~INTELLIGENCE SUMMARY~~

(~~Erase heading not~~ required.)

Army Form C. 2118

Place	Date	Hour	Summary of Events and Information	Remarks and references to Appendices
Hebuterne	June	15	Quiet day & night.	
	—	16.	Inter-company relief. Quiet day but hostile machine guns very active during the night.	
	—	17.	Our artillery active, little hostile reply. Large quantity (?) English aeroplanes crossed german lines.	
	—	18.	Our artillery again active, also enemy.	
	—	19-21.	Nothing to report	
COUIN	22.		Moved to COUIN in same huts as previously occupied.	
—	23 - July 1st.		Training	

Instructions regarding War Diaries and Intelligence Summaries are contained in F. S. Regs., Part II. and the Staff Manual respectively. Title Pages will be prepared in manuscript.

WAR DIARY
or
~~INTELLIGENCE SUMMARY~~
(Erase heading not required.)

Army Form C. 2118

145th MGC

Place	Date	Hour	Summary of Events and Information	Remarks and references to Appendices
COULONVILLERS	June 1.		Paraded at 5.45 AM & marched to St RIQUIER training ground. One Section was attached to the Bucks Battalion who were attacking ARGONVILLERS. Remaining Sections paraded with limber & had long morning at extended order drill. Returned to billets at 1 PM.	
	– 2nd to 4th		Training on St RIQUIER AREA.	
	– 4th		Moved to a farm N.W. of GAPENNES, a march of 5 miles, – very poor reception by the two families living there. Accomodation for the men poor & in consequence a large number of men bivouaced out.	
	– 5		On Training ground from 6-30 to 12.30 AM.	
	– 6th to 10th		Training on St RIQUIER area.	
	– 10th.		Paraded at 4.30 a.m & marched to Mézerolles, where we spent the night. Billets fairly good.	
	11th.		Paraded at 5.30 a.m & marched to Couin, where we spent night in huts.	
	12th		Marched to trenches & relieved 143rd Brigade M.G.C. Very bad weather & artillery quiet. Enemy machine guns active in the evening	
	13th.		Quiet day, but enemy's heavy mortars very active from direction of 16 poplars about 11 p.m	
	14th.		Quiet day.	

145th Brigade.

48th Division.

145th BRIGADE MACHINE GUN COMPANY

JUNE 1916

145 Bde M G Coy

Vol 5

Army Form C. 2118

WAR DIARY
or
~~INTELLIGENCE~~ SUMMARY

(Erase heading not required.)

Instructions regarding War Diaries and Intelligence Summaries are contained in F. S. Regs., Part II. and the Staff Manual respectively. Title Pages will be prepared in manuscript.

Place	Date	Hour	Summary of Events and Information	Remarks and references to Appendices
BEAUVAL	May 21		Brigade Church Parade at 10.0 AM.	
	21–28		Training – 5 hours per day – Firing on range, Physical Exercise, Selected squad drill, Arms Drill, Semaphore, Indication & recognition.	
	31		Moved to COULONVILLERS – Brigade march – Started 4.0 AM & arrived 11.50 AM. Very few fell out – One hours Halt for breakfast just outside BEAUMETZ. Men in Barns.	

1875 Wt. W593/826 1,000,000 4/15 J.B.C. & A. A.D.S.S./Forms/C. 2118.

Army Form C. 2118

Instructions regarding War Diaries and Intelligence Summaries are contained in F. S. Regs., Part II. and the Staff Manual respectively. Title Pages will be prepared in manuscript.

WAR DIARY
or
INTELLIGENCE SUMMARY
(Erase heading not required.)

Place	Date	Hour	Summary of Events and Information	Remarks and references to Appendices
HEBUTERNE	May 16		as the trench had been blown in & most of the garrison killed or wounded. Troops came up over the open ground through the German Barrage & attacked the enemy who were retreating to their own lines & inflicted considerable damage on them. Machine guns supported the Infantry by firing on the German front line, but the Artillery fire was weak. There were many casualties on our side.	
			The Company was relieved by the 145th Bde Machine Gun Coy & moved to the huts at COUIN. No casualties.	
	17.		Men rested all day.	
BEAUVAL	18		Company paraded at 5.45 AM & met the Brigade just outside COUIN & marched to BEAUVAL. Very hot day & as all men wore Steel helmets, many fell out. The Brigade was inspected by the Corps Commander just outside Marieux. All men reported in billets by 12.10 PM.	
	19.		Cleaning guns, remainder of day resting.	
	20.		Parades during the morning, including Physical Training, inspection of kit and feet. The Divisional Band played for 2 hours in the Square	

1875 Wt. W593/826 1,000,000 4/15 J.B.C. & A. A.D.S.S./Forms/C. 2118.

Instructions regarding War Diaries and Intelligence Summaries are contained in F. S. Regs., Part II. and the Staff Manual respectively. Title Pages will be prepared in manuscript.

WAR DIARY
or
INTELLIGENCE SUMMARY
(Erase heading not required.)

Army Form C. 2118

Place	Date	Hour	Summary of Events and Information	Remarks and references to Appendices
Hebuterne	13		Nothing to report on our Front. K & J Section heavily shelled before breakfast. Our new M.G. position in Pelissier almost complete. Rough Sketch (detailed illustration is being forwarded to M.G. School G.H.Q.)	

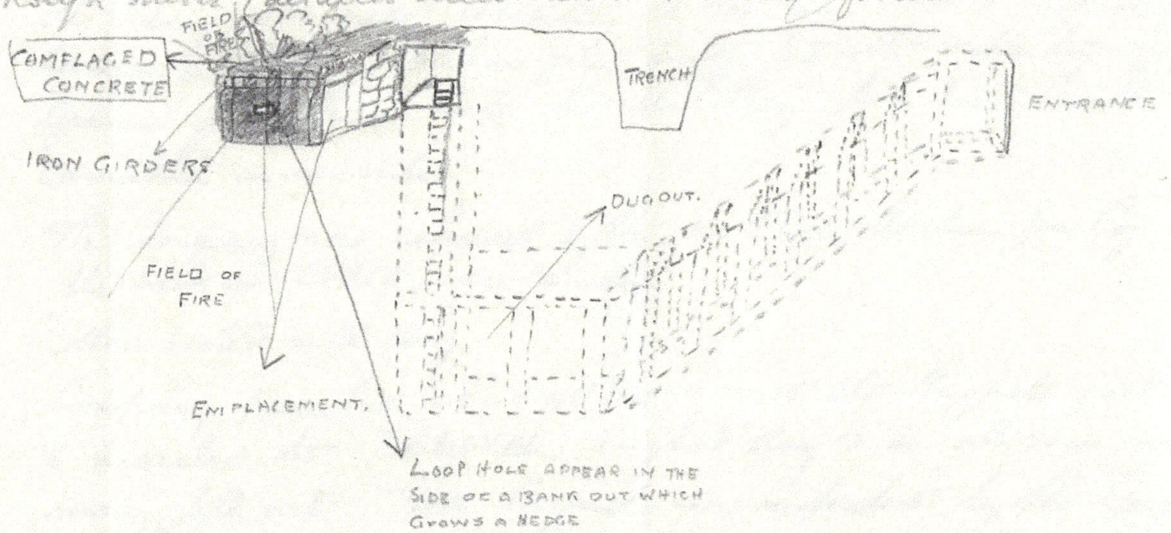

Place	Date	Hour	Summary of Events and Information	Remarks and references to Appendices
	14		Nothing to report.	
	15		Weather bad. Wind S W	
	16		At 12.30 AM. the enemy opened an intense bombardment along the whole of our front & continued for 2 hours. The German entered our front line trench SE of HEBUTERNE, & encountered little or no opposition, to the	

1875 Wt. W593/826 1,000,000 4/15 J.B.C. & A. A.D.S.S./Forms/C. 2118.

145 Bde

145 Bde M G Coy — Army Form C. 2118

Vol 4

WAR DIARY
or
INTELLIGENCE SUMMARY
(Erase heading not required.)

Instructions regarding War Diaries and Intelligence Summaries are contained in F. S. Regs., Part II. and the Staff Manual respectively. Title Pages will be prepared in manuscript.

Place	Date	Hour	Summary of Events and Information	Remarks and references to Appendices
HEBUTERNE	1916 April 25		The Company was relieved as a whole by the M.G. Company of the 144th Inf Brig after doing continuous duty in the line since February 2nd, went in to rest billets at Bayencourt	
	26		The Company was inspected at 12.15 pm by Lt Green. Our C.O. Capt B Long went to Hospital with German measles, Lt Green becoming temporary O.C.	
	27		A grouping practice with rifles was fired by all ranks. Overhaul of the whole company in progress.	
	28		Nothing to report	
	29		do	
	30		do	
	May 1st		Received orders at 9 pm to relieve the 144th Brigade M.G. Coy by 3.0pm 2nd inst	
	2		~~2nd inst~~ B.M.G.C.C of 167th Brigade was shown over our positions. It is probable that we are going to be relieved.	
	3		Enemy very quiet on our Front	
	4		do. A deserter came over belonging to the 2nd Guard Res.	
	5		The MG Coy of the 167th Brigade relieved us of J+K Sections. Our disposition is 6 guns in the line, 2 in support + 8 in reserve at Sailly	
	6		Nothing of interest to report.	
	7		It is probable that there is a change of troops opposite as affairs have been very quiet since our return	
	8		Nothing to report	
	9		do	
	10		do	
	11		do	
	12th		A very quiet Day on our Front	

145th Brigade.

48th Division.

145th BRIGADE MACHINE GUN COMPANY

M A Y 1 9 1 6:

Army Form C. 2118.

Instructions regarding War Diaries and Intelligence Summaries are contained in F. S. Regs., Part II. and the Staff Manual respectively. Title pages will be prepared in manuscript.

WAR DIARY
or
INTELLIGENCE SUMMARY.
(*Erase heading not required.*)

Place	Date	Hour	Summary of Events and Information	Remarks and references to Appendices
			<u>Copied from first page of succeeding War Diary.</u>	
HEBUTERNE				
	April 25th	1916	The Company was relieved as a whole bynthe M.G. Company of the 144th Inf. Brig. after doing continuous duty in the line since February 2nd. Went in to rest billets at BAYOUCOURT	
	26th		The Company was inspected at 12.15 p.m. by Lt.Green.Our C.O..Capt. B.Long went to hospital with German Measles, Lt.Green becoming temporary C.O.	
	27th		A grouping practice with rifles was fired by all ranks. Inoculation of the whole company in progress.	
	28th		Nothing to report.	
	29th		do.	
	30th		do.	

D. D. & L., London, E.C.
(A8004) Wt. W1771/M2-31 750,000 5/17 Sch. 52 Forms/C2118/14

Instructions regarding War Diaries and Intelligence Summaries are contained in F. S. Regs., Part II. and the Staff Manual respectively. Title Pages will be prepared in manuscript.

WAR DIARY
or
INTELLIGENCE SUMMARY
(Erase heading not required.)

Army Form C. 2118

Place	Date	Hour	Summary of Events and Information	Remarks and references to Appendices
HEBUTERNE	Apl 16		French aeroplane flew over lines all night. Very light night. Enemy shelled New trench at 10.45 PM & 11.30 PM. Brigade ordered us to place 9 guns to cover front German line from Serre Rd to GOMMECOURT & fire intermittently throughout the night. Guns in position at 12.15 AM. Weather improved & several aeroplanes of ours flew over their lines throughout the day.	No. 1299 Pte Reece P. 1st Bucks (Wounded slightly)
	17.		Quiet day owing to bad weather. During the night a few minenwerfers were fired by the enemy. The 6" Howitzers replied on the S.W. Corner of GOMMECOURT with 5 shells.	
	18		Experiments being made in firing Vickers guns without the muzzle cups. Guns fired well, although a little slower.	
	19.		Nothing to report.	
	20		do	
	21		do	
	22		Hostile Artillery was very active: about 800 shells fell along our ~~front~~ casualties very slight. Enemy machine guns active on Hebuterne	
	23		Hostile artillery again very active: about 1200 shells fell along our front. Three of our guns traversed Gommecourt Village intermittently all day	
	24		Nothing of interest occurred	

1875 Wt. W593/826 1,000,000 4/15 J.B.C. & A. A.D.S.S./Forms/C. 2118.

Army Form C. 2118

WAR DIARY
or
INTELLIGENCE SUMMARY
(Erase heading not required.)

Instructions regarding War Diaries and Intelligence Summaries are contained in F. S. Regs., Part II. and the Staff Manual respectively. Title Pages will be prepared in manuscript.

Place	Date	Hour	Summary of Events and Information	Remarks and references to Appendices
HEBUTERNE	Apl 9th		of Shrapnel + bursts of machine gun fire. The trench was finished at 7.30 AM. + the total casualties were 2 men killed, 1 Officer & 13 men wounded.	
	-10.		Indiscriminate shelling during the day. At night the wiring of new trench was strengthened + revetments continued. Besides shrapnel, the enemy put several 5.9 shells on Sitter trench. There were a few casualties.	
	-11		Wiring & revetting of new trench continued from 8.0 PM. During the early part of the ~~night~~ night, several salvoes of Shrapnel & an occasional minenwerfer were fired on the working party. After 10.30 PM all was quiet. Only one man was wounded. The machine guns were again in position to repel any rush on the part of the enemy	
	-12		Very quiet all day & night.	
	-13		All leave stopped, those at present on leave recalled by wire. A patrol came up to new trench, one German was shot & his body brought in, others were wounded. Several salvoes + at times heavy shelling on new trench at 11.25 pm. 11-55 PM., 2.30 AM & 3.5 AM.	
	-14.		Very strong wind + much rain. During the night at 10.45 PM + 11.30 PM, our Artillery fired rapid for 5 minutes on front trenches facing our new trench.	
	-15		Few shells on the Village.	

1875 Wt. W593/826 1,000,000 4/15 J.B.C. & A. A.D.S.S./Forms/C. 2118.

Instructions regarding War Diaries and Intelligence Summaries are contained in F. S. Regs., Part II. and the Staff Manual respectively. Title Pages will be prepared in manuscript.

WAR DIARY
or
INTELLIGENCE SUMMARY
(Erase heading not required.)

Army Form C. 2118

Place	Date	Hour	Summary of Events and Information	Remarks and references to Appendices
HEBUTERNE	Apl 6		fired, in some cases 4 at a time. All was quiet on our own frontage, except that a large number of flares were sent up, until a little after 10·PM, when several shrapnel shells were fired on the SAILLY-HEBUTERNE Road, just above the ridge.	
	7.		Several 5·9 Shells fired on K Sector.	
	8.		Enemy aeroplane dropped 2 bombs, which landed just behind the 4.5 Howitzers. No damage done. One hole made by these bombs was 6 ft deep & 10 ft diameter. Indiscriminate shelling during the day. & on the trenches between the left Battn of this Bde & the next Battn, the Germans were registering on the 2nd line. A report was received from Brigade that a raid on the trenches of K Sector might be expected. Three machine guns were laid on the German Front line trenches between GOMMECOURT & NAMELESS FARM from CATMILL, THE MOUND & in the house behind Billet 14, with men on duty all night. No raid was attempted.	
	9		At 8·0 PM a party of 1500 men were detailed to dig a trench from the front of our line. This number included the covering party of several hundred men. The actual trench dug was between points K 16. a 9.0. K 17.a. 00.75. K 11 c 22 & K 10.d.4.5. The enemy sent off several salvoes of	

1875 Wt. W593/826 1,000,000 4/15 J.B.C. & A. A.D.S.S./Forms/C. 2118.

Instructions regarding War Diaries and Intelligence Summaries are contained in F. S. Regs., Part II. and the Staff Manual respectively. Title Pages will be prepared in manuscript.

WAR DIARY
or
INTELLIGENCE SUMMARY
(Erase heading not required.)

Army Form C. 2118

Place	Date	Hour	Summary of Events and Information	Remarks and references to Appendices
H.Q. BUTERNE	APRIL. 1.		Weather getting warm. German aeroplanes including a twin engine biplane over our lines.	
	2.		Intermittent shelling on both sides. C Section with exception of PASTEUR trench handed over to 144th Bde. This included all new machine gun emplacements & mined dug-outs. One Section went to BAYENCOURT, leaving 3 sections in the line. Section at BAYENCOURT will be relieved each 6 days.	
	3.		New emplacement in house near Billet is completed. This is built from the ground to the eave of the house & allows of firing over the village into GOMMECOURT with safety. German active with Minenwerfer on the Warwick Brigade.	
	4.		Nothing to report	
	5.		A few shells on the village.	
	6		A draft of 8 men from each Battalion attached to this Company for instruction in the Vickers guns for 14 days. This is now a permanent arrangement & affords a common sense arrangement in securing immediate reinforcements for working the guns in case of loss in personnel. Twenty four men reported at HQ at 8.30AM & 8 men to the Section at BAYENCOURT. At 8.55 PM a heavy bombardment was started by the Germans on the 31st Div who are on the right of the 144th Bde. This lasted for 1½ hours. One noticed the exceptional number of minenwerfer	

Herewith A.F.C 2118.

B Williamson 2/Lt

for OC.

M.G. Company

145th Infy Brig

145th Brigade.

48th Division.

145th BRIGADE MACHINE GUN COMPANY

APRIL 1 9 1 6

WAR DIARY
or
INTELLIGENCE SUMMARY
(Erase heading not required.)

Instructions regarding War Diaries and Intelligence Summaries are contained in F. S. Regs., Part II. and the Staff Manual respectively. Title Pages will be prepared in manuscript.

Place	Date	Hour	Summary of Events and Information	Remarks and references to Appendices
HEBUTERNE	Mch 23		Quiet day	
	24.		Heavy fall of snow during the night of 23rd & early morning. Quiet day.	
	25.		Leave stopped (no reason given). New Respiratory Tubes issued to Machine Gunners. Day very quiet. The new position at WAGRAM practically finished & progress with MARIE LOUISE & VERCINGETORIX considerable. Quiet night	
	26		Little shelling on either side. Steel helmets (50) issued to men.	
	27.		Six O.R. Reinforcements arrived from GRANTHAM. Little Artillery fire.	
	28.		Very quiet day, with exception of 3. 5.9 shells on centre Battalion	
	29.		Eleven Machine guns trained on GOMMECOURT WOOD & PARK & firing 1 belt per ¼ hour consecutively. Enemy machine guns replied on village, also a few 5.9 shells on trenches E of HEBUTERNE. Machine Gun Coy H.Q. moved to Brigade old H.Q's, as the latter moved to SAILLY on Monday 27th. Snow falling	
	30th		One of our aeroplanes shot down by the enemy behind their lines.	
	31st		All stand to in the early morning, several movements sent out on front lines. Fourteen machine guns concentrated on GOMMECOURT WOOD & VILLAGE, firing one belt at 10.15 PM & another at 10.30 PM. No reply.	

1875 Wt. W593/826 1,000,000 4/15 J.B.C. & A. A.D.S.S./Forms/C. 2118.

WAR DIARY

or

INTELLIGENCE SUMMARY

(Erase heading not required.)

Army Form C. 2118

Instructions regarding War Diaries and Intelligence Summaries are contained in F. S. Regs., Part II. and the Staff Manual respectively. Title Pages will be prepared in manuscript.

Place	Date	Hour	Summary of Events and Information	Remarks and references to Appendices
HEBUTERNE	Mch. 19		At 2 AM a very heavy bombardment was begun by the Germans on the left Battn of the 144th Bde & touching our right Battn. & continued for one hour. Several gas shells were used, & although it was not considered necessary to order helmets to be put on, there was a distinct smell of gas like the smell of mustard & cress & had the effect of sickness on one. Our guns (machine) were brought from the Post back to the H.Q. The guns on the SQUARE & PELISSIER started firing on their night lines & the gun on VERCINGETOREX was fired from the new emplacement. All stood to for two hours, when practically all shelling had ceased. The firing of our artillery almost surpassed that of the Germans.	
	20		Quiet night. Arranged bombardment by 10th Corps Heavy Artillery, How. & Field guns on first & second German lines opposite left Battalion of 144th Brigade.	
	21		An extremely quiet day. Leave to England opened.	
	22		A raid was carried out at midnight by the 5th Glosters with object of capturing a prisoner. The Artillery were to put a barrage on the second line & the machine guns were to provide a barrage for the flanks – thus making a barrage on three sides of a square, the open side being the point of entry of the raiding parties. The enterprise was not successful the raiders failing to cut thro' the wire before being perceived. The Artillery barrage was poor & insufficient for the purpose. Our task was accomplished rounds being expended.	

1875 Wt. W593/826 1,000,000 4/15 J.B.C. & A. A.D.S.S./Forms/C. 2118.

WAR DIARY
or
INTELLIGENCE SUMMARY
(Erase heading not required.)

Instructions regarding War Diaries and Intelligence Summaries are contained in F. S. Regs., Part II. and the Staff Manual respectively. Title Pages will be prepared in manuscript.

Place	Date	Hour	Summary of Events and Information	Remarks and references to Appendices
HEBUTERNE	Mch 14.		Clear day. Several Balloons up behind German lines & 3 German Aeroplanes over our lines for some time during the morning, with the result that our Batteries were heavily shelled later in the day. At 5 o'clock 8 Machine guns were turned on to GOMMECOURT WOOD & VILLAGE & fired 500 rounds each. This wood had been left untouched for 5 days & the result was no doubt satisfactory to us, as the Germans replied with Artillery & machine gun on to the 2nd line & village for some time afterwards.	
	15.		Considerable Artillery activity on our part, about 100 shells fired on strong points of enemy's lines. Company H.Q. were moved to dug outs in another part of the village, where easier communication & a safer means is secured of reaching the guns.	
	16		Machine guns firing consecutively from 10 AM to 5 PM. Artillery activity on both sides.	
	17.		Nothing to report	
	18.		Several large calibre shells (5.9 or 8.0) fell in the village near the church & in the Keep. Four machine guns fired on GOMMECOURT & four on BOIS ROSSIGNOL at 6.15 PM. Germans replied with 77 mm shells on second line trenches, & machine gun fire on the village.	

1875 Wt. W593/826 1,000,000 4/15 J.B.C. & A. A.D.S.S./Forms/C. 2118.

(3)

Instructions regarding War Diaries and Intelligence Summaries are contained in F. S. Regs., Part II. and the Staff Manual respectively. Title Pages will be prepared in manuscript.

WAR DIARY
or
INTELLIGENCE SUMMARY
(Erase heading not required.)

Army Form C. 2118

Place	Date	Hour	Summary of Events and Information	Remarks and references to Appendices
HEBUTERNE	Mch 10		Our guns seemed to be replying vigorously	
	11		German shelling the left Battalion trenches & the outskirts of village. A few shells fell near our Headquarters by the Pond. No reply on the part of our artillery. Two machine guns firing from a shellhole near PAPIN. (K15d31) on the CHEMIN CREUX K17 b1.9 & communication trenches leading to LA LOUVIERES FARM K18.c.2.5. About 7.30PM several 4.2 Shells landed near our H.Q at the centre of the village. The shelling is again becoming very irritating & nerve racking	
	12		Clear day & sun shining. Continued programme for Lewis & Vickers guns. One belt from 14 Vickers guns & 1 drum from 6 Lewis guns fired on front, second & third German lines behind SERRE & north to GOMMECOURT at 10.30 PM. & a similar amount at 10.50 PM. All guns fired well, with one exception, which was due to gun being cold. Enemy put up a number of Verylights & replied with 3 machine guns on our front line & village, but reply very weak.	
	13.		A beautiful clear morning & weather more like summer. During the morning, our artillery were active & the Germans replied chiefly on the village itself about 12.30PM. Concerts have been arranged for the men up in the trenches & a cellar has been fitted up to hold 100 men below Billet No . The VARLETS are giving the first concert.	

1875 Wt. W593/826 1,000,000 4/15 J.B.C. & A. A.D.S.S./Forms/C. 2118.

Army Form C. 2118

Instructions regarding War Diaries and Intelligence Summaries are contained in F. S. Regs., Part II. and the Staff Manual respectively. Title Pages will be prepared in manuscript.

WAR DIARY
or
INTELLIGENCE SUMMARY
(Erase heading not required.)

Place	Date	Hour	Summary of Events and Information	Remarks and references to Appendices
HEBUTERNE	Mch 6.		they are so frequently changed. It is a bad policy	
	-7		Very quiet.	
	-8.		Machine guns trained on Sunken Road & 16 Poplars & firing from 6 PM to 6 AM the following morning. The previous night one of the Bucks Officers' patrols had a most successful encounter with a covering party of the enemy at this point, their casualties amounting to at least 15, & on our side only 3 were slightly wounded & then returned to duty the same day.	
	-9		Machine gun programme with 10 guns firing on various parts of the enemy lines at 4.15 PM. Enemy machine guns have been laid on the village, but all bullets go very high. There was a little shelling on various parts of the village, but no concerted action on enemy's part. Three of their machine guns replied to ours, but they have not up to the present had more than 3 firing at one time. A new position for indirect fire on the Sunken Road K17.b.1.9. from Poplar K.15 b.5.5 was used & found very useful. No screen necessary.	
	-10.		More snow during the night & the trenches in the support line in places is 3 feet deep. Nine machine guns fired 2 belts each on BOIS ROSSIGNOL at 3.30 PM with the usual result, that one expects when firing in this direction, of salvoes of 77 mm shells on the front & support line. A scheme is being drawn up for using Bombers, Lewis Rifles, Mortars & machine guns collectively for meeting counter attacks on trenches ~~captured~~ taken & being consolidated by the infantry. At 11 PM a heavy bombardment began on the British Trenches SE of COLINCAMPS, which lasted 1½ hours.	

1875 Wt. W593/826 1,000,000 4/15 J.B.C. & A. A.D.S.S./Forms/C. 2118.

148 Bde [illegible]

Instructions regarding War Diaries and Intelligence Summaries are contained in F. S. Regs., Part II. and the Staff Manual respectively. Title Pages will be prepared in manuscript.

WAR DIARY
or
~~INTELLIGENCE SUMMARY~~
(Erase heading not required.)

Army Form C. 2118

Place	Date	Hour	Summary of Events and Information	Remarks and references to Appendices
HEBUTERNE	Mch. 1.		Programme of machine gun fire from 2.30 to 6 PM. No reply on the part of the enemy. The enemy does not appear to use more than 1 or 2 guns at a time. Machine gun was mounted in the Cahaw Trench from 6.15 to 7.30 AM. No distinct target fired at but GOMMECOURT WOOD was swept & corner of ROSSIGNOL WOOD.	
			First draft of 4 men arrived from Grantham to replace casualties sustained in Marie Louise position 10th ult.	
	Mch 2		A gun mounted at 6 am in trench Macdonald in the hope of a direct target – a hope not fulfilled. Programme of fire carried out in the forenoon on GOMMECOURT WOOD. At 6.30 pm two guns swept the Sunken Road behind the enemies lines	
	Mch 3		A programme of fire on enemies Dump on the right of GOMMEWOOD PARC carried out all through the night – the target was located from aeroplane photographs. Two interested spectators attended in the persons of Non conformist & R.C. padres. Enemy not very active perhaps due to the fact of the heavy fighting at Verdun.	
	4th		Programme of previous day repeated. Gun transferred from Fauriner position to Fort Briggs where a site has been chosen which commands the Fourmier ridge. During the night & until 3 pm snow fell heavily.	
	5th		Nothing to report.	
	6th		A further fall of snow during the night, but sun shining & much hot during the day. Very little activity on either side.	
			Owing to the frequent change of teams in the trenches, it has been found impossible to keep guns under the direct charge of their own [illegible]. This has proved most unsatisfactory & a long list of deficiencies will no doubt be sent in after one relief from the trenches for a rest. It has been found impossible for the team commander to check every item on taking over, with the result that losses are frequently arising. No team now takes a pride in its own guns, as	

145th Brigade.

48th Division.

145th BRIGADE MACHINE GUN COMPANY

MARCH 1 9 1 6 ; ;

To Officer
i/c
A.G. Office
Base

Enclosed 1st instalment of War Diary from this Co. for the months of JAN & FEB.

Maurice C Cooper Lt
for O.C.
M.G.C.
148th Infy Bde.

McL 1.1.6

Army Form C. 2118

Instructions regarding War Diaries and Intelligence Summaries are contained in F. S. Regs., Part II. and the Staff Manual respectively. Title Pages will be prepared in manuscript.

WAR DIARY
or
INTELLIGENCE SUMMARY
(Erase heading not required.)

Place	Date	Hour	Summary of Events and Information	Remarks and references to Appendices
HEBUTERNE	23		During the night the enemy shelled the 12th Brigade on our right, to which our artillery replied. The 12th Bde now form part of the 48th Div.	
	24.		Very heavy frost during the night & slight fog in the early morning, which prevented any observation, consequently little shelling.	
	25.		Snowing heavily all day. Very quiet all day.	
	26		Nothing to report	
	27.		Fine clear day & thaw setting in. Wind has veered round to S.W. Artillery activity on both sides. Two of our machine guns firing short bursts on enemy's support lines during the afternoon. The enemy replied by shelling our front line.	
	28.		Raining most of the day. Our machine guns carried out a programme on the village & second line of Germans. Shelling on both sides throughout the day. At dusk the Germans replied with machine guns on the village.	
	29		Enemy aeroplane dropped two bombs on HEBUTERNE about 8.45 AM, no damage done. This the first occasion on which their aeroplanes have done this. Machine gun programme with 10 guns carried out during the afternoon. Considerable artillery activity on our right.	

1875 Wt. W593/826 1,000,000 4/15 J.B.C. & A. A.D.S.S./Forms/C. 2118.

Army Form C. 2118

WAR DIARY
or
INTELLIGENCE SUMMARY
(Erase heading not required.)

Instructions regarding War Diaries and Intelligence Summaries are contained in F. S. Regs., Part II. and the Staff Manual respectively. Title Pages will be prepared in manuscript.

Place	Date	Hour	Summary of Events and Information	Remarks and references to Appendices
HEBUTERNE	Feb 18.		was moved into the Mound (R.6), left position giving enfilade fire on the German Trenches. Everything was quiet again by 3.30 AM.	
	19.		Very heavy bombardment of the 12th Brigade on our right by the German was opened about 6.30 PM. Considerable activity was shown by enemy machine guns, during the night & particularly at "Stand to". Great improvement in the weather & this allowed of substantial progress being made with new emplacements.	
	20.		Baths at BUS allotted to the Transport section. The men are feeling the lack of clean underwear very much. Only 50% of clothes are issued to those using the baths during the morning & none during the afternoon, & the consequence is that during the long tour of the trenches, very few of the men are able to get a change of clothing.	
	21.		Quiet day.	
	22.		Snowing most of the day. & quiet on the front.	
	23.		Still snowing. Machine guns traversed the whole of the German Front line from 6 to 6.30 AM. This was in return for their activity in traversing our lines at "Stand-To" each morning. Work still proceeding on the new emplacements, & one in VERCINGETORIX practically completed. This one replaces the position at MARIE LOUISE which was completely destroyed by a German Shell.	

1875 Wt. W593/826 1,000,000 4/15 J.B.C. & A. A.D.S.S./Forms/C. 2118.

Army Form C. 2118

WAR DIARY
or
INTELLIGENCE SUMMARY
(Erase heading not required.)

Instructions regarding War Diaries and Intelligence Summaries are contained in F. S. Regs., Part II. and the Staff Manual respectively. Title Pages will be prepared in manuscript.

Place	Date	Hour	Summary of Events and Information	Remarks and references to Appendices
HEBUTERNE	1916 Feb 14.		One officer of the company sent back to rest at COURCELLES every 6 days, & to look after the Transport now stationed there.	
	15th		Our guns shelled the Germans the whole of the day, with little reply on their part.	
	16th		Enemy inactive. New dispositions on Brigade front, which allow of one Battalion being always at rest.	
	17th		A few shells on front line, but on the whole very quiet; probably due to very bad weather.	
	18th		In the early morning about 1.30 AM the Germans commenced a heavy bombardment of the trenches on our left with guns of every size up to 5.9, heavy trench mortars, grenades & Minenwerfer. The moon was practically full & a very clear night. All officers got out of bed & the Brigade [illegible] given. The left Battalion of the Brigade stood to. The bombardment continued for an hour, our guns replying to a small extent, only field guns & one or two heavy shells were sent over. It is not known if the Germans left their trenches, but our artillery raised a tir de barrage on the German lines. The Vickers gun at Cut Mill fired several belts & a reserve gun	

WAR DIARY
or
INTELLIGENCE SUMMARY
(Erase heading not required.)

Army Form C. 2118

Instructions regarding War Diaries and Intelligence Summaries are contained in F. S. Regs., Part II. and the Staff Manual respectively. Title Pages will be prepared in manuscript.

Place	Date	Hour	Summary of Events and Information	Remarks and references to Appendices
COUIN	1916 Feb 1		which resolved itself into a School of amusement. Four guns with teams took over G. Sector of the trenches from the Machine Gun Coy in the line.	
—	2.		Relieved the 144th Bde Machine Gun Coy in the trenches with a prospect of a long stay. Our guns took up the same positions.	
HEBUTERNE	3		New positions sited & work started	
	3rd–6th		Nothing of any importance occurred	
	7th–9th		The village very heavily shelled with shells of large & small calibre & all cellars were used at various times during the day. There was very little reply on the part of our guns.	
	10th		MARIE LOUISE Gun & team shelled very heavily & unfortunately several casualties from a direct hit on the emplacement. All men belonged to the Section 2, consisting of the draft from the 1st Bucks Battalion.	Cpl Watkins (since wounded) Pte Wright, James, Brunton, Baker } Killed
	11th		The deceased were buried in HEBUTERNE cemetery by Rev Capt Holmes. The village still being shelled, but not with the same intensity.	
	12th–13th		During the two days about 1000 shells were dropped in & around HEBUTERNE	

1875 Wt. W593/826 1,000,000 4/15 I.R.C. & A. A.D.S.S./Forms/C. 2118.

MACHINE GUN COMPANY
145th INFTRY BDE

Army Form C. 2118

Instructions regarding War Diaries and Intelligence Summaries are contained in F. S. Regs., Part II. and the Staff Manual respectively. Title Pages will be prepared in manuscript.

WAR DIARY
or
~~INTELLIGENCE SUMMARY~~
(Erase heading not required.)

Place	Date	Hour	Summary of Events and Information	Remarks and references to Appendices
	1916			
COUIN.	Jan 11th		Official date of formation of the 145th BRIGADE MACHINE GUN COMPANY	
	17th		Drafts from the four Units of Brigade joined up & were billeted in the wooden huts erected in the grounds of the Chateau belonging to the Marquis de LOUVENCOURT.	
	18th–21st		Arranging details of management.	
	21st		Relieved the 144th Brigade Machine Gun Company in the trenches at HEBUTERNE	
HEBUTERNE	21st–27th		Nothing of importance occurred.	
	27th		Returned to huts at COUIN.	
COUIN.	29th	-	New Vickers Maxim Guns received. Instructors came from the 143rd Bde M G Coy to explain the working of the new gun to the N.C.O's & the N.C.O's then instructed their own teams.	
	31st		The football team of this Company played D Co of the 1/5 Glos. Regt in the Brigade football league winning by 2 goals to NIL.	
	Feb 1st		The old converted Maxim guns returned to Ordnance. Officer's chargers arrived. A school of riding was started for the Officers during the afternoon	

1875 Wt. W593/826 1,000,000 4/15 J.B.C. & A. A.D.S.S./Forms/C. 2118.

145th Brigade.

48th Division.

Company formed in France 11.1.16.

145th BRIGADE MACHINE GUN COMPANY

11th JANUARY to 29th FEBRUARY 1 9 1 6

1

Dec '1917

145th

Machine Gun Coy

Jan 1916 → Oct 1917

48TH DIVISION
145TH INFY BDE

145TH MACHINE GUN COY.

JAN 1916-~~D C 1917~~

1917 OCT

TO ITALY